GOLDEN INTERLUDE

GOLDEN INTERLUDE

The Edens in India
1836–1842

JANET DUNBAR

ALAN SUTTON

Alan Sutton Publishing Limited
Brunswick Road · Gloucester

Copyright © Janet Dunbar 1955

First published by John Murray 1955
This edition published 1985

British Library Cataloguing in Publication Data

Dunbar, Janet
Golden interlude : the Edens in India 1836–1842.
1. Eden *(Family)*   2. India—Biography
I. Title
929'.2'0954   CS1209.E3

ISBN 0-86299-229-X

Cover picture: Lilium Auratum *by John Frederick Lewis*
Birmingham Museum and Art Gallery

Printed in Great Britain

CONTENTS

ILLUSTRATIONS

* *Reproduced by courtesy of the
Commonwealth Relations Office, India Office Library*

Illustrations

DRAWINGS IN TEXT BY FANNY EDEN

SKETCH MAP BY E. G. MORTON

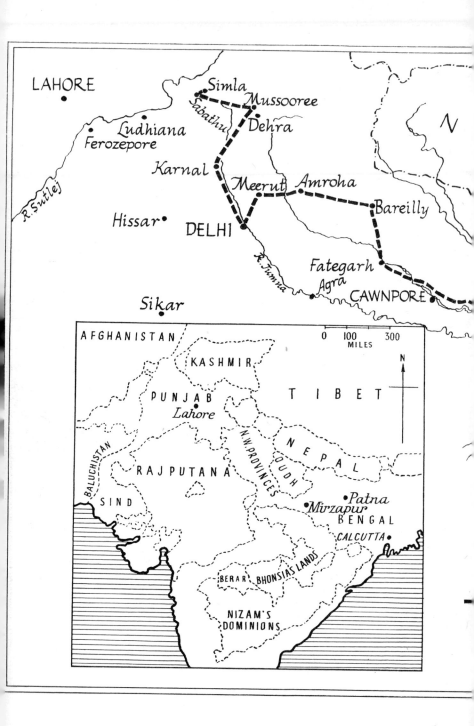

N E P A L

Gandak R.

Ghaghra R.

Ballia

Ghazipur

Dinapore

Barh

PATNA

Monghyr

Rajmahal

R. Ganges

Khulna

ALLAHABAD BENARES

Chunar

Mirzapur

CALCUTTA

Sundarbans

Mouths of
the Ganges

N

Mahanadi R.

— — Main Journey Up The Country
(Calcutta to Simla detours not shown)

0   40   120
Miles

E.G.M.

INTRODUCTION

IN the year 1835, George Eden, 2nd Lord Auckland, was appointed Governor-General of India.

An able politician—such was his reputation—he had been President of the Board of Trade, and was now First Lord of the Admiralty. He belonged to one of the great Whig families, and he and his sister Emily were friends of Lord Melbourne. When, after a short reign, the Tory government gave place to the Whigs in 1835, and Melbourne again became Prime Minister, he cancelled the Tory appointment in India and offered the Governor-Generalship to Lord Auckland.

It was considerable promotion, and Lord Auckland was pleased. To his sisters, Emily and Fanny, it was a calamity. They lived with him, all three being unmarried and their parents dead. Emily was thirty-eight and Fanny thirty-four. They were cultivated women who led a very full and happy existence, moving in the highest society, on terms of close friendship with the prominent Whig families, and taking pleasure in frequent visits to Bowood and Longleat, Chatsworth and Knowsley and many of the other great country-houses. Above all, they were part of a large, close-knit family of sisters and brothers, nieces and nephews, cousins and near connections, with whom they kept in touch by visits and regular correspondence.

Lord Auckland's appointment to India put an end to this pleasant, stimulating life. The society in Calcutta would be of a very different kind: stiff, military and official. As the Governor-General's sisters, they would have to entertain and be entertained; it would be a new, hedged-in world of *sahibs* and *memsahibs* whom they did not know. The physical discomforts which lay ahead—the five-months' voyage under sail, the extreme heat in which they would have to live for five or six years—were distasteful to contemplate, but could be endured. What they found almost unbearable was the prospect of such a long separation from the friends, sisters and brothers to whom they were devotedly attached. It was now that they realised to the full how much their lives were built on the solid foundation of mutual interests and affection between them and their friends and relations.

It did not occur to them to refuse to accompany their brother. They had lived with him since their parents' death many years before; he depended on them to manage the domestic side of his life. Besides, Emily would have been wretchedly unhappy away from George. Ever since girlhood she had idolised her brother. They understood each other very well; in a large family of varying temperaments, these two were cut from the same piece of cloth. They shared the same strong political views, especially on the Reform question; and of late years Emily had been an influential hostess for George. It was therefore inevitable that she should continue to be his hostess and companion, in a country which she disliked even before she saw it, in a climate which filled her with dread by its repute. With them would go Fanny, their youngest sister, who had lived with them for fourteen years.

This account of Emily and Fanny Eden mainly covers, in detail, the extraordinary six years, 1836–42, which they spent in India. They found themselves in a world of dramatic contrasts. There was the Anglo-Indian life of dinners, receptions, balls and theatricals: a tiny society, toy-sized against a fabulous background of jewelled magnificence, where princes hung themselves with diamonds and caparisoned their horses with emeralds, where temples were sheeted with gold, and agate fountains played in marble courtyards. They spent over two years in a journey to the north-west, and found yet another world: a nightmare where men killed their wives without question, where women sold their children for a handful of rice, where superstitious rites demanded human sacrifice at seed-time.

It was an India over which hung the menacing shadow of Russia. Europe had for long been watching that incalculable empire rolling eastwards in Asia. Part of Persia had already been swallowed up; the Ottoman Sultan had been attacked. Was India to be the next victim? Russian emissaries were already in Afghanistan—and Afghanistan bordered the north-west frontier of India. The Governor-General's earliest instructions were to build up a rampart of friendly buffer-states between India and Russia. He could not foretell that his over-zealous reading of those orders was to lead him into one of the most disastrous minor wars in the history of British arms.

Emily Eden, many years after her return from India, published selections from the vast number of letters which she sent home between 1835 and 1842. There came into my hands, some time ago, four privately-bound volumes of letters which were thought to be more of Emily Eden's correspondence, hitherto unpublished. They turned out, on being transcribed, to be letters from Fanny, written in the form of a journal to an intimate friend in England.

Hitherto, one had only caught glimpses of Fanny through Emily's eyes—and critical eyes they could be on occasion, too. To Emily, Fanny was 'one of the people who cannot exist without constant excitement.' Even after six further years of closer acquaintanceship, enforced by their elevated position in India, the brilliant, opinionated elder sister was no nearer to understanding Fanny's sense of adventure and quick acceptance of the odd, unexpected happenings of life. The discovery of these new letters is extraordinarily interesting to me, at any rate, for they bring out the inner relationship between these two sisters, so different in nature, who were bound by the tenacious Eden affection and sense of family duty to spend most of their lives together. Fanny reveals herself as gentler in temperament, more perceptive than the other, and she has a charming wit which is not inferior to the humour of the more celebrated sister.

Three of the journals cover many of the same events which Emily describes in her published letters. The fourth journal is an account of a tiger-shooting trip to the Rajmahal hills which Fanny joined, armed with a sketch-book instead of a gun. While admitting that man-eating tigers had to be destroyed, she found more pleasure in riding on her elephant through the rose-covered jungles which hid the great beasts. She passed through villages where no white woman had ever been before, seeing primitive India through the eyes of a friendly, sympathetic *memsahib*, completely different from the stock type of those days. This is an account at first-hand of what must have been a unique experience for a high-bred Whig lady not long out from home. I am including part of the Rajmahal journal, and a number of Fanny's sketches. All four journals are illustrated with scores of drawings, some in pencil, others in pen-and-ink and coloured chalks. Fanny was not such a finished artist as Emily, and her drawings of figures are not always successful; but her landscapes and buildings have an evocative quality: she makes you see what she saw.

I should have preferred to present the sisters through the medium of their letters only; but these would not have made a connected story. Emily and Fanny Eden wrote hundreds of letters from India, and got into the habit of duplicating some of these, with slight variations, for different sets of friends and relations. I soon found that, in order to make a coherent picture of their life in India, I had also to use sources other than the letters. I have, however, woven their own words and phrasing into the narrative, wherever possible, and have also quoted directly from unpublished material.

The Edens usually spelt Indian names phonetically in their letters and journals. I have left these in the original versions whenever they are directly quoted, but have followed modern standard spelling in the narrative.

ACKNOWLEDGMENTS

THE manuscript journals which the present Lord Auckland lent me were the inspiration for this book, and I wish to record my gratitude to him. The journals have since been acquired by the India Office Library.

I am greatly indebted to the Right Honourable Sir Anthony Eden, who gave me access to family letters and papers which enabled me to fill in much of the background of the sisters' lives.

Mr. Oswald Eden Dickinson helped me considerably with information; Mr. M. H. B. Lethbridge, late I.C.S., gave very useful assistance with the transcription, and Mr. Arthur Hughes, late I.C.S., made many suggestions regarding the spelling and possible meaning of Indian words in the original letters.

My daughter, Mrs. Ralph Merrifield, accorded valuable help in transcribing part of the journals in the early stages.

I wish to express my appreciation of the help afforded me over a long period by the Librarian and staff of the India Office Library, and especially by Mr. D. Matthews. I wish similarly to thank the staffs of the British Museum Reading Room, Map Room and Manuscript Room, and the ever-helpful Librarian and assistants of the Richmond (Surrey) Public Library.

The portrait sketches of Emily Eden and William Godolphin Osborne are reproduced by kind permission of the Right Honourable Sir Anthony Eden. The portrait of George Eden, 2nd Baron Auckland, is taken from a miniature in the possession of Mr. O. E. Dickinson. The sources of the other illustrations are given under the captions.

For FRANCES

1

EARLY YEARS

EMILY EDEN was born in Old Palace Yard, Westminster, in 1797, the seventh daughter of William Eden, 1st Baron Auckland. Fanny was also born in the Westminster house, in 1801. She was the eighth daughter and youngest child of this family of fourteen children.

Their father was a son of Sir Robert Eden, of West Auckland, in Co. Durham; their mother, Eleanor Elliot, a sister of the first Earl of Minto. Both parents were people of outstanding personality. William Eden held diplomatic posts in America and Ireland, was Minister-Plenipotentiary to the Court of Versailles before the Revolution, and later Ambassador to Spain and to Holland.

Mrs. Eden accompanied her husband to all his foreign posts, and several of her children were born abroad. William Eden relates in his diary how they travelled with all their children, nurses and servants —a party of forty; while their chaplain, surgeon and midwife followed a day behind. His wife was a devoted mother, but she took her full share in the social life inseparable from a diplomatist's duties. He wrote to a friend:

'Mrs. Eden is just returned from passing nearly a week . . . [at] the Court of Versailles without feeling a moment's discomposure. . . . We have now as many nations in our Nursery as were assembled at the Tower of Babel.'

It was said that she made domestic life quite fashionable, in an age when children were left almost entirely to the care of nurses and servants. Mrs. Eden also kept a diary, in which she lovingly noted down details of her children's nurture and upbringing: 'Out of fourteen I suckled thirteen. Eleven of the children had smallpox during their wanderings, also cowpox, whooping-cough, measles and scarlet fever.'

She was receptive to new ideas, too. When Fanny was four years old, Mrs. Eden wrote in her diary: 'At the end of the year Robert and Fanny were inoculated for the smallpox, which took no effect.'

Emily and Fanny, like their sisters before them, were educated by their mother and by governesses. They had an excellent education. Besides formal lessons, they were encouraged to read anything they wished.   They were taken to the play, and taught to have an intelligent interest in foreign affairs.   At the age of eighteen Emily could write: 'Poor Beckenham is gone mad about the corn laws,' and know clearly what she was writing about.   And later in the same year, referring to the Battle of Waterloo, which had just been fought, she was able to view this Europe-shaking event with an objectivity far beyond her years: 'I am tired of rejoicing and lamenting over this news which, upon the whole, strikes me as very melancholy, though I know that is a very wrong feeling.'

By the time Emily was eighteen and Fanny fourteen, Lady Auckland (as she had now become) had replaced the governess by a tutor, who had charge of the education of Robert, the brother who came between them in age.   He was a thorough tutor.   Writing on one occasion to George, who was in France at the time, Emily told him all the home news and added: 'Madden has given us so much to do, we have not a minute's spare time.   We are duller than a hundred posts about Astronomy, and if you can find any planets for us in Paris, we shall be obliged to you, as we cannot find one on the globe, and Madden only laughs at us.'

Emily wrote long letters to George when he was away; her preference for this brother was apparent at an early age.   It was plain, too, that she was George's favourite in the family.   She understood his brand of whimsical mockery, and replied in kind.   He, in turn, respected her considerable gifts of good conversation and political *nous*. He expressed this appreciation in a typical way when he once wrote to her from a country-house where he was staying:

'To console us for not having you, we have an Emily here who has something of the fooley in her, but she unluckily is a dullfooley.'

The Edens lived at Eden Farm, the house near Beckenham, in Kent, where their parents had settled after the years abroad.   In 1814 Lord Auckland died, and George succeeded to the title, and began to take his political career seriously.

Lady Auckland did not long survive her husband; she died four years after him.   Fanny and Emily, the only unmarried daughters, were faced with the decision of what to do about the future.   It was not a difficult decision; the answer was inevitable.   They would go and live with George.   In London, alas!   George had to be in London a good deal, and he could not afford to keep up an establishment in town and a house in the country; he and his sisters had each only a limited income.   He let Eden Farm to a rich Kentish widow who agreed to take it on his own terms: a seven-year lease at £600 a year. That, George reckoned, would give them the prospect of being settled and comfortable.

The next step was to find a house in London for the three of them. After looking at several, they found one which they liked in Grosvenor Street. Emily and Fanny left their country home with its gardens and meadows, and came to live in London. They thought it a poor substitute for Kent. There were no groves of trees to turn brown and yellow in October, and the people in the streets looked cold—not at all as fresh and merry as they should, in crisp autumn weather. True, there were near relations in London. Their sister Louisa called, but as she talked about nothing except patterns of cloth and new clothes for her children, it was not very interesting. The sister they would much rather have been near was the eldest, Eleanor—dearly beloved Eleanor, nearly twenty years their senior and the most understanding of women. She lived at East Combe, near Charlton in Kent, not a day's driving distance from Eden Farm. Now that they were no longer able to visit her frequently, as had been their habit, they had to content themselves with writing every week.

Eleanor Eden, as a girl, had been in love with William Pitt, but the affair came to nothing, and in 1799 she married Lord Hobart, who became the Earl of Buckinghamshire a few years later. Lady Bucks, as Eleanor was known to her friends, was the one to whom all the rest of the family turned in joy or in grief. Calm, patient, infinitely kind, Eleanor never failed to be interested in everything that Emily or Fanny did.

'My Dearest Sister,' Emily wrote to her, at the end of a day that had been full of annoyances, 'I am going to write you a long letter, and I shall be like a ginger-beer bottle, if once the cork is drawn. I shall spirtle you all over. . . .'

There were two other people for whom Emily could draw the cork and be her trenchantly candid self. One was Theresa Villiers, the sister of George Villiers who later became the 4th Lord Clarendon. Theresa was witty, beautiful, clever—and as good and true as she was lovely. Her family doted on her. Anyone with less force of character would have been hopelessly spoilt, but Theresa was unspoilable. She had been endowed with a quality of spirit which kept envy at a distance. Emily had known her from girlhood, and they had begun writing to each other at an early age; they could both express themselves well on paper, and enjoyed each other's letters.

The other close friend was Pamela FitzGerald, a daughter of the Lord Edward FitzGerald who had been in the Irish Rebellion of 1798, and forfeited his estates in consequence. Pamela had a fascinating personality. Gay and warm-hearted, she possessed a courage which was never crushed. And she had need of courage, right through her life; her childhood had been one of insecurity and continual uprootings as she was sent first to one relative and then another. She married Sir Guy Campbell in 1830—a happy marriage which was to stand the test of continual financial buffetings. They lived part of the year in Ireland, where Pamela brought up a rapidly expanding family on a steadily diminishing income. She educated them herself until they were at an age for a tutor; she was a woman of wide learning and cultivated tastes.

Emily was greatly attached to both these friends, and wrote to them frequently. Different as they were from each other, they shared many things in common with Emily Eden; the same kind of humour, a sense of the ridiculous, the same zest in the everyday happenings of life. When they gossiped in their letters it was without malice; their wit was sharp, but it was never dipped in acid.

Fanny, too, had her intimate friends. She had often travelled from Eden Farm to visit them in London; now she could see them more often. There was Caroline Montague, with whom she often liked to pass the day shopping or walking; and the Countess of Derby, when she was in town. This last was a curious friendship, for Lady Derby was over forty years older than Fanny. She had been Eliza Farren, the actress, and she was as slim and elegant at sixty as she had been in her young days. Fanny was never conscious of the difference in age; they both had natural high spirits, and there was a very real affection between them.

It was with the Grosvenor family, though, that Fanny felt most at home. Lord Robert—Emma—Eleanor—they all welcomed her as if she had been one of their own; there were times when she felt as much of a Grosvenor as an Eden. She could always count on the kindest of welcomes at Grosvenor House, and she gave them unstinted love in return.

Living in London had its compensations, in spite of the lack of a garden. Emily entertained for George, and she and Fanny were entertained in turn by the best society. It was mostly Whig society, of course. Emily shone in that *milieu*; she could argue about politics with men of the first ability, and hold her own. Fanny was a Whig,

too, but she disliked arguing. She was more detached than her
sister about politics, and was apt to smile when the conversation
grew too warm. Politics, she felt, were not articles to be
passionate over. What was required was coolness. With cool
consideration came common-sensible-ness, a quality Fanny much
admired.

It was useless to argue with Emily about arguing, so Fanny talked
about dancing, and bonnets, and gowns, and the latest babies in the
family. When she went away on country-house visits, she wrote long
letters to her sister; merry, bubbling letters which always made Emily
miss her. Fanny might be regrettably like quicksilver at home, but
when she was not there—well, one was very conscious that she was
not there.

When Emily was away visiting, she was equally aware of there being
no Fanny at hand, and was soon mending a pen to write to her younger
sister. The only time she did not miss Fanny was when she herself
was away with George. Then she did not miss anybody. George's
company had always been sufficient in itself.

One of the advantages of living in London was the ease with which
they could get away from it. There were many invitations to the
country; to stay with the Lansdownes at Bowood, or the Baths at
Longleat, or—more unwillingly—with the Duke of Devonshire at
Chatsworth. Mere magnificence never impressed either Emily or
Fanny; they valued character, good humour and good heart above
everything else. They liked the Duke of Devonshire, but they did
not at all care for the way he took pleasure in making his guests do
what they didn't want to do.

Then there were brothers and sisters to visit. Robert had been
ordained and had a living at Hertingfordbury. Caroline was married
to Arthur Vansittart, and had quantities of children. Charlotte had
married Sir Francis Godolphin Osborne, and her brood was particularly
unruly; especially William, the third son, who liked to play practical
jokes. William had stayed at Eden Farm as a boy of ten, and Emily
had allowed her irritation with him to break into a letter to a friend:

'I was so cross and stupid with a pain in my ear which I have
had this week, and in such a fury with Willy Osborne, who made
a point of dropping his shuttlecock on my paper every minute,
that I was obliged to leave off writing in order to fight with him;
and when that battle was ended, he insisted on playing blind man's
buff.'

Mary had married Charles Drummond, and was filling her quiver every year.

'The work of education goes on from morning till night,' wrote Emily from Mary's house in Essex. 'Six small Intellects continually on the march, and Mary, of course, is hatching a seventh child. I own I am glad I am not married, it is such a tiresome fatiguing life. Though as a visitor I delight in the children, yet I would not be so worn and worried as their mother is on any consideration. I think she fidgets too much about them, but a large family is a great standing fidget of itself, and I suppose one would be the same under the same circumstances.'

It was not the first time Emily had declared that she was glad she was not married, or that she was perfectly content in her single state and had no intention of changing it. She enjoyed the friendship of many prominent men, and rumour had from time to time matched her with several of them—even with Melbourne, after the death of his wife. But Emily laughed rumour away each time. She had once been in love, in her younger days. Not many people knew about her sentimental attachment to one of the sons of Spencer Perceval, the Prime Minister who was assassinated in 1812. Young Mr. Perceval was an indecisive young man, and he had not declared himself; it had caused her great unhappiness at the time. Emily never spoke of it. As she passed from her twenties into the thirties, her relations with men became more and more securely founded on the talent she possessed for friendship.

Rumour had also been busy with Fanny.

'How do Fanny and Edward Drummond go on?' wrote Pamela FitzGerald to Emily in 1819. 'I hope she still thinks him pleasant. Don't rob her of those comfortable illusions; any bulwark against bore is a blessing.'

Two years later she was writing again: 'Does Fanny still keep up "brother and sister" with Edward Drummond? I don't think even Fanny could do it. . . .'

Edward Drummond was Private Secretary to Sir Robert Peel, and a family connection through Mary. Fanny was apparently quite able to keep up 'brother and sister' with him, for she never showed any sign of deeper affection.

In spite of their predilection for the single state, Emily and Fanny took the greatest interest in the love affairs of their friends, and were not averse from putting a finger in a match-making pie themselves,

now and again.   All through their lives they were happy in the marital
happiness of others, and grieved whenever that happiness was broken
by death or misfortune.

So the years went on, pleasantly enough, in London and the country.
Besides his position at the Board of Trade, George held a minor
Admiralty appointment, that of Auditor of the Accounts at Greenwich
Hospital—an appointment carrying a salary and perquisites which
came to £600 a year in all.   He performed the routine duties of the
post with his usual punctiliousness; but an unexpected variation came
in 1828.   Like many seemingly unconnected events, this was to have
important results for Emily and Fanny, as well as for George.   During
the last three months of 1827, Thomas Austin, clerk to the Deputy
Treasurer of the Hospital, embezzled upwards of £3,000, and fled to
Ireland with his loot.   Emily wrote to Theresa Villiers from East Combe:

'The investigation of the whole business has been put into George's
hands, and there is so much that is disagreeable in it, besides confining
him to Greenwich, that he has been very low, poor fellow.   But like
a sensible man, he sent for me to keep up his spirits. . . .'

The investigation took a long time.   George had the use of apart-
ments at Greenwich, and Emily stayed there with him for some weeks,
coming to town for social engagements but always glad to return to
George.   He disliked living anywhere but in London, and was
impatient to be done with the wretched business of the dishonest clerk.
As the weeks went on, and he had to spend more and more time at
Greenwich, Emily suggested that they might let the house in Grosvenor
Street, and take Park Lodge, a nice little place that was vacant in
Greenwich Park, quite near to George's office.   George hated the idea
and said so.   But he could not afford to give up an appointment of
£600 a year, and he now realised that he would have to spend more
time than he had formerly done at Greenwich.   Emily quietly went
on making arrangements for taking the nice little place, buying furniture, and engaging servants.

The house was ready the following year.   After a last winter spent
in London, Emily and Fanny were delighted to leave Grosvenor Street
for good, and return to the country to live.   George had been made a
Commissioner of Greenwich Hospital, and was resigned to the new turn
his affairs had taken.   After all, Greenwich was not very far from London,
and so long as Emily and Fanny were content, George was ready to
admit that a house with a garden was an agreeable place to live in.

*   *   *   *   *

The garden at Park Lodge soon became a passion with Emily. She had green fingers. Her back ached and her hands were grimed, but there were soon hedges of sweet-peas, and beds of yellow carnations, roses and sweet-williams. George caught the fever, and bought his own watering-pot, so as not to be scolded for borrowing Emily's.

Fanny settled down again with great satisfaction to country life. She helped in the garden, read a great deal, visited her friends and invited them to the new home in return; and generally went on her own, self-contained way, aware that she was affectionately tolerated, but was not an essential part of the life of this brother and sister with whom she lived. She did not see so much of the Grosvenors now, but she wrote to them often. Then, it was not a difficult journey from Greenwich to East Combe, and Fanny paid frequent visits to the much-loved Eleanor. She and Emily also stepped into a Margate steamboat one day and took a trip to Broadstairs, to visit their sister, Caroline Vansittart, for a few days. Caroline had fourteen children, but she found time to arrange excursions to Ramsgate and Dover, and she took Fanny sailing to find a shell beach which was locally famous. Emily preferred dry land. She disliked being on the sea, as she always suffered from acute seasickness. If it was all the same to everybody, she said, she never wanted to leave dry land at any time, for any reason.

Back at Greenwich, they resumed a now familiar and comfortable pattern of life. They were both fond of sketching, and Emily had become very accomplished with both chalks and water-colours. Fanny freely admitted to having less talent, but that did not prevent her from getting a good deal of enjoyment out of drawing and colouring anything that took her fancy. They took a house in town for the winter, as the drives from Greenwich were becoming cold and dark, and George had many duties to attend to in London. Emily and Fanny divided their time between Greenwich, visits to friends and relations, and staying with George in town. They were with him in April, when the Reform Bill passed its second reading in the Lords and was at last carried. They were delighted at their party's success—though to Emily it seemed like a gigantic game of chess, with the advantage going first to one side, and then to the other.

That summer at Greenwich should have been perfect, with new plants coming along, and the established flowers blooming as never before. But the news of a glorious promotion was inflicted upon them on Epsom Race Day—the one day they had set apart for a holiday, with a visit to the races, and a whole afternoon later in that excellent little garden.

The news was that George had been appointed First Lord of the Admiralty. They would have to leave Greenwich and go back to live in London—for good. The day was not much of a holiday after that. They went to the races, as they had intended; but as for gardening, what was the good of cultivating flowers for other people's nosegays? The roses were all out, and the sweet-peas, and the orange trees. The whole garden looked lovely; but Emily sat on the verandah, crying, and George was nearly as low in spirits as she was. George was not one to allow the loss of a garden to depress him for long, however. The new appointment was a good one, and he was now assured of a retiring pension. He had been offered the appointment because of a reshuffle in the Cabinet—the result of an uproar over the Irish Church Bill.

'The Government is on the brink of dissolution,' wrote Charles Greville in his Journal on May 27th.

There was certainly turmoil in the Cabinet, several of its members resigning over the Appropriation clause in the Bill, which dealt with the surplus revenues of the Established Church in Ireland. In the resulting patch-up in the Cabinet there were some new appointments, the most unpopular being Lord Auckland's promotion.

'Though I like him personally,' Greville went on, 'it certainly does appear strange and objectionable. He has neither reputation nor political calibre to entitle him to such an elevation, and his want of urbanity and forbidding manner seem to render him peculiarly unfit for the post they have conferred on him.'

Six months later, Greville handsomely owned himself in the wrong, noting that 'Auckland turned out a very popular and, I believe, very good First Lord of the Admiralty. I have heard many praises and not one complaint of him.'

If George was aware that he had no outward graces to commend him to those who did not know him well, he showed no sign of it. Unperturbable as ever, he prepared to take up the appointment, though he knew that the Government was seething with internal troubles and might fall.

The months which followed were the most uncomfortable that Emily or Fanny had ever spent. Having parted with the Greenwich house, they prepared to move into the huge residential quarters of the Admiralty. But the state of the Government was so precarious that they could not make a definite migration until the political situation was clearer. They were not able to move back into the Grosvenor Street house, which had been sold. They had no home. Emily talked of setting up a tent under a hedge. They finally took a cottage on Ham Common, near Richmond, which belonged to an elderly relation, General Eden. Emily was in poor health; it was a very hot summer and she hated heat. It took quantities of steel draughts, together with the fresh air at Ham, to bring an improvement. She also had a new companion, a little black King Charles spaniel, still a puppy, whom she called Chance. It was pleasant walking on the Common, or in Richmond Park, with Chance. There were friends in the neighbourhood to call upon too; and one day there was a royal luncheon party and a visit to Hampton Court with the King, who was being entertained by the Earl of Albemarle at his house, not far away. Emily and Fanny liked King William, even though he was occasionally a little ridiculous. He insisted on showing them every picture in the Palace at Hampton himself, and telling a story about each—generally an improper story.

A good deal of their time was occupied in writing letters and sending family news to relations and connections. Emily was always relaxed and happy with a pen in her hand. She had sometimes thought of writing a novel, and now that she had so much time to spare she began to draft out a plot and work on the first chapters. Theresa Lister★ was writing a novel; it was fun to exchange comments and compare notes.

She did not see much of George. Emily had lost both his society and the garden at Greenwich, the two charms of her life, as she called them. George had begun his new duties as soon as possible, as was his wont. He had already made the First Lord's accustomed tour of the Ports, and was calmly continuing with other Admiralty business, in spite of the chaotic political situation. He came down to Ham Common to see them whenever he could, but he had very little time; when he had finished his long and strenuous day at the Admiralty he generally had to go on to the House. The Whigs were divided within their own party. Several Ministers had resigned, and gossip had it that there were going to be changes.

It was at this time that the first possibility—the incredible, appalling impossibility—of India came to the two sisters. In October, 1834, Emily wrote to Theresa:

'There was a great *sough* of India for about a fortnight, but I always

★ Theresa Villiers had married Thomas Henry Lister in 1830.

said it was too bad to be true, which is a dangerous assertion to make in most cases; it only hastens the catastrophe. But this was such an extreme case, such a horrible supposition, that there was nothing for it but to bully it; and the danger is over now. Botany Bay would be a joke to it. *There* is a decent climate to begin with, and the fun of a little felony first. But to be sent to Calcutta for no cause at all! At all events, I should hardly have got there before George got home again, for I should have walked across the country to join him, if I had gone at all. I think I see myself going into a ship for five months! I would not do it for £1,000 a day. . . .'

At the end of the summer, Emily and Fanny left Ham Common and returned to London. They surveyed the inconvenient Admiralty kitchens, and wondered how they were going to furnish the immense reception rooms. But they could not do very much, for the Government was rocking and was likely to fall. Events moved fast. The Whigs went out of office. Emily and Fanny were now without a permanent home; their household goods and furniture were packed and stored. They visited their sisters and stayed with their friends, and watched the statesmen and politicians playing general post.

Sir Robert Peel had formed a Tory government, but it did not last long. By April, 1835, Peel was forced to resign, and Melbourne again became Prime Minister. The upheavals of the previous months had had a sobering effect on the Whigs. Lord Melbourne began his second Administration with a reshuffled pack of Ministers, and he proceeded to make new appointments. He cancelled the Tory nominee in India, Lord Heytesbury, and offered the Governor-Generalship to Lord Auckland.

*   *   *   *   *

'I never knew before *really* what it was to have no time,' Emily wrote to Pamela Campbell. 'You cannot think what a whirl and entanglement buying and measuring and trying-on makes in one's brain. Poor Goliath himself would have been obliged to lie down and rest if he had tried on six pairs of stays consecutively. . . .

'It is so irritating to want so many things, and such cold articles. A cargo of large fans; a *silver* busk because all steel busks become rusty and spoil the stays; nightdresses with short sleeves, and net nightcaps, because muslin is too hot. Then such anomalies—quantities of flannel which I never wear at all in this cool climate, but which we are to wear at night there, because the creatures who are pulling all night at the Punkahs sometimes fall asleep. . . . Then they wake and begin pulling away with such fresh vigour that you catch your death with a sudden chill. . . .'

It relieved her to write to Pam of these absurd details; it cushioned the deep-seated dread of the inevitable partings which lay ahead. The days fled by. Fanny went down to East Combe to stay with Eleanor and Emily followed in September, to say good-bye and bring Fanny back with her. It was a painful farewell. Eleanor had been both mother and sister to them and they loved her with the tenderest affection. When, under God's providence, would they all meet again?

The following day they travelled down to Portsmouth with George and William Osborne, to look at the *Jupiter*, the vessel which was to carry them to India. William, their sister Charlotte's son, had secured the position of Military Secretary to his uncle; he had already been in India with his regiment, the 16th Lancers, and was glad to return to a life where there would be plenty of opportunity of hunting tiger and wild boar. William was now thirty; a nonchalant young man with a taste for practical jokes.

The *Jupiter*, Emily observed, was as comfortable as a ship could be, no doubt. Its master, Captain Grey, escorted the party over the vessel, which was a tall-masted frigate that had been converted into a troopship, with special quarters furbished up for the new Governor-General and his sisters. Had Emily liked ships, she would have liked this one. But there was a smell of new paint and tar which made her feel very sick. It was not an auspicious omen. Fanny was unaffected by the smell. She and William examined everything with alert interest. If this was to be their home for the next five months, Fanny wanted to have a good look at it.

They returned to London to make their last arrangements for departure, and it was now that Emily nearly gave way to despair. She felt as if she could cut somebody's throat quite through. It did not matter whose throat—it would be a sort of savage relief. The whole business was so much worse than she had expected, and that was saying a great deal.

A letter from Lord Melbourne brought an added bitterness. She realised afresh, as she had realised from the beginning, that it was not only her family and intimates she was going to miss, but also those friends of distinction and high intelligence whom she had been used to meet in the political and social worlds. Melbourne wrote:

'My Mother always used to say that I was very selfish, both Boy and Man, and I believe she was right—at least I know that I am always anxious to escape from anything of a painful nature, and find every excuse for doing so. Very few events could be more painful to me than your going, and therefore I am not unwilling to avoid wishing you good-bye. Then God bless you—as to health, let us hope for the best. The climate of the East Indies very often re-establishes it.

I send you a Milton, which I have had a long time, and often read in. I shall be most anxious to hear from you and promise to write. Adieu.

Yours,

MELBOURNE.'

There was also a letter from the King, which Emily liked because of the beautiful handwriting. William the Fourth said the expected polite things about Lord Auckland, but he also complimented Emily and Fanny for not consenting to be separated from their brother by the fear of the climate or the remoteness of the destination. 'So affectionate a brother,' continued his Majesty, 'deserves the devotion he meets with.'

The last few days in London were full of official farewell visits and other annoyances. Fanny went on with her packing, and Emily was in a fair way to going quietly and genteelly mad. Her only comfort was that if she had been preparing to see George off instead of sailing with him, how very much worse it would have been.

They were ready to leave at last. On September 30th they travelled down to Portsmouth and put up at an inn, where they had to endure the usual drawback of inn beds—insects of no pleasing description. To add to Emily's irritation, there was a tribe of Sir Johns and Sir Henrys, friends of George's, who kept bursting in with offers of dinners, which were declined. The wind was in the wrong quarter, dead against them, so there was no chance of departing at once. They crossed over to Ryde, in the hope of finding a cleaner and quieter inn, and settled down to wait for a fair wind. Fanny and William Osborne went out sailing in a small boat. Fanny wanted to test her seaworthiness. She had already made up her mind that she must grow to like what she had to endure. Emily walked on the quay, wishing they were away, longing to stay.

On Saturday, October 3rd, the wind changed, and Captain Grey decided to set sail. Fanny, Emily, George and William embarked, together with Dr. Drummond, the physician officially provided for the voyage. They also took with them their six personal servants, all of whom were to become very much part of their lives in India. George's valet, Mars, was a French paragon of correctness; he was assisted by a second attendant, Giles, a wiry, practical man. Emily's English maid, Wright, sedately efficient, got on surprisingly well with the half-Portuguese, half-native *ayah*, Rosina, also engaged to wait on the senior Miss Eden. Fanny had brought her own maid, Jones, whose rosy Englishness could bring the most outlandish situation down to normal, as Fanny was to find on many occasions. The servants' party was completed by a French negro chef, St. Cloup, a temperamental genius of a cook.

And, of course, there was Chance, Emily's spaniel. All the Edens were devoted to animals; but Chance was different from any dog that had ever been in the family before. He was Emily's constant companion, and appeared to take an almost human interest in what went on around him. William Osborne's half-dozen greyhounds, which he had brought with him for hunting, were likeable enough, but could not compare with Chance.

Besides the Governor-General's party, there was a troop of soldiers on board, bound for Calcutta. The holds of the ship were full of provisions, live as well as packed. Sheep, pigs and poultry—they all had to be carried, so that the travellers could have fresh meat on the long, uncertain voyage.

The sails were set, the wind blew fair, and the *Jupiter* moved away from the quayside, out of the harbour, and presently into the open sea.

The voyage to India had begun.

2

THE VOYAGE

IT may have been that trial sail with William at Portsmouth, or a naturally strong stomach, but Fanny soon had the satisfaction of finding out that she was a good sailor. From the very first day on board she was able to be her naturally active self, walking with William on the deck or playing chess with him, reading and writing, playing with Chance or with the greyhounds. When she wanted more sedentary occupation she sat working at her wool embroidery, a horse and rider stitched on fine canvas, which was to be a horse-cloth.

The one thing that worried her was something she had not expected; incessant noise in her cabin. For the first three nights she was kept awake by the continuous creaking of the bulkheads. Here was an affliction which it would be difficult to get used to, for she had always detested noise.

George, detached and philosophical about his comforts or lack of them, had brought Hindustani grammar-books, and set himself regular hours of study each day. Beyond occasional giddiness when the ship rolled, he, too, discovered that he had good sea-legs, and he soon established a routine of work designed to catch his nephew in its net occasionally—without much success. William considered he had as much Hindustani as was necessary for the present. He also declared that he was seasick. It was a special and particular form of seasickness which, alas, took the contrary and alarming line of extreme hunger. So it was meritorious in him to struggle against the complaint by going down to the cockpit to dine with the midshipmen at twelve, coming up to have a few mouthfuls with his aunts at one, joining Captain Grey at luncheon at two, and picking a bit with the officers at three in order to be tolerably well for dinner at six.

One could never do anything with William. He got his own way by the simple method of making people laugh. Always sure of himself, always self-possessed, he hid the real abilities which he possessed behind a devil-may-care manner which often verged on impudence.

Fanny laughed with him and at him. He was only a few years younger than herself, and his lively high spirits kept her amused. In spite of the difference in their temperaments, they both had a streak of adventurous fun which made them natural companions. With his Aunt Emily, William kept up a jocular but wary relationship. His continual jokes were never particularly subtle, and there were times when he annoyed Emily as much as he had done on the occasion of the shuttlecock twenty years before. William at thirty was as liable to infuriate her as William at ten, and well he knew it. He might invent a peculiar brand of seasickness for himself and go in for outrageous antics under cover of this special malady, but he did not poke fun at Emily's misery during the ten days across the ocean to Funchal.

It was genuine misery. Those first days of the voyage were as terrible as Emily had feared. She was seasick for hours at a time, unable to eat anything except a little arrowroot. The *Jupiter* turned out to be a rolling, heaving ship; if Emily could have scuttled her or blown her out of the water, she would have done so and swum home.

Nobody could do anything to help, however much they tried. Rosina, the *ayah*, slept on the floor of Emily's cabin, wrapped in a heap of Indian shawls, with her black arms, covered with bracelets, crossed over her head. Chance was in and out of the cabin, frisking with the midshipmen, chasing a rabbit which they had got out from its hutch for his amusement. Emily sipped her arrowroot, and schooled herself to wait through the long hours of wretchedness.

The *Jupiter* made Madeira on Tuesday, October 13th, and the Governor-General's party landed for several days' stay—Emily certain that she would never be brought aboard again except by a guard of marines.

They were the guests of a Mr. Stothard, a wealthy wine merchant who had a large house in Funchal. George had been told by the London half of Mr. Stothard's firm to make that gentleman's house his headquarters in Funchal, and the wine merchant calmly accepted the fact that he had four personages, a physician, a ship's captain, six servants and a dog quartered on him without warning.

Fanny and Emily found Madeira as delightful as a place out of a book of travels. Everything *looked* tropical. Funchal was a paradise of gardens full of palms and banana trees, and orange trees heavy with fruit. Dusky, laughing women who might have come out of a Murillo picture sat plaiting their hair by the roadside, or walked barefoot between the trees. They made an entrancing picture to Fanny and Emily.

Mr. Stothard's hospitality was thoughtful as well as open-handed.

He provided the party with palanquins and ponies to take them up the narrow streets of the almost perpendicular town, streets which would not admit a carriage. And one day they rode for three miles into the hills, between hedges of fuchsia and myrtle and great pink cactus flowers. It was like a hot-house at home in England, only on a grand scale.

They enjoyed everything, and were more than sorry when the short stay was over. Mr. Stothard had been a perfect host; Emily hoped everybody would buy his wine. Fanny would have given a great deal to be able to stay in Funchal, but, as usual, made terms with the inevitable, and re-embarked on the *Jupiter* without repining.

On Friday, with the fair island behind them, they were once more under way, their course set for Rio de Janeiro.

Fanny had never before realised the vast monotony of the sea. Her problem was to keep herself occupied. William sometimes came along for a game of chess, when he was not larking with the older midshipmen, who could entice him down to their quarters by holding up a lighted cigar from the farthest point of the ship. George was immersed for hours in his Hindustani grammar. Fanny did not intrude unnecessarily on her sister; she made no demands on Emily for anything more than the normal, taken-for-granted relationship which had always existed between them.

For real friendship Fanny turned to her letter-writing. These were to be letter-journals, she told Eleanor Grosvenor. All the time she was away from England, she would write of her life in daily letters, sending them home whenever the opportunity offered. Eleanor might keep them, if she wished. One day, perhaps, they would sit together once more, and talk and laugh at these ancient traveller's tales.

By the end of October, they were within ten degrees of the Equator, with the thermometer at eighty in the coolest period of the twenty-four hours. The heat, as well as the perpetual ship-noises, made sleep nearly impossible. The creaking of the bulkheads and staircases grew so intolerable at last that Captain Grey was forced into taking some active measures, for no two people could hear each other speak in the same cabin. The carpenters were sent up to do what they could to lessen the noises, which they managed to bring down to a more endurable level.

Emily's seasickness had abated since they left Madeira, and she was able to dine with the others on most days. But she found it a detestable life. She could not read or write for five minutes without feeling giddy, and when the ship rolled, was forced to remain completely idle. She wondered whether George would have come if he had known the full extent of the horrors of the voyage. She asked him constantly: "Do you give it up?" hoping that he would say "Yes" and let them go home again.

But George could not and would not give up the Governor-General-ship before it had even begun. Emily was perfectly aware that it gave her great relief to pour out complaints in unmeasured language to Theresa or Pamela. The *Jupiter* was making an uncommonly prosperous voyage, and she knew that she had ten times as many comforts as most people had at sea.

They crossed the Line on the evening of Friday, November 13th. The Governor-General's party went up on deck to see the festivities, which had been in preparation for days.

Amphitrite, a very tall sailor, looked handsome in one of Wright's gowns and Emily's caps. Another sailor, dressed as Neptune, made a speech to George and presented Emily and Fanny with two white pigeons. The sisters thanked the men—then got out of the way as fast as they could before the shaving and ducking began. They did not find it amusing to watch the victims of this sport being tossed into a water-filled sail and half-drowned, or nearly choked with pitch, or shaved with a razor which was as jagged as a sharp saw. They thought it a savage process, and wondered Captain Grey did not stop it. Once the ceremonies were over, the ship's company resumed their normal duties, and William Osborne began to fall into deep fits of boredom. George, in his bland, detached way, continued in the private routine of study and leisure which he had set himself. The only time he fidgeted was when the wind fell and the ship could not make its seven knots.

The heat, though it brought discomfort, was not the fiery furnace they had always supposed it to be. On the day when they should have been actually under the sun, standing in their own shadow, Fanny and Emily were glad of warm gowns.

'Never think of pitying the naked negro panting at the Line,' wrote Emily to her eldest sister. 'If he pants, it must be for some clothes.'

She found tropical skies drab-coloured, with a dirty yellow look towards sunset; and as for thunder and lightning, she would be ashamed if she could not make a better storm out of a sheet of tin and a tallow candle. What astonished Emily most about the heat at the Equator was her sister's excellent health and vitality in such a

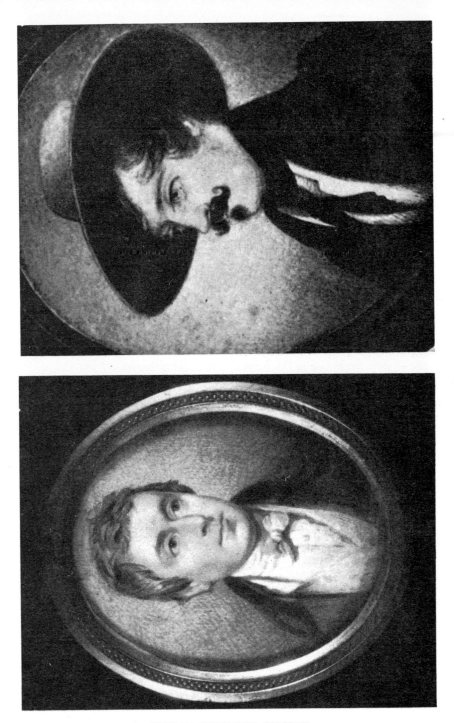

WILLIAM GODOLPHIN OSBORNE
GEORGE EDEN, 2ND BARON AUCKLAND, CREATED EARL OF AUCKLAND

EMILY EDEN
From a chalk drawing by [H. B. Zinder?]

temperature. Fanny had never been robust as a child, and her quick-silver nature had often responded with alarming results to extremes of weather at home. Now, when Emily lay writing on a hard couch in a cabin of the rolling ship, Fanny would be out in the open, watching the crew of 250 men at their exercises. There she would stand, or follow them at a short distance, while the sailors dragged ropes, chains and blocks, and the seniors screamed orders, and the petty officers blew whistles.

William could find no such interest in the daily round of a ship's crew. He had got tired of horse-play with the midshipmen, and was bored with everything else. He hated life at sea, and did not mind saying so on every suitable and unsuitable occasion.

On Monday, November 16th, they discovered America. They had been hunting about for it all the previous day, but the weather was hazy, and they could not see the land. When they at last sailed into the harbour at Rio, they were enchanted by the prospect. Spread before them was a beautiful panorama of wooded, rocky, mountainous islets—scores of them, as many as there were days in the year.

The Governor-General and his sisters were received by the Admiral of the station, Sir Graham Eden Hamond. He was their father's godson, and so was full of civilities for personal as well as for official reasons.

There was no possibility of their sleeping ashore. Rio had not a single hotel, and the Admiral had to tell them regretfully that mosquitoes and all sorts of vermin would make the inns impossible. The only thing to do was to use the *Jupiter* as their hotel; and as a ship at anchor was very different from a ship at sea, they decided it would serve very well. George had a barge of his own on board, independent of the captain's gig, so Fanny and Emily were able to come and go as they pleased. The harbour was full of shipping, and the English, French and Brazilian admirals all hoisted Lord Auckland's flag. Then they saluted and the *Jupiter* replied, until Fanny and Emily were nearly deafened. They were thankful to get into the town with George, after he had discharged his courtesy visits.

It was odd, reflected Emily, how short a time surprise lasted. Here they were, in a South American town where the streets swarmed with slaves wearing the same quantity of clothes that Adam wore when he left Paradise, and yet the sight of all these undressed creatures was not at all startling after the first moment. They might have come out of the pictures in a book.

Emily and Fanny liked Rio. They found it very dirty, but much more amusing than Funchal; the slaves made such cheerful hallooing noises as they dragged the carts about, or carried loads on their heads. The one drawback was the excessive hospitality pressed upon the visitors. The Admiral gave a ball for them—the last thing they wanted, in that heat. Still, endless balls lay ahead in Calcutta, so they decided it was as well to get used to them.

A single day was saved from the general wreck, one of those days which made up for the incessant strain of appearing to enjoy the heavy gaieties. They avoided all official hosts, and took the barge to a quiet little bay further down the coast. George had ordered horses, and Captain Grey took the four of them—Fanny, Emily, William and George himself—on a ride that he had known in former times.

Up, up into the high mountains they rode, and felt that Nature could do no more in the way of beauty. Clouds, mountains, trees, butterflies, waterfalls—such a combination! They sometimes stopped to walk, and sometimes to sit and sketch. Time flowed along in contented silence—but they had to turn their horses to Rio again, before the dusk descended. It was a day Fanny and Emily would always remember; a cool place in the mind to which they could return in the brassy heat which lay in wait for them in India.

The *Jupiter* left Rio in fine weather on Saturday, November 21st, and made eighty miles the first day. The winds were fair, and the going steady, but in the middle of the following week they ran into a heavy swell, and two days later a gale blew up. Within a few hours it had whipped the sea into a churning mass, carried away two of the ship's sails, and filled the cabins with water.

Fanny disliked the turmoil, but she was not afraid, and held on to her cot and the furnishings of her cabin. Emily was extremely wretched. She had been sick for days, but was so tired of the roaring round her that on the third day of the storm she got up, put on a dressing-gown, and rolled into George's cabin. By a lucky combination of lurches she landed on one end of his sofa, and George tucked himself up on the other end. Then the ship took one of her deepest rolls. Two heavy boxes broke from their lashings and began dancing about among George's boots and shoes. The spar that kept his books in against the wall gave way, and the volumes poured out on the floor. George made a grab at the bell to summon Mars, and in a few moments the valet came in—sitting down, which was the only way of moving that day.

"*Encore un déménagement!*" he said, as he tried to pick up the books. "*Eh bien! C'est une manière de voyager, mais si c'est la bonne . . . ?*"

The next roll of the ship brought William Osborne sliding in—also sitting—and saying: "More fun! No dinner today. That last lurch sent the cook into the sheep-pen, and the sheep are too frightened to help him out."

Fanny joined the party in George's cabin for dinner; a dish of macaroni, put on the floor, like everything else, and served, with his usual dignity, by the seated Mars.

The gale turned out to be the one black patch of the voyage. By the time they had been three weeks out of Rio, they had had great varieties of weather, calms and fine sailing. When the winds were fair, the *Jupiter* went flying along as steady as a church. There was plenty of entertainment on board. The midshipmen made a little theatre on deck, and acted several plays, including the serious drama, *Ella Rosenburg*. This would have been very affecting, if the heroine's cap with attached oakum plaits had not kept falling off, much to 'Ella's' annoyance.

Some of the sailors could sing old English glees, which Fanny and Emily loved to listen to as the men sat on the long evening watch. One night Emily asked for *Home, Sweet Home*, but she did not try that again—it was playing with edged tools. Better to listen to them telling stories to each other, or to watch them dancing their nautical reels to the music of 'young Paganini,' the ship's fiddler.

Not a single vessel had passed them on the sea; they had not even seen a sail in the far distance. Were they only a few days from Africa? Fanny did not believe it. She was sure the ship's chronometer had gone wrong, and offered Captain Grey the loan of her little Swiss watch, the size of a shilling. Captain Grey looked half-affronted, but acknowledged the little joke.

William was living in a state of farcical despair. He went about insulting all the sailors with his horror of the ship, and gravely consulted Dr. Drummond about his health. Dr. Drummond, who was rather solemn, said he could not see exactly what was the matter.

"Matter enough!" said William. "I've got the Jupiters. I'm a creak, Doctor, nothing but a creak. Listen to my neck when I turn it!"

There were times, thought Fanny, when she felt she was actually creaking herself.

Africa came in sight on December 14th. Fanny took her first view of it at five o'clock in the morning; it looked very much like the Cape of Good Hope on a map. When they got nearer, Table Mountain, with other hills ranged beside it, sharpened into a wall behind the town —rugged and handsome.

At the foot of the mountain Capetown spread out, white and clean, very Dutch-like. Emily had now come on deck, and she said she believed this clean look to be a 'deceptious appearance'—in which she turned out to be right.

The *Jupiter* had been twenty-three days coming from Rio, the usual length of the passage. In spite of the gales and the tossings about, the whole party found themselves in astonishingly good health. The sea air had helped Fanny's recurrent headaches, and Emily, subject to agues and many other minor ailments, declared herself very well. George had grown fatter.

They took a house for the few days they expected to stay in the port, and after putting some books and writing cases on the tables, tried to make it as much like a Broadstairs or Tunbridge Wells house as possible. But it was not like Broadstairs or Tunbridge Wells. There was a great deal of negro jabber going on under the windows, and on the first night or two they were much devoured by every species of small creature. They saw cockroaches on the walls, and other, horrider insects came out in the night and made sleep impossible. Captain Grey sent them brass bedsteads from the *Jupiter*, so *that* inconvenience did not occur again.

In spite of the devastating heat, they paid official calls with George. It grew cooler in the late afternoon, and then they began to enjoy the Cape. They went for long drives up-country, passing tracts of dense shrub aflame with yellow flowers. Fanny would have liked to stay for days, to sketch the hills rising suddenly from the plains, and the negroes in sugar-loaf hats driving their teams of twenty oxen in the long, low Cape wagons.

The time passed all too quickly. They drove to Constantia to pick out the wine they were to take with them. George bought several Cape horses, which were better than Arab horses for ladies' riding, and persuaded Captain Grey to find room for four of them in the *Jupiter*.

Both Fanny and Emily now dreaded the prospect of the next stage of the voyage: the unbroken passage from Capetown to Calcutta, which might take anything from twelve to fourteen weeks. The few acquaintances they had made at the Cape suddenly seemed like old friends. And when again would they be able to enjoy an abundance of apricots, strawberries, peas and new potatoes?

They wrote ten letters apiece, to be carried by the *Liverpool*, homeward bound from Capetown. Then, after a stay on land which had lasted a week, they embarked once more on the ship and turned their faces towards India.

★　　★　　★　　★　　★

The next three weeks were the longest Fanny had ever known. No more storms burst upon them, but the heat was growing stronger, especially at night. Fanny sat on the lee-side of the ship with Emily; all the doors and windows around them were open, but nothing would induce a draught to blow through. They had to make up their minds that this temperature was what they would have to endure in Calcutta.

Then came a sudden, unlooked-for accident; an 'adventure' as Emily called it, which mercifully stopped short of tragedy. On January 26th, as they were once again nearing the Line, a squall swooped out of the cloudless blue and carried away the ship's main-top mast. It was a fine day, with no wind. But, as so often happened near the Line, there was squally wind in the upper atmosphere.

Fanny and Emily were coming away from breakfast, when they heard a tremendous crash. They ran up to the deck, which they found heaving with a mass of collapsed ropes and canvas.

There was a cry of "Man overboard!" which put everybody into a fever. But it was only a hat; the owner was caught in one of the lower sails, and escaped with stunning and bruising. He was reckoned fortunate, for all the officers who had ever seen a similar accident with a topmast said they had never known it without great loss of life and serious wounds.

Fanny and Emily were now able to watch a supreme example of Captain Grey's seamanship. The mast was four feet in circumference where it had given way, and it was snapped off almost as clean as if it had been cut with a knife. Captain Grey's presence of mind was striking. Within two minutes he had given the order: "All hands clear wreck," which brought every human being up from below. Each man was immediately in his place working away at disentangling ropes and furling sails. Within five hours everything was in its place and the mast mended. The sails were set once more, and the *Jupiter* continued on her way.

January came to an end; the last weeks of the voyage stretched wearily ahead. They had hoped to reach Calcutta by the middle of February, but a check came as they neared the Line once more. The ship had been within a hundred miles of the Line for days, but had not been able to cross it.

They tacked about, waiting for a favourable wind, averaging a bare thirty miles a day. It was tantalising to lose the precious time, for the extreme hot weather began in Calcutta in the middle of March, and George was anxious that they should have two or three cool weeks to break them in to the climate. If a fair breeze came, they might reach Calcutta within ten days; but some of the ship's officers gloomily forecast a further month on the water.

The sea looked like a plate of silver that had been cleaned by a remarkably good under-butler. And such heat! The thermometer at eighty-eight under the awning, with the nights as hot as the days. The officers had come to an end of their fresh meat, and the midshipmen to an end of their fresh clothes; the freehold of two dirty shirts for one clean one was offered and refused. When it grew dusk, the young men would appear in their hot blue uniforms, white trousers having become so scarce.

Fanny and Emily hardly knew how to get through the still, oppressive days. They could not read or sew; their only relief was in writing letters home. If Emily wrote to Lady Bucks, Fanny's letter would be addressed to Robert, or Caroline or Louisa. Family letters were passed round at home, so it did not matter greatly who gave an account of their days. Emily did not trouble to brighten the record. They all knew that she was prone to vent surface grumbles and tempers when she felt like it; and on these calm-locked days she seemed to feel *scrapey* all day long.

'We tack about first to the east and then to the west,' she wrote, 'trying to screw a little northing out of them—like people who can't get to sleep, and try first one side to lie on, and then the other.'

Fanny sat alone writing to Eleanor Grosvenor. She could forget the tedium and the discomfort with this friend; her pen glanced and sparkled, lightly skimming the boredom, the clammy heat, the sense of solitariness which sometimes came upon her. Fanny and Eleanor could talk together on paper as easily as they had gossiped when they had walked in the flagged, flower-bright garden at Greenwich, or toasted themselves in front of the fire in Eleanor's London morning-parlour.

The sheets of paper grew into packages, ready to be addressed and sent over to any homeward-bound brig that might come in sight. But when would that be? Emily was for sticking a letter in a bottle; at least their friends would know where to look for them!

At last, at long last, they woke one morning to find a jungle in sight. The date was March 2nd, and they had been seventy-two days out of sight of land. Every moment was interesting now. Before the end of the afternoon there were steamers in sight, not only coming to tow them to Calcutta, but bringing the *Zenobia* which was to take their letters to England. Best of all, one of the steamers would be bringing them letters, some of which had been waiting for them since November, having come by the overland mail. The *Jupiter* had been in telegraphic communication with Calcutta all day, and this was the one piece of news which mattered most. The pilot was already on board. He told them that they had been given up for lost, they were so much overdue. They hardly listened; the steamers were coming near.

Fanny and Emily never forgot the delight, the heart-aching joy of seeing the parcels of letters come out of the *dak* boat. There was a package for Fanny, and ten letters for Emily. She wrote home later:
'I locked my cabin door, flumped myself down on the bed, and absolutely wallowed in my letters like a pig.'

Besides the mail from England, there was a letter from a Mrs. Robertson at Calcutta, who said that Emily had been very kind to her, playing cat's-cradle with her many years before in an English country-house. Emily and Fanny were touched. It would be pleasant to find someone disposed to be kind in a land of strangers. Emily decided that for the future she would play at cat's-cradle with all the little girls she met.

Another steamer arrived to assist the *Jupiter*. There was also the *Soonamookie*, the yacht which the Governor-General would use for his term of office. It was manned by Hindus in splendid dresses, and brought one of the aides-de-camp who had been attached to the acting Governor-General, Sir Charles Metcalfe. With him was Captain Byrne, who was formally in charge of the establishment at Government House.

Captain Byrne was an official-looking man with impeccable manners. Emily and Fanny looked at him with interest, as he would be one of their companions for the next five years. They neither liked nor disliked him at first sight; he made no great impression on them either way. They could not know, as they all stood bowing and making polite conversation, that they would spend many hours of those five years trying to outmanoeuvre and outwit this pattern of pomposity and correct behaviour.

The steamers began to tow the *Jupiter* up the river. Captain Grey had set his heart on landing them at Calcutta, so George did not board the yacht. They made good progress on that and the following day. On March 4th, however, there came a check. One of the steamers towing them had to swerve to avoid a brig at anchor; she was caught in an eddy, and drove the *Jupiter* and the other steamer aground. The *Soonamookie*, which was being towed astern, ran against the *Jupiter* and broke some of her railings. It was quite a collision.

After two hours of delay they were obliged to take to the steamer and give up the *Jupiter*. It was the greatest mortification to all parties, especially to Captain Grey, and to the officers and midshipmen, who had volunteered to man the barge and row the Governor-General and his sisters ashore. But there was no help for it. George and William got into full dress, and Fanny and Emily changed into their best gowns. It was difficult to look smart and keep a composed demeanour in such heat, but they must try. They gave presents to the quarter-masters and coxswains, and thanked all the sailors in general who had been so kind on the voyage. The steamer seemed cramped, and even noisier than the sailing vessel had been. The last part of the voyage was made against the tide. There were no arm-chairs or sofas on board, so they stood by the rail, or sat on hard chairs; and at last came in sight of the roofs and trees of Calcutta.

It was Emily's birthday. She was thirty-nine. Nobody, she reflected, knew or cared about it except herself, who would rather be a year younger each time than a year older. Surely that would be a worthy reward for each year passed in this place?

The steamer came to a slow stop in the harbour. At the landing-stage, squares of troops stood at attention. There were waiting carriages, groups of officers and officials, impressive uniforms. George was nervous, but, as usual, outwardly calm. Accompanied by William, Captain Byrne, and an aide-de-camp, he went on shore. Fanny and Emily followed, hoping that they would soon be bundled off in one of the carriages; but they had to wait until George had inspected his guard of honour and walked down the lines of troops.

It was over at last: the saluting, the sharp noise of arms being presented, the unsmiling bows and courtesies of these soldiers and civilians.

The arrival

Fanny and Emily, escorted to the carriage behind George, felt indeed that they were strangers in a strange land. The *Jupiter* lay behind them, homelike and friendly, in spite of her misdemeanours. Before them was a shimmering haze which was the air they would henceforth have to breathe; through it they could see the gleam of white buildings, reflecting the heat. This was what must become the known, the familiar.

They had arrived in India.

3

CALCUTTA

IT was like something out of the Arabian Nights. So thought Fanny.
She had never before seen anything so magnificent as her first sight
of Government House in the moonlight, its halls illuminated, the
steps of the portico crowded with turbaned attendants in white muslin
dresses.

Eighty people had been invited to dine with them, but the formal
reception was omitted owing to the lateness of the hour, and they
thankfully retired before midnight.

Everyone in the Governor-General's party had a separate suite of
rooms. Fanny and Emily were in opposite wings. Fanny was a
little alarmed at the first sight of her own boudoir. It was, she
reckoned, very much the size of the Picture Gallery at Grosvenor
House. Three large windows at one side overlooked the city, and
three more at the other side gave a view of the great gate and entrance
to the house. At one end, sets of folding doors opened into the bedroom and bathroom, and at the opposite end three more doors led to
the dressing-room and passage.

It took her some days to get used to being so far away from Emily.
When Fanny went to pay her sister a visit in the evening, she was in

peril of stepping upon the living bales of muslin which were sleeping about the galleries. It was just as if they were all acting in a long opera, Fanny decided. Only it was an opera which promised to go on for five years . . .

Within two days, each had an establishment of servants. Emily, being the senior sister, had rather more than Fanny. Her personal attendant was a kindly *kitmutgar* who spoke English—an advantage he had over the other servants. He and four more glided behind her whenever she moved from one room to another; and there was a sentry at her dressing-room door who presented arms whenever she went to fetch her pocket-handkerchief or her keys. Then there was a tailor with a long beard, who mended her habit-shirts and her petticoats; an extra *ayah* to assist Wright and Rosina as dressers, and a very old woman who seemed to be a personal under-housemaid. Besides these there were two bearers with a sedan-chair at the bottom of the stair-case, in case she should be too idle to walk.

Fanny could never become accustomed to being followed about everywhere by two or three bearers, though she was glad that Jones's dignity was enhanced by a new assistant in the form of an *ayah*, Myra. There were also three outriders whom she shared with Emily, to escort them on excursions.

George's retinue was, of course, far more formidable than theirs. He was unable to stir without a tail of fifteen joints after him. William, too, had a respectable supply, though he reduced it to three when he went out alone. When he accompanied his uncle to the Council Chamber, he had to be careful to collect his full number, or Captain Byrne would have had something to say.

What Fanny and Emily liked best was when they all met by accident, with their entire tails on.

They went to church in state on the Sunday following their arrival, driving with George in a carriage with five guards galloping by the side. Three velvet chairs had been placed in the middle of the cathedral aisle, with an open railing round them and a space railed off behind for the aides-de-camp. All the pews were made with open railings, and the ladies of Calcutta were able to get a good view of the Governor-General's sisters—the first hostesses to appear at Government House since Lady William Bentinck, two years before. Metcalfe, the provisional Governor-General, had not been married; unofficial wives did not count.

Fanny and Emily sat on either side of George, hoping they looked

29

cool and elegant, though they did not feel so. They were quite aware of the stares; and they were doing a little quiet scrutinising on their own account. Some of the ladies had come without bonnets, and all fanned themselves unceasingly with large feather fans. Otherwise it was very much like an English church, with a fashionable congregation and the service very well chanted.

On the following morning they had a great many visitors at Government House. The aides-de-camp handed in the ladies and gave them chairs, and in due time handed them out again. The visits were not of long duration, though they seemed to last hours while they were in progress. Fanny and Emily hoped their callers would not compare notes as to what had been said, for some of Emily's topics had had to serve many times over, and Fanny had run out of small talk at a very early stage of the reception.

George held his first levee the next day. He received seven hundred gentlemen, and was perfectly ready to go on in the afternoon to the Chowringee—the Regent's Park of Calcutta—to leave cards on Sir Henry Fane, the Commander-in-Chief of the garrison. Sir Henry was giving a ball in their honour that evening, so they did not remain; they drove back immediately to dine and to dress for their first official appearance at a social event.

Wright and Jones had been unpacking and pressing gowns all day. Emily was in some anxiety over her *toilette*. Would her best blonde come out of the box quite yellow, and patterned by the cockroaches? That was what often happened to gowns which had suffered a long sea-voyage. But the fine laces and muslins which Wright lifted carefully out of the tin-lined boxes were quite fresh; they had been well packed in London. It was a great relief.

She and Fanny were ready by ten o'clock. They joined George and William in the carriage, and almost at once found themselves in the centre of an immense procession of aides-de-camp, servants and guards, with ten men running before the carriage holding flaming torches aloft.

The ball, when they got there, was much like a London ball; but the uniforms made it look more dressed, and there was more space for dancing than there would have been in a London ballroom. The couples whirled away as if they were not living in a furnace-like temperature; and instead of resting between the dances, which would have been the sensible thing to do, they walked round and round the room.

There seemed to be few unmarried young ladies, Emily noticed, though there were several young brides. Everyone appeared to dance on to a most respectable old age; mothers of grown-up sons and daughters never missed a quadrille or waltz. And what pains they had taken with their gowns! Emily was impressed as well as amused. She could see that here in India there was no reason for a woman to become a dowager. Not all the men were young, either. It could not be such a bad climate, or the old gentlemen who were figuring away on the floor would not be so active.

She herself, and Fanny, and George had all had enough by midnight. William stayed on to represent them, with the utmost willingness. One of their new aides-de-camp escorted them to their carriage, and murmured that he would not be coming home with them. Emily and Fanny were sure that he was going to slink back to the ball, to have a few further dances.

★   ★   ★   ★   ★

Lord Auckland was a servant of two masters: the Whig party in England and the East India Company. His had been a political appointment made by a Whig Prime Minister; if the Whigs went out of office he would be recalled. But after the government upheavals of the past two years, the glass seemed set fair for a normal term of office for Melbourne's administration, and the Governor-General expected to remain in India for six years.

He was not unaware of the difficulties which lay ahead of him by reason of physical geography alone: England was a four-months' voyage away. The Governor-General was in India to carry out the commercial policy of the East India Company, and to keep within the framework of the political policy of the home government. At the same time he would be expected to act on his own initiative if the need arose. Should the Court of Directors or the Board of Control at home disapprove of his actions—well, he was there to be blamed as well as praised.

'I am called upon to decide questions which may involve war or peace, ruin or safety, honour or disgrace,' he was to write angrily to the Board of Control two years later. 'And who knows till it is tried what is an important measure?' It was not very consistent to attempt to govern India from England when it took the best part of eight months to send dispatches home and get a reply.

Auckland realised within a few weeks of his arrival that he might be called upon to make many decisions on his own responsibility, and risk the authorities at home not approving of them. There were, for instance, a large number of domestic and social reforms which he intended to carry out: particularly reforms in the education of the natives. He had decided ideas on that question, and he could only hope that the Company would support him when he put his ideas into practice.

The East India Company had become a great power in central Asia. The group of English merchants who had sent out ships in the sixteenth century with a charter from the first Elizabeth had been concerned with wresting some of the trade from similar French, Dutch and Portuguese adventurers who had established stations on the coasts of India. Within two hundred years the Company had grown into a vast empire, with its own army, and territory which it administered through civil officers recruited from home. They found a sub-continent in a state of medieval anarchy, netted by treachery and intrigue, without codes or laws. The Company brought trade, and prospered. Its stations multiplied. Together with merchandise it brought English ideas of law and order, and was able to enforce them.

It was not, of course, a story of altruistic conquerors, or lay mission-aries. Many of the young men who went out to India as cadets in the Company's service 'shook the pagoda tree, and the rich fruit fell into their laps.' The day of the incorruptibles had not yet come.

By the end of the eighteenth century the home government saw that it was time for them to take a hand. India had become far too important to leave in the hands of an enormous trading concern, which itself was growing in influence every year. London instituted a Board of Control, which would work closely with the Court of Directors— the governing body of the Company. The political conduct of affairs passed to the Board, leaving commerce to the Court. The Governor-General of India was, from now on, jointly responsible to the Board of Control and the Court of Directors for the government of India. To assist him, he had a body of Ministers in Council, civil and military, who met regularly in Calcutta. There were also trained advisers, political and private Secretaries who knew the country and could speak Hindustani and Persian.

Lord Auckland's predecessor in the office had been Lord William Bentinck, a man with enlightened ideas on most native questions. When he had gone home two years before, he had left Charles Metcalfe, a former senior Minister, as provisional Governor-General. Metcalfe had vigorously put some of Bentinck's ideas into practice, and Auckland hoped to extend and expand these reforms still further. He looked forward to his term of office. At the very outset of his stewardship, he determined to leave behind him some contribution to the good and happiness of India.

★　　★　　★　　★　　★

It was nearing the end of March, and the hot weather had come. For two weeks Fanny and Emily had been trying to get used to living in an oven, and at the same time fulfilling a daily programme of duties which they might just have been able to get through comfortably in a nice, bracing frost at home. Now the torrid summer of mid-India was upon them. Until then, the early morning air which had come in through the open windows and doors had been comparatively cool; but if they were to breathe any fresh air at all in the hot weather, they would have to be out by five o'clock.

They soon established a new routine. As soon as they rose, they went riding, so as to be back before the sun had much power; then they came down to breakfast in the great dining-room, with the doors and windows closed against the growing heat. From then until luncheon at two o'clock it was only possible to sit quietly sewing or reading. After luncheon, Emily went to her sitting-room and Fanny to her own boudoir; they could now take off their gowns and relax for several hours. At half-past five the cool time of the day set in, and it was possible to go out driving. All European Calcutta was to be met driving on the Esplanade, sitting behind turbaned postillions and coachmen. There might also be a nice English *britschka*, with good horses and a tribe of running footmen by its side; and in it one of the native princes, dressed just as he was when he first came into the world, sitting cross-legged on the front seat very composedly smoking his hookah.

The household dined at eight o'clock, but it was rarely a family affair. There were usually dinner parties, when up to fifty people sat down to table in the great marble hall. Well-dressed women of various breeding, correctly uniformed men—and hardly a dozen all told who had anything in common with Fanny and Emily. Yet the niceties had to be observed, and conversation to be manufactured, somehow.

Every Monday and Wednesday evening the Governor-General's sisters were at home to anybody who was on the Government House list. The aides-de-camp settled this list between them, and Emily hoped that they would have the sense to place upon it all the ladies most agreeable to themselves. Callers who gave due notice were also received on Thursday mornings, but Fanny and Emily soon found three receiving periods in the week too exhausting, for there were now schools to visit and fancy fairs to open. They changed the Monday and Wednesday visitations to a single evening, and were thenceforth at home to the list only on a Tuesday. Thursday mornings were still reserved for newcomers presenting letters of introduction, or anyone else who wished to see them.

It was all very formal and very dull. The callers looked extremely fashionable, came in immense numbers, sat down for five minutes, and, though there might be forty in the room at once, never spoke to each other unless they were acquainted. However, it was a cheap way of getting through all the visiting duties of life at one fell swoop.

There was a good deal of gossip, but Emily and Fanny did not know the people sufficiently by name or by sight to attach the right history to the right face, even if they wanted to hear it. In any case, they could not get into any intimacies, had they wished it, for the whole patronage in that immense country was in the hands of the Governor-General, and the slightest hint of undue friendliness towards any one person on the part of his sisters would have put the rest of society into a fume. It was too hot, said Emily, for superimposed fuming. . . .

The real misery of their new existence was the separation from home and friends. Outwardly composed, civil, unflagging in what was required of them, Emily and Fanny were unhappy. They longed for the companionship of their own friends at home, for the understanding between kindred spirits which had such long roots in the past.

'I was suddenly picked out of a collection of brothers, sisters and intimate friends,' wrote Emily to Pamela Campbell, 'with heaps of daily interests and habits of long standing, devoted to the last night's debate and this morning's paper, detesting the heat of even an English summer, worshipping autumn, and rather rejoicing in a sharp east wind; with a passion for sketching in the country, and enjoying an easy life in town. With all this we are sent out of reach of even letters from home to an entirely new society of a most second-rate description, to a life of forms and aides-de-camp half the day, and darkness and solitude the other half. And to a climate! . . . It is so very HOT I do not know how to spell it large enough.'

She had lost George as a companion; she never saw him now except in a crowd. He opened schools, made speeches, went to the opera,

CALCUTTA FROM THE SEA

A VIEW OF GOVERNMENT HOUSE FROM THE COURT HOUSE STREET, CALCUTTA
A VIEW OF BARRACKPORE HOUSE, WITH THE REACH OF THE RIVER

appeared at balls; all on top of the official work which occupied him most of the day. He never felt tired, did not mind the heat, filled all the hours fuller than they could hold, and slept well at night. But he still talked to her about the work which closely interested him, whenever they could get an hour together. George had always had in Emily a ready anvil on which he could hammer out ideas, and he found her a sympathetic and percipient listener to his plans for educational reform.

He was particularly anxious to start new schools where anybody who wished could send their children. The present system was a dual one. There were native schools which taught in classical Persian, and turned out scholars in that tongue; and European schools which taught in English, and supplied the clerks and other inferior officials who were useful in the local Civil Service. A very few establishments, like the Hindu College in Calcutta, produced native teachers and lawyers, who imbibed European ideas, and were suspect by their own countrymen in consequence.

George wanted to extend the system considerably, on the lines already begun by Bentinck and Metcalfe. He had long taken the view that the natives must be helped to understand their own conditions, and in time to take over their own schools and courts. This could only be done by adequate education, and education George intended them to have in great numbers, so far as it lay within his powers. The first thing was to persuade the native schools to teach in the vernacular, so that children could learn quickly. He had already arranged for a proper series of vernacular class-books to be written and distributed; and he also wanted to have appropriate European books translated into the vernacular, in order to give young people some idea of other lands, and so substitute knowledge for the ignorance and prejudice which made the native fear the stranger.

He was opposed at every turn. The existing native teachers were determined to maintain their classical teaching, and several Ministers in Council upheld them. Why meddle with the existing system?

George was perfectly aware of the powerful hold which tradition had on the native, simple and subtle alike. He had no wish whatever to cut off the teaching of the past. But with it, he declared, must go teaching which would fit children for the present. Only by learning quickly and easily in their own vernacular tongues would they be able to understand the world in which they had to live. He intended to found colleges for the training of school-teachers in different parts of

the country.   Battles had already been fought in Council over an
allocation of the Indian income towards wider education, and George
was prepared to fight many more, should it be necessary.   Native
school-teachers, doctors, judges: these men were essential for the well-
being of India, and wherever he went, he was going to insist on something being done towards their training.

So argued George, in Council and out of it.   When the Court of
Directors wrote to say that his predecessors had spent enough, and
more than enough, on native education, and that unreasonable expenditure must stop, the Governor-General wrote forcible letters in reply,
pointing out that a small number of Europeans could not go on
administering this enormous country for ever, and that it was essential
to extend the system of native education.   Already at the Hindu
College there were a number of promising young men who would
form a *cadre* of potential school-teachers, as well as others who were
students of medicine and law.   There should be Hindu Colleges of
this kind all over India.

Both Emily and Fanny took the deepest interest in George's reforms,
and never missed an opportunity of visiting the existing schools, or
attending meetings when the formation of new ones were being discussed.   It was a secret relief to each of them that they had something
on which they could both work whole-heartedly and with one mind.
In so many other ways there was a chasm of constraint between them
that neither could bridge.   The Governor-General's sisters were able
enough to share their duties, but they could not share their loneliness.

Their relationship was what it had always been—calm, rational, full
of the Eden family affection.   There was never the slightest quarrel
or strained relationship between them; they accepted each other with
the tolerance and understanding of well-bred people who had lived
together all their lives, and knew each other's qualities and failings.
But they were no more friends in the real sense of the word than they
had been in their younger years.   Emily had grown more dogmatic,
Fanny more reflective; Emily more impatient, Fanny more withdrawn.   They could support each other in the ordinary business of life
—they could bear with bores, smile over a parvenu's pretentions or a
fashionable's too-tight sleeves.   What neither could do was to reveal
her innermost self to the other.   Only the few close friends at home
had keys to those locked chambers.

Fanny felt as solitary in the magnificence of Government House as
did Emily, but she did not echo Emily's outbursts of hates and despairs.

When the heat and the perpetual formalities of official life tried her too hard, she found relief in writing home to the Grosvenors:

'There are moments when a feeling of desperation comes over me to think that I must dream this dream, so distinct from all my past life, for five years. But I mean to make the best of it.'

She made that resolve before the end of her first month in Calcutta, and she kept to it during the entire time that she was in India.

★   ★   ★   ★   ★

If the middle of the week was almost unsupportable in Calcutta during the hot weather, the long week-ends at Barrackpore more than compensated

Barrackpore was the Governor-General's country-house eighteen miles up the river from Calcutta, and Fanny and Emily fell in love with it. A charming place, like an English villa on the banks of the Thames, it had the added attraction—in spite of its immense rooms—of being only large enough to hold Emily, Fanny, George and William. The aides and Secretaries and others in George's *entourage* slept in small thatched cottages built round the park. Even when they had to ask local magnates and their wives to stay, there was no need to see them except at luncheon and dinner; for the visitors, too, were lodged in guest-bungalows. It was all very satisfactory.

The park was green and fresh-looking, with a flower-garden which filled Emily with joy. This was indeed something to which they could look forward between Monday and Thursday in baking Calcutta. And when George began to renew his old interest in gardening, Emily was more pleased than ever. She decided that she would make an entirely new garden further off, in another part of the park, so that she and George would have a private place in which they could walk and talk, and plan fresh arrangements of seed-beds and flowers.

There was also a private menagerie in the grounds. It had been much neglected, but there was a foundation of a leopard and two 'rhinocerouses,' to which they could without trouble add a few monkeys and birds. Myriads of fireflies and parroquets flew about the park, and—less pleasant—jackals roamed at night and snarled at the animals in the cages. Sometimes the jackals slunk through the guest-bungalows. One night a visitor's little dog was rescued from the very jaws of a jackal, who had picked it up as a nice morsel. Emily kept a very strict eye on Chance after that. It would hurt Chance's pride as well as his fat little person if he were picked up to make a jackal's dinner.

It was cooler in Barrackpore than in Calcutta, but still much too hot to walk. Emily soon got used to being carried about the grounds in her sedan. Fanny tried that at first but found it too tame. There were elephants to ride, and Fanny decided to learn to sit on one.

This was not so easy as it looked. Frightened out of her life, with the eyes of the bodyguard upon her, Fanny waited with apparent calmness while one of the towering creatures was brought past her and halted. She scrambled like a cat up the ladder, which was necessary even though the elephant knelt down, and sat herself with great dignity and presence of mind in the howdah. Then she and George, who had mounted on another elephant, took a ride round the park, being, she guessed, quite twenty feet above the level of the sea—a thing that seldom happened in Bengal. There were, it was true, little hills in the park, but these were man-made. In a previous Governor-General's reign someone had said "Make a hill," and a hill had been made. Then another, and another, until the park was diversified by undulations which made it resemble, in some measure, an estate at home.

The sisters found that no request of this kind was considered out of the way. Emily wanted a large pond for fish and water-lilies in her new garden, and Captain FitzGerald, one of the civil engineers attached to the household, made two.

The house itself was not in such a satisfactory state as the grounds and gardens. Emily thought the furnishings and hangings shabby, and the furniture worse than that of any average London hotel. It was not surprising. Everything brought to India was so perishable that even one year of neglect could reduce a house and its appointments to decay. Sir Charles Metcalfe had not used the place very much, and it looked drab. After a talk with George about expenses and what they could afford, Emily and Fanny decided on replenishments, and looked forward to arranging their new possessions.

It would have been perfect if they could always have lived at Barrackpore. Surely George could Governor-General there as well as at Calcutta? It would save so much fuss, too. No servants were kept at Barrackpore; the whole establishment had to be transported in a fleet of boats on Thursday, and taken back again to Calcutta on Monday morning. Four hundred servants, down to the tailor squatting in the passage, peering through his spectacles at the sewing on his knees. True, there was no confusion, as there would have been in England. Here, each servant took charge of one thing only, and did it thoroughly and exactly to the minute. And their feet didn't creak, like their English counterparts'. But moving a household of four hundred people in open steamers up and down the Hooghly when it happened to rain was not a comfortable experience. Why not remain here during the entire hot weather? *Need* they live in Calcutta at all?

These were but rhetorical questions, as Fanny and Emily well knew. George did not mind Calcutta. He did not mind the heat, or the glare, or the mosquitoes. Emily was of the opinion that the mosquitoes did not even bother with George, there being his sisters to devour. As far as George was concerned, he liked Barrackpore well enough; but he had no regrets when Monday morning came. Immediately the party embarked on the *Soonamookie* for the return journey to Calcutta, George disappeared into his cabin with William and his Private Secretary, Mr. Colvin, and soon they were absorbed in business.

There was plenty to keep them occupied in routine matters of administration alone. Colvin had to keep a record of every senior official, 'writer' and cadet in the Company's service, and to let the Governor-General know in good time when substitutes were needed for men going on leave. Reports came in constantly from agents in distant posts; one of these was exploring the possibilities of growing tea in Assam, with the help of Chinese experts. All matters of day-to-day business—mixed with an absurd amount of nonsense which Mr. Colvin tried to keep down to reasonable proportions: the complaints of minor officials over slights, imagined or real, in the matter of precedence; the demands of opportunists and place-hunters seeking favours.

The devoted Secretary dealt with as many questions himself as he had time for. He knew that the real problems which faced the Governor-General were of a different kind altogether, and were becoming increasingly complex, requiring a clear mind and freedom from minor worries of administration to grapple with them.

★   ★   ★   ★   ★

The country was ostensibly at peace. Lord Auckland's predecessors had sent trade missions to the Punjab, Afghanistan and Persia—the great states on the north-west frontiers of India. The missions had indeed been concerned with commercial relations, but not entirely so. Since the beginning of the century, when the French and the Russians had been pushing acquisitive hands further and further eastwards, England had been watching India's north-west borders. After Napoleon's downfall, the French were no more to be feared. There remained Russia: the huge, mysterious empire of the Tsar, which had already swallowed up all the Persian possessions on the south of the Caucasus, as well as part of the Ottoman empire, and was obviously seeking another mighty mouthful. The trade missions had found Russian agents in favour at the Persian court, and Russian influence seeping into Afghanistan. All Asia was aware of this growing Russian penetration into the states bordering India.

Lord William Bentinck had left a Minute for his successor.

'From the days of Peter the Great to the present time,' he wrote, 'the views of Russia have been turned to the obtaining possession of that part of central Asia which is watered by the Oxus, and joins the eastern shore of the Caspian. The latest accounts from Kabul state that they are building a fort between the Caspian and Khiva. This is the best line of their operation against India, but it can only be considered at present as a very distant speculation. . . .'

There was a chain of British trading stations along strategic routes out of India to the north-west: stations which had had teeth built into them, until they had grown into small forts. If attack was to come, some preparation was being made to meet it.

Lord Auckland and his advisers hoped that the threat of aggression would continue to be a distant speculation, but nobody could be sure. Before he had left London, he had had long discussions with Sir John Cam Hobhouse, the President of the Board of Control, and had received perfectly explicit instructions. He was to do everything in his power to build a rampart of friendly states round the north-west provinces of India. This meant alliances with the rulers of those territories.

The most important was Ranjit Singh, the ruler of the Sikh kingdom of the Punjab, the old Lion of the North. Ranjit had had his own period of acquisitiveness; he had taken Peshawar from the Afghans, and had only recently been sharply pulled up by the British for 'casting covetous eyes on territories in the possession of his neighbours, the Amirs of Sind.' He had been bidden to keep his hands off his neighbours' possessions and stay on his own side of the Sutlej river. The hard-headed old Sikh had accepted the instruction; the British were more useful to him as allies than enemies. So the Punjab could be more or less depended upon.

The great problem was Afghanistan. It had no established ruler with whom a binding alliance could be made. For centuries the various tribes in its wild mountain highlands had fought each other for supremacy; it was not fifty years since they had become united under a single monarch. Even that had not unified the country. Shah Shuja Mirza, one of the sons of this king, had struggled as far as the throne after his father's death, but he had not lasted long. The great clans fought each other for supremacy, and in the end one man, Dost Muhammad Khan, of the dominating Barkzai clan, rose to supreme power. Shah Shuja fled to Ranjit Singh's dominions and settled down into a comfortable captivity.

It soon appeared that Dost Muhammad was a warrior who also had a shrewd political sense. He sent a letter to the new Governor-General of India, congratulating him on his safe arrival. He hoped Lord Auckland would advise him how best to govern Afghanistan—and how to get Peshawar back from the Sikhs. The Governor-General answered in equally friendly terms. He thanked Dost Muhammad for his good wishes, said he hoped shortly to send a commercial mission to Kabul, and ended with the firm statement that it was not the practice of the British Government to take sides in disputes between independent states.

George could not have replied otherwise; he had clear instructions from the Board of Control in such matters. But he was aware that Dost Muhammad was obstinately set on regaining Peshawar; just as Ranjit Singh was mulishly determined not to let it go. He hoped that an experienced and persuasive agent like Alexander Burnes would make Dost Muhammad see that it would be wise to keep friendly with a great and prosperous trading nation, and not go hankering after lost possessions.

The Governor-General certainly had enough to keep him absorbed as he worked with Mr. Colvin in the cabin of the *Soonamookie*, or presided in the Council Chamber at Government House.

★　　★　　★　　★　　★

Calcutta society had taken kindly to the Governor-General's sisters, and had settled down to thinking of the Governor-General himself as a mild, amiable gentleman unlikely to overstep the bounds of well-signposted duties. Then the great shoe question suddenly disturbed the military messes and the drawing-rooms.

It cropped up at the Hindu College examinations, held in the marble hall at Government House. At the end of the examinations prizes were awarded to the best boys who recited English poems and acted scenes from Shakespeare. There were forty-five boys in the College, most of them of the highest caste, and every respectable native in Calcutta came to the show.

They came in shoes. European opinion was startled, and soon sharply divided. Sir Charles Metcalfe, in spite of his otherwise en- lightened ideas, had never allowed the natives to come into the hall with their shoes on. But there were a number of Europeans now who thought that the natives were sufficiently well-informed to feel the degradation of this order. They wished to have Indians treated with more civility and respect. Lord Auckland agreed with this point of view, and rescinded Metcalfe's order.

The charm of being allowed to come before the Governor-General in shoes brought an immense concourse of natives together—all wear- ing new, stiff European shoes. Many of the men found it difficult to walk in them, but they persevered. Slowly, haltingly, they passed before the Governor-General in their white muslin dresses, wearing brilliantly gleaming turbans which would have made the fortune of a milliner at home. It was one of the prettiest sights Emily and Fanny had seen in Calcutta—in spite of the incongruous shoes.

The weather grew steadily hotter. Emily had had several attacks of sickness; violent pains followed by agues which sent her into the depths of depression. She tried to get Dr. Drummond to attend to her, as she had found him such an excellent doctor on the voyage. George, too, would have liked to keep the doctor as his private physician; but by some rule of the Company they were unable to have him, and were informed they must have a local doctor instead.

This turned out to be a little man who looked rather like the poet, Tom Moore. When Emily had one of her attacks he gave her calomel and opium, and came to see her every hour—an attention which it was usual to pay to the Governor-General's family. It was a particularly inconvenient attention to Emily, who felt it was but civil to invent a new symptom every time he appeared. His nostrums had some effect, but Emily would have given a good deal for the unfussy common-sense of Dr. Drummond.

The *Jupiter*, still at Calcutta refitting, was due to sail for home in the middle of April. Captain Grey and his officers came to Government House and to Barrackpore, enjoyed themselves at balls and private theatricals, and played cricket against the Calcutta Eleven—a sight which Emily and Fanny found pretty and English, reminding them of Princes Plain.

Fanny tried not to think of the *Jupiter* returning to England. She and Emily concentrated on the practical occupation of buying trinkets and embroideries to send back to their family and friends. 'There is to be seen at our jeweller's a pearl, a single pearl set as a mermaid, with an enamelled head and a green tail, which I had some thoughts of buying and presenting to you,' Fanny wrote to Eleanor Grosvenor. 'Forty thousand pounds was all they asked for it. Very cheap, the man said.' She had to content herself with sending two Chinese screens, and promised to find something Indian worth sending later, when she had a chance to travel. In Calcutta she and Emily found that there were only things which could be got in London at a quarter of the price, on the principle that nobody got good fish near the sea.

Emily had one piece of good fortune before the *Jupiter* went off. She was able, after all, to secure Dr. Drummond as her medical adviser. She had consulted with Dr. Nicolson, the most influential of the faculty in Calcutta, as to the best man to appoint to the household. He suggested Dr. Drummond, and when Emily told him of her difficulties with the Honourable Company, he laughed and went off to consult the proper authorities. He came back armed with precedents—and permissions.

The *Jupiter* sailed, and the last link with home was loosed. Emily and Fanny went down to the landing-place and watched her out of sight: the tall, blowing sails growing smaller until they merged into the distance. Then they turned back to their six years of India.

By May the temperature had reached ninety-five degrees. Everybody said it was one of the hottest seasons they had known. Emily and Fanny lived in darkened rooms, and wondered how they could survive through each succeeding day.

They were at Barrackpore on one particularly baking Sunday when Emily was accosted in the breakfast-room by a clergyman, a visitor from Calcutta who was staying with them for the week-end.

"Pray, Miss Eden, are you aware that your *malis* are at work this morning?" he asked.

Emily was duly shocked, but as she did not know who or what *malis* were, she could not do much about it. They were, she was informed, the gardeners. Emily found it difficult to deny that her *malis* had such un-Sabbatarian habits, for unluckily they began to pick away with their pickaxes under the window at that very moment.

She said that she would mention it to Lord Auckland, and he would doubtless speak to the *malis* forthwith.

At breakfast, however, Major Byrne briskly took up the question. Byrne had recently been promoted, and was more efficient than ever. Of course the *malis* were at work, said Byrne. For more than half of each week they were absent at their own religious festivals, and would starve if they were not allowed to work on the days which they thought lawful. The reverend gentleman found himself without an argument; he was no match for Major Byrne. Fanny and Emily would have enjoyed listening to an argument between them on the point, but it was difficult to fix their attention on anything outside the mere effort of existing, and they did not put in a word.

The heat—the heat—the heat. It would have been some slight comfort to be able to stay at Barrackpore all the time, for at least the park and gardens brought an illusion of coolness, and sometimes there was a river breeze. But George returned to Calcutta each Monday morning as faithfully as ever, and Emily and Fanny felt bound to go with him.

The doors and windows in Government House were kept tightly closed, except where *tatties* hung in the apertures: rush mats kept sprayed with water, the evaporation lowering the temperature by a few degrees. Large punkahs were constantly kept going, but the resulting draughts seemed nearly as hot as the still air. The only exertion Fanny could bring herself to was writing letters home. The sisters did not see each other in the afternoons; absolute solitude, said Emily, was necessary for everybody during some part of the day, and she closed the door of her sitting-room against all comers. Fanny did not retire, but preferred to sit in the great marble hall. Sometimes William was free from his duties and would join her; they would play a game of chess, or William would stretch himself out in a long chair and do nothing. He was not good at small talk, nor was he fond of serious conversation. But he was easy and companionable when he felt in his usual spirits; and even in moods of depression he never took himself too seriously. Fanny was content with him as he was.

Upstairs, in the huge sitting-room with its view over the lawns and flower-beds, Emily lay on her sofa and tried to imagine coolness. She thought of spring in England. Her favourite picture was of the dear little chimney-sweeps knickety-knocketing their brushes and shovels about the streets, and Pamela Campbell, her carriage boiling over with children, giving the urchins halfpennies and begging them not to be run over.. Emily, too, once gave halfpence to chimney-sweepers in Arcadia, long ago. . . . There were so many hours to fill in this odd, unnatural life. Sometimes she could lull herself into a daydream, and almost persuade herself that she was in Grosvenor Street, and that Theresa would soon be calling to pass the morning with her. Then she would rouse up in a fever of desperation because it was not true.

Yet a good many of her thoughts were pleasant, and still could bring some echo of happiness. She lived in her memories. Walking with George in the garden at Greenwich. Playing in charades at Bowood, to amuse the Lansdownes. Listening to Robert preaching his first sermon at Hertingfordbury—a sermon which she had written for him. How dreadful it had been when she had sat in the pew listening to him, and had detected a disguised quotation from Shakespeare in one of the most impressive passages! And how dear Robert had laughed over it afterwards. Emily laughed over it now. There were golden days with Eleanor at East Combe, after driving along the lanes from Eden Farm through the Kentish countryside. Did one have to leave Kent to know how much one loved it? Ah, no. Emily had always savoured good things at the time; when she had been happy, she had known it. There had ever been the greatest happiness at her eldest sister's house.

The pain of her intense loneliness crept into her letters:

'I think I won't write any more, but just drive quietly to East Combe, sit down in the breakfast-room on that low chair, take *The Favourite of Nature* out of that bookcase by the fireplace, open the window wide for some real fresh air, and have a good gossip while you arrange your flowers. O dear, dear, but it is no use talking; only I do live in England for hours together, though you don't perceive me.'

Self-pity did not creep into many of her letters to East Combe, however; Emily got into the habit of setting down every detail of her Indian life which might amuse and interest them at home. The details were growing more and more magnificent. There was the day an ambassador arrived from one of the chief native princes. George and his officers had to encase themselves in full dress immediately after breakfast—with the thermometer at ninety-four degrees.

Major Byrne filled the ballroom with soldiers, attendants and the entire Government House band. Soon there arrived fifty of the ambassador's servants with baskets on their heads containing fruits, preserves, barley-sugar and sugar-plums. Then came a silver howdah, something like an overgrown coffin lined with velvet, thought Emily.

She and Fanny watched the scene from an upper window, craning to see what came next. Five silver trays piled with fine shawls. Gold stuffs on the following tray, glinting in the sun: what unparalleled trains they would have made at a Court drawing-room! There followed trays of bracelets and armlets, and ornaments for the hair; necklaces of pearls and emeralds which looked unreal, the stones were so large.

Fanny and Emily left the window and slipped downstairs, to have a closer look, and hid themselves behind pillars in the great hall—keeping out of sight, because the native notabilities looked upon those valuable articles, women, with scorn. They watched the gifts being spread on a large Venetian carpet before George's throne-like chair of state. George came in, and sat majestically down, while an immense body of servants, all smartened up with new liveries, arranged themselves behind him. Major Byrne and the other aides-de-camp in attendance began to fan themselves with their cocked hats, without much result; they looked hotter than they had done before.

The ambassador now arrived—an old black gentleman in a scarlet turban, short-waisted muslin gown and petticoat, and bare feet. This was an occasion when George had to obey Byrne's decree, and receive an ambassador who had taken off his shoes. The visit lasted only ten minutes. The moment the little man had taken his leave and gone, Major Byrne swept up the shawls and ornaments, goldstuffs and necklaces, and carried them off. Emily and Fanny watched him in despairing resignation. He was only doing his duty, the shocking man. They knew the Company's inflexible rule: no gifts to be accepted and kept by a servant of the Company. And George was its foremost servant in India.

In principle, they approved of such a thoroughly English rejection of the bad old ways in the bad old days. The long era of bribery and corruption was long over; the pagoda tree had been shaken by greedy European merchants for the last time decades before. The Honourable East India Company had grown into a service which followed the rule of law, and was not based on the exchange of favours. Its servants had not only to be above corruption, but to let all men see that they were so.

Major Byrne did not miss a trinket, a shawl, or a gem. These would be put in the Company's coffers, some of them to be presented, in turn, to other rajahs or nawabs. Only the trays of fruits and sweetmeats were left behind; Byrne gave these to the servants.

Fanny and Emily did not even get a taste of barley-sugar—which they could have put up with, in lieu of emeralds.

*   *   *   *   *

The rains came at the end of June, and as this made the hitherto unwatered roads passable, the sisters were able to take drives through lanes and by-roads which gave them a different picture of the town. European Calcutta, they found, was very like St. John's Wood; the houses were built in the same style and the gardens were set out to the same pattern. Then came an abrupt change. The native parts of the town were so thronged that it was difficult to drive through them. Groups of men squatted at the doors of clay huts, some of them with wild, handsome countenances. Every now and then a Chinese, with his twinkling eyes and yellow face and satin dress, stalked along among these black, naked creatures.

When the carriage got right out of town, the road was straight and shady. A few scattered savages at the doors of their huts, with boys climbing up the cocoa-trees, were the only human creatures they met. It gave Fanny a curious, dream-like feeling to drive back from these scenes to the opulent luxury of Government House.

Sometimes they went further afield. Once Emily and George drove off to a salt-water lake four miles distant. It looked, thought Emily, like an unfinished bit of creation before the land and sea were put in their proper places.

Then there was the evening when Fanny and Emily went riding with George and William on four of the horses they had bought at the Cape —mettlesome animals who were apt to shy at anything unexpected. They had not been out long before a thunderstorm came on, and they were drenched in a half a minute. It was like taking a shower-bath on a large scale, horse and all.

A few minutes later they met thirty-three elephants in a narrow lane. It was not an amusing moment. No elephants were allowed to come within a certain distance of Calcutta, because most horses reared and plunged at the sight of them. Fanny's and George's horses had a particular objection to elephants. All the *syces* set off screaming at once: the usual reaction of these grooms when faced with an awkward situation. Fanny begged, in a tone of most dignified cowardice, to be allowed to get off her horse. She followed behind George and the others on foot, while the elephants crashed through the hedges on either side, under the proddings of their *mahouts*.

In spite of her caution, Fanny liked elephants. She felt she could make a friend of an elephant. Already she had a respect for their intelligence and resourcefulness; a respect, she regretfully observed, that she could not extend to tigers, alligators or snakes.

By July the weather was slightly cooler; it was possible to have the windows open during the heavy rain. It was also possible to breathe out of doors without gasping with one's tongue hanging out, like Chance. That little black angel had the audacity to dote on India, and had never enjoyed better spirits, or a more imperious temper. He was once nearly carried off by vultures, and he and William's favourite greyhound both narrowly escaped the snap of an alligator's jaws while they were swimming in the Ganges. He gave his own particular servant a fright that time. Chance had learnt from the natives to eat mangoes, and was suspected of smoking his hookah whenever he got comfortably alone with the tailors. He had become very much of a personage in the Governor-General's household.

Now that the rains had laid the dust, Fanny and Emily got out as much as possible. William had bought a pony-trap with wicker sides, a light conveyance which would go on roads not wide enough to admit a carriage. When they went off in the pony-trap and discovered green lanes bordered with bamboo and cocoa-trees, and old mosques with tanks full of pink lotus flowers, George laughed and said they talked as enthusiastically as if they were at Matlock. But Fanny and Emily were glad to escape from the Course with its tiresome crowd of carriages and Europeans. George could laugh, if he wished. It would have done him good to have come with them on their jaunts.

They had to admit, however, that George was quite well, and uncommonly happy in his own way. He was in his office from six in the morning till six at night, and then was ready for any further duties, social or otherwise, that might be required of him. He never grumbled, never complained. There were moments when Emily could have shaken George.

The rains brought a coolness which was a relief after the weeks of torrid heat, but there were disadvantages. It was the season when books and pictures became mildewed and blistered. Fanny discovered a monster of a fishy-looking insect inside the glass of a print of Eleanor Grosvenor, beginning to eat Eleanor up; the greedy creature was removed just in time. A near relation of this little horror, a centipede, began to invade the living-rooms; the aides killed one close by Fanny's foot at a ball in the marble hall.

The greatest trial was with their clothes. They had both brought out a large supply of gowns and bonnets and linen. But there was even more changing of garments expected of them here than they had anticipated, and they had been insufficiently warned of the devastating results of the rainy season on materials. Stuffs grew rusty overnight, and gowns developed spots and patches which disintegrated into holes at a touch. The local milliners and shopkeepers would not open the tin-lined boxes of goods which filled their storerooms, knowing that their stocks would be ruined in a matter of days if brought out and exposed to the air.

The rains themselves seemed to the sisters to be outlandish in their extravagance. There was a day at Barrackpore when the downpour turned into sheets of solid water. It was as if the river had got out of its bed and was walking about in the park. Fanny and Emily stood at a window watching the lawns turn rapidly into a lake. The driving wall of water actually washed the fish out of Emily's ornamental tanks; the fish hopped about on the grass, with screeching servants paddling about trying to catch them.

The rains, too, brought out new insects. One was the elephant-fly, which was about the size of a bantam's egg and was so hard that stepping upon it did not hurt it, and so strong that if one put a plate over it the creature scuttled across the room, plate and all. Then came a variation of an old enemy—one from which they had often fled on their way across the world. Emily went into her dressing-room one evening to find it invaded by a set of flying-bugs, which bounced against her whenever she moved. They did not bite, but their smell sent her running out again.

There was always someone at hand to help deal with these and other horrors, but the two sisters got into the habit of taking particular care where they walked, sat, or put anything down. As a set-off to the discomforts which were peculiar to the climate, they knew that they had every luxury which the wit of man could devise. They were, too, acquiring the habit of the European in India of denying themselves nothing—a habit which they feared would be awkward later on, when they returned home.

Their life had now become established in a regular pattern. They had got used to a multiplicity of servants, to being followed about everywhere by a *jemadar*, a kind of lieutenant over the others who was instantly before them when they expressed the slightest wish. When they were not out at balls or themselves entertaining at late parties, they dined at eight, played at écarté on the verandah afterwards, and retired to bed at ten. There were times when the extraordinariness of it all struck them with the same force as it had done at the very beginning. Emily wrote to Theresa:

'I could not help thinking how strange it would have seemed at home. [Today] was a rainy day, so all the servants were indoors. The two tailors were sitting in one window, making a new gown for me, and Rosina by them chopping up her betel-nut. At the opposite window were two Dacca embroiderers working at a large frame, and the sentry, in an ecstacy of admiration, mounting guard over them. There was the bearer standing upright, in a sweet sleep, pulling away at my punkah. My own five servants were sitting in a circle, with an English spelling-book, which they were learning by heart; and my *jemadar*, who, out of compliment to me, has taken to draw, was sketching a bird. Chance's servant was waiting at the end of the passage for his "little excellency" to go out walking, and a Chinese was waiting with some rolls of satin that he had brought to show.'

A group like that, in spite of its strangeness when compared with the servants she had known at home, always stimulated Emily's talent for sketching. Both she and Fanny had been taught by the best drawing-masters in their youth, and they turned to the pencil as naturally as they did to the pen. Emily derived great happiness from her talent. When she was in good health, and the heat did not entirely deprive her of the will to move, she spent several hours of every day at her drawing-books.

Getting paper was a difficulty. She had brought out a good supply, but it did not last long—especially when the ladies of Calcutta discovered that Miss Eden was adept at catching a good likeness, and even cleverer at copying an existing portrait. One wanted the picture of a sister she had lost touched up—and, in fact, renewed, as the damp had utterly destroyed it. Another had a picture of a brother in England, in a draped cloak; the picture had only been lent her, and he was such a darling and she had not seen him for years, and if Miss Eden would have the goodness to copy it. . . . Emily could not refuse such requests. There were no professional artists in Calcutta, except one who painted second-rate signposts, and she felt it a duty to help anyone to a likeness of a friend at home. It was one of the few things it was possible for her to do directly for people. Many of the letters home asked for more drawing-paper to be sent out. She and Fanny could sometimes buy Chinese rice-paper, but it was more suitable for

Chinese paints than for pencil and chalk or for ordinary pen-and-ink sketches. Besides, it was very expensive.

They had to watch their personal expenses. Both Emily and Fanny possessed small private incomes, which were supplemented by George, so there was no need to practise very close economy. But they always had to consider what they could afford to buy; they felt they must save a certain amount towards their later years.

George received a handsome salary and large allowances, and for the first time was able to put money aside. If they lived to return home, considered Emily, they would be very much better off than they could ever have expected to be had they remained at Greenwich. The Governor-General's place was undoubtedly very well paid; and it might well be, for his was a hard-working situation in a cruel climate.

She and George had already been able to make some definite provision towards their return home by buying a house in London, so they would have a home waiting for them. It was at Kensington Gore, in Knightsbridge, and Emily and Fanny often had it in mind, though they had never seen it. Any choice piece of embroidery or native craftsmanship which they could afford was bought for their little house at home. They often talked of it, and made plans of how they would arrange the rooms, with this screen there, and that cabinet in a position where the inlaid wood could be seen to good advantage. . . .

And then they would fall silent, remembering that it was yet but 1836.

* * * * *

Calcutta society was excited. It was shocked, too. The Governor-General was going to dine with a native; so ran the rumour.

George was not unduly worried by what Calcutta society thought when he wished to pursue a course of action which he felt was a desirable one. George said that the staring *round* look which everybody's eyes had was not, as was always supposed, occasioned by the heat and the shrinking of the eyelids. It was caused by the knack they had of wondering at everything. The least deviation from everyday routine put them out.

Dwarkanauth Tagore had asked the Governor-General and his sisters to go and see the villa which he had built, a villa in a regular English style. The Governor-General was delighted to accept the invitation, and forthwith named the following Monday.

The party went in particular state. William drove Fanny in his phaeton; Major Byrne was in one cab, and Captain MacGregor in another. Even Dr. Drummond had an equipage to himself for the occasion. George and Emily were impressive in the government coach, with quantities of servants running beside it.

Dwarkanauth's villa was delightful. He himself spoke excellent English, and he knew how to give a party. There were elephants on the lawn, boats on the lake, ices in the summer-house, and beautiful pictures and books to look at in the well-furnished rooms. George and his sisters enjoyed themselves immensely, and made all the noise and clatter they could when they returned to Government House, so as to impress the visit on all those who happened to be interested.

The following day, there was more fuel for the shockable. A French company of actors had just landed from the Mauritius, and Emily sent for the manager and engaged his troupe to diversify the next Tuesday evening. She and Fanny had introduced dancing into their receiving periods, to make them a little more lively. The prospect of a professional theatrical entertainment, for a change, was enchanting.

The news flew round. The local newspapers, which always kept a close eye on Government House, thought such an entertainment quite proper. A section of Calcutta society decided to disapprove.

'The odd thing is,' wrote Fanny to Eleanor Grosvenor, 'that some of the very strict ones, who will not come to our Tuesdays when there is dancing, do not think the plays so bad. It does seem very odd that mothers of families should not see how absolutely *right* it is that the numbers of boys who are here (exposed to every possible temptation, and in a country where it is a fashion to seem dissipated and extravagant), should be, if possible, kept in good society, and under the eye of people on whom their promotion depends. And if dancing here from nine to half-past eleven, without cards, without supper, without even wine, amuses them, and keeps them in the society of respectable people, it surely must be better than shutting up the House, and saying it is *wrong* to be amused. . . . We had a large dinner in the evening. I wish that were reckoned immoral, but the very strictest make no objection to dinners.'

Captain MacGregor undertook to have a little theatre fitted up in the ballroom of Government House, and it turned out very well, with dressing-rooms and a place for the orchestra. Everything was ready by Monday. Then Emily's troubles began. The French actors became temperamental and objected to the placing of the lamps for lighting the stage. The Government House band chose to give themselves airs, and declared that they could not play music for vaudevilles. Emily lost her temper and turned on the bandmaster.

"I have not an idea what you mean!" she scolded. "The Governor-General must have whatever music he chooses to order, and it is your fault if the band can't play it. It is a great disgrace for you if, when Lord Auckland wishes for some vaudevilles, you cannot play them."

This unexpected attack had an immediate effect, and when Emily and Fanny went quietly into the ballroom next morning to watch the actors rehearse, the jolly little songs of the farces were being smartly accompanied by the band.

It was therefore tantalising to learn later in the day that the *jeune première* had got a fever, brought on by rehearsing in the heat, and that there was no possibility of a performance that evening.

Major Byrne and Captain MacGregor had the task of preparing the guests for a change of plan. There would be dancing instead of the theatrical entertainment. And as it was by far the largest party that had ever come to their Tuesday evenings, Emily and Fanny decided that being shocked did not keep people away from French farces.

The *jeune première* was sufficiently recovered to play on the following Tuesday, and there was, again, a numerous company. The stage was now splendidly lighted, as one of the great chandeliers of the ballroom hung over it, right in the middle. The farces were acted as well as Emily had ever seen such plays done in Paris or London. True, more than half the audience did not understand French, but those who did laughed a little more in consequence, to show their superiority.

Much of the restful charm of Barrackpore was disappearing as the summer wore on, for now that the Governor-General and his sisters were established, their social duties grew heavier. The week-ends could no longer be counted upon for a rest. There were people of consequence who had to be invited to Barrackpore; Sir Henry Fane and his family, or visiting bishops and other clergy, or officials who came with letters of introduction from the Directors of the East India Company.

Emily and Fanny played their parts as hostesses with their usual ease and friendliness, but before long they both knew that it was going to take all their will-power to keep up this appearance of composure. They were never able to relax now. From a ceaseless round of duties in Calcutta they came to a houseful of week-end visitors at

Barrackpore. They had to find entertainment for these visitors; and cards and games soon palled.

One evening they had a puppet-show, which was a success. There were fifty puppets at a time on the miniature stage: tiny figures dancing nautches or riding on elephants. The native showmen who manipulated the puppets were excellent mimics; Emily thought them as good as the Italian *fantoccini*.

The animals, wild and tame, provided some diversion. The menagerie had grown. There was an old tiger, and a young one who was beginning to turn his playful pats into good hard scratches, and so would have to be given a cage of his own. A leopard, two cheetahs, two small black bears, and two porcupines had also been added, besides an assortment of sloths and monkeys. Best of all, there were birds— tiny exotics, and two Siamese partridges, wonderful birds with rich brown crests and scarlet legs, which someone had brought from China.

Chance, of course, was the acknowledged *doyen* of their animal world, both at Calcutta and Barrackpore. He had become so Indian-ised that if he could have barked out orders, they would probably have been in Hindustani. William Osborne had taught him a great variety of tricks, which he displayed at dessert every evening. This not only made conversation, in a country where that talent did not abound, but it surprised people not used to such a highly educated dog. One lady at the Barrackpore dinner-table was so taken with a fit of laughter at seeing Chance lie down on his back and feed himself with his hind paw, that she did not recover her gravity for the remainder of her stay.

They all had need of whatever laughter came their way. August was a failure as far as the rains were concerned. It was like living in a hot poultice. Dr. Nicolson had warned them that in the winter it would be like living in a cold one, but that was something to look forward to. Their main concern at present was to get through this truly devilish stretch of super-hot hot season, remain decently clothed when gowns tended to fall to pieces on being shaken, and to maintain some kind of dignified front against the ever-wondering eyes of the Calcutta ladies.

Fanny had established a private correspondence with China, which she hoped would produce great things in the way of clothes. If the articles should turn out to be contraband, that, she considered, would give an added zest to the transaction. The Chinese made silks with embossed flowers on them, so stiff and grand they would sit up alone

54

in a chair. To appear in one of those silks would make all the Calcutta ladies fall down in separate fainting fits; because, being in Asia, they thought it incumbent upon them to wear only what came from Europe.

Fanny never looked at the thermometer now, for fear the shock would be too much for her; but whenever she had reason to believe, from her own feelings, that it was not higher than a hundred degrees, she intended to come rustling down in a China silk, with the walk and bearing of a mandarin, and give the Calcutta world something to talk about.

★   ★   ★   ★   ★

It was November, and the gay season had begun.

Regular balls and private theatricals began to fill up social life once the cold weather had come. That, considered Emily, was only a courtesy term. When the old residents asked if it did not remind her of an English November, she would have liked to show them a good Guy Fawkes, and the boys purple with cold, beating their sides, and the squibs and crackers fizzing along the frosty ground. She did not deny that the weather had improved; but she still was not able to live five minutes without a punkah, and without having the blinds kept closed as long as there was a ray of sun.

'You have no idea what sallow figures we all are,' she wrote home. 'In another year . . . I shall believe we are all our natural colour. The new arrivals sometimes stagger us, but we simply say, "How coarse!" and wait with confidence for the effects that three weeks' baking will have. A delicate tender yellow is the sure result.'

Emily and Fanny being halfway in age between the mamas and daughters of Calcutta society, were expected to give entertainments agreeable to both generations. Formal dinners were an ever-recurring infliction, and dances where the energetic fifties and sixties insisted on frisking with the younger set, provided more cynical amusement than pleasure.

Encouraged by the two ladies at Government House, the bachelors of Calcutta gave a ball, to which Emily and Fanny brought two quadrilles of young ladies—without their chaperones. Sixteen young ladies, with no sharp-eyed mothers to watch them. Emily and Fanny had selected sixteen partners for them with care, and if that did not settle at least six of them happily, it would be a great waste of trouble, red velvet and blue satin.

Both Emily and Fanny had a tenderness for young people, and thought it was a dreadful life for them in India. They came out from England looking so fresh and pretty, and eager to be amused. They found that for months at a time they had to be shut up in dark rooms with no occupation for twenty-three out of the twenty-four hours. There were no gardens, no villages, no poor people to visit, no schools to teach, no poultry to look after—none of the things they had been used to doing at home. Very few of them were at ease with their parents, having been sent to England when they were children.

Gardening, cottage visiting, a village at the end of a country lane—these came to mind every time Emily and Fanny received a new arrival from home. The first sharp pangs of homesickness had been dulled, but the sight of a fresh-complexioned girl among all these yellow faces usually brought a flash of pain as well as pleasure.

One day early in December they had an extraordinary piece of luck. They met someone who had actually met their sister Eleanor, and who knew East Combe, and Eden Farm, and many of their neighbours.

An Army captain who had been invited to stay at Barrackpore brought with him his eighteen-year-old wife, newly come from England. Emily and Fanny were first attracted to the young couple because he was nearly seven feet tall and she was tiny, hardly coming up to his elbow. But she more than made up for her lack of inches by good humour and high spirits. And then, she came from Blackheath!

Her value rose from that moment. She knew Lady Buckingham-shire, whom she considered beautiful and amiable, and she had once been to East Combe, having been taken there by the doctor to be vaccinated from the gardener's children. What a climax of interest, to meet at the furthest extremity of the globe a girl who had been vaccinated by the Eden family doctor from Eleanor's gardener's children! It made her second cousin to Fanny and Emily on the spot. Even George and William were stirred by this new link with home. William tried to make her recollect a favourite tradesman at Black-heath, which she could not do. George then said, "But were you never at Trill's?"

"Oh, Lord Auckland, do you know Trill's? What a good shop it was, was it not?" said the Captain's little wife.

This was almost the first time she had dared to speak to George, and it made them all laugh. Commonplace as the remark was, they found something cheering in the sound of Trill's. Only the day before, Wright had said, with a deep sigh: "To be sure, what a different place this would be if we had but Trill's shop within reach." A devoted lady's-maid who went trapesing out to India with her mistress had many haberdashery problems to solve in a country that knew no Trills.

A cargo of ribbons, pins and tapes might have paid for itself twice over if some enterprising merchant had sent one out. It was a wonder then no American traders had thought of it; they thought of so much else that was useful. Besides cheap—and pirated—editions of English books, they sent cargoes of ice and apples. These were luxuries which brought high prices. True, Fanny and Emily found the apples horrid, tasting of the hay in which they had been packed. But the Europeans who had been twenty years in India, who had left their homes at an age when munching an apple was a real pleasure, flew at the mucky, hay-covered fruit—and fancied themselves young, and their livers the natural size, as they ate it.

The gaieties at Government House continued through most of December. Emily and Fanny heard a rumour that the military thought they were not being sufficiently noticed by the Miss Edens. That meant a ball had better be given for the affronted gentlemen.

It was a very grand ball, to make up for the apparent neglect. The front of the house, and the road and bridge outside, were illuminated by native lamps—wooden saucers with a flame of coconut oil burning in them. Emily and Fanny had arches of flowers put over the stair-cases and in the ballroom, and provided a sitting-down supper, which was much thought of. Calcutta co-operated by sending sixteen dancing ladies, besides plenty of gentlemen. Diplomatic invitations had also been accepted. General Allard, a Frenchman in the service of Ranjit Singh, came with some of his officers. There was a Danish contingent from Serampore. It was not for nothing that the Eden ladies were daughters of one of the most accomplished of eighteenth-century ambassadors.

The first Christmas in India was the first real landmark that Fanny and Emily could feel they had passed. The previous Christmas they had been at sea. Now that 1836 was on the point of turning into 1837, it looked as if the calendar was at least taking one step onwards; they could even look forward to next Christmas, when they expected to be on the first part of a great journey to the north-west provinces.

On Christmas Day they went to church with George and William. They were both in low spirits. Fanny had not been feeling well for some weeks, and Emily had had a long bout of headaches, and was in Dr. Drummond's daily care.

The church service brought some comfort to the sisters as they knelt down side by side, each isolated in her own little cell. The familiar words of the communion service brought their family and friends very close at that moment. They felt, as they had rarely done before, that they were indeed part of the great fellowship of Christians, commemorating the birth of the same Saviour, with the same rites, on the same day. It brought those at home very near. But one part of the service was entirely thrown away on Emily, she told her sister Eleanor in her next letter.

'I beg to observe [that] the Psalms, as usual, did not agree with my complaint. "Hearken, oh daughter, and consider; incline thine ear; forget also thine own people, and thy father's house." I never think David quite understood what he was writing about. The more I hearken and consider, the more I feel that my own people and my father's house are the very points I never can forget. I never thought so much of them before.'

The new year that stretched before them promised to be different from the past nine months in India, which seemed in retrospect to be more like nine years. For one thing, there was the northern journey to prepare for. But there was to be a much earlier break in the pattern of their official life in 1837; for Fanny, at any rate.

'My dear, here is such a plan, such a sublime plan burst upon me!' she wrote to Eleanor Grosvenor. 'It will eventually conduct me either to the bottom of a tiger's throat or the top of a rhinoceros' horn. . . . They do say—it is hardly possible to believe them—that there are *hills* in Bengal, not more than 140 miles from here; and the unsophisticated population of those hills is entirely composed of tigers, rhinoceroses, wild buffaloes, and, now and then, a herd of wild hogs. There, I'm going to live for three weeks in a tent. I shall travel the first fifty miles in a palankeen, and then I shall march. It takes a full week to travel a hundred miles in that manner . . . as our beds, armchairs, tables and clothes all travel on the heads of human beings.'

Emily wrote more details to Theresa Lister. Fanny, she told Theresa, was going on a tiger-shooting expedition with William into the Rajmahal hills; they would be joining a Mr. and Mrs. Cockerell, who made one of these hunting trips every year. Mrs. Cockerell was a sharp little woman, almost pretty, and very ill-natured—or so Emily had heard. But Fanny would not see too much of her, for Mrs. Cockerell was a keen tiger-huntress, and so would be out on her elephant with the men; while Fanny would be able to sketch all day long if she wished. It would be a very good change of scene for her, and something out of the common course of life, Emily thought. And it would make an amusing recollection in after-life, when they returned to England.

'William won't hear reason as to the horrible dangers he is going to take me into,' Fanny wrote home. 'The other two ladies regularly get upon their elephants and go tiger-hunting every day; they talk of the excitement of the tiger's spring, and the excellent day it was when they saw eight killed. I happen to be very much afraid of a cat—I may say, a kitten. If I were to stay at home while the others were out, a stray tiger would just walk in and carry me off. As George encouragingly observed this morning, "I see him moving at a round trot with you in his mouth, like a goose thrown over a fox's back."'

William Osborne was already making plans to join the Cockerells. It was going to be a nice little march, he observed to Fanny. No fuss or trouble at all. He had written already for elephants, and they need only have a guard of twenty men. Fanny had better take Jones, in case she should be ill, and the *ayah*, Myra, to be a companion for the English maid. Then, with Fanny's own sixteen bearers, she would only want ten or twelve more to carry her things. Of course, her *kitmutgar* would also have to go, to wait on her at dinner, and *peons* to pitch her tent, and her *jemadars* to look after them all, and her washerman and tailor. Those few, with his own tail of servants, would do very well.

Fanny ventured to suggest that she was not likely to want any clothes made for the three or four weeks they expected to be away.

"Oh, but tailors are always of use," said William. "I remember the time a tiger fastened on my elephant's trunk, and so nearly clawed me out of the howdah. My tailor saved the elephant's life by sewing up the wound."

Fanny was secretly alarmed at the tiger-shooting part of the trip, but the prospect of a few weeks in real hills, with real scenery to sketch and William to look after her, made her decision to go an easy one. She laughed at Dr. Drummond, who disapproved of the proposed jaunt on account of her delicate constitution. And when he got together all the most frightening documents he could find about tigers and jungle fevers and laid them on the table before her with a solemn air, she laughed even more.

They were to set off in the middle of February. The six weeks before their departure were chequered by the kind of events Fanny and Emily had already inured themselves to accept; the sudden death of friends, ships foundering in sight of land, the constant danger to their beloved pets from the semi-wild animals and the snakes which infested Barrackpore.

The loss of Dr. Bramley, head of the Hindu College, affected them both with real sadness. He was one of the few people with whom they had been able to achieve some intimacy; a cultivated man who was regarded by everyone with affection and respect. He sang well and played on the flute; a delightful guest to have. One day he developed a bad headache, and less than a week later he was dead of fever.

'You cannot imagine how the ranks close in after a death,' Emily wrote to Pamela. 'The most intimate friends never stay at home above two days, and they see everybody again directly. . . . I should have thought grief might have taken just the other line, but I suppose they could not bear it *alone* here. . . . Dr. Bramley had more warm friends than anybody here, but there was not one who stayed away from the races after his death.'

Then there was the awesome spectacle of the *Gregson*, which was burnt down to the water's edge just as it got out to sea. All the passengers were saved in the ship's boats, and were brought back to Calcutta; but every article on board was lost. How many of their letters home had been on her, wondered Fanny and Emily. An immense packet had been sent by the *Victoria* three months before, and that vessel had been burnt out at the Mauritius. It was very depressing.

The first week in February brought a near-catastrophe which shook William Osborne's habitual nonchalance. It happened at Barrackpore. William and the aides-de-camp, with a sprinkling of male guests, had settled themselves on the lawn for an hour's smoking and political argument after the ladies had gone to bed. Behind them was a row of servants, and behind the servants about twenty jackals.

Fairy,* who had been curled up on William's knee, jumped off. There was a little shriek, which they took to be a cat screaming. A moment later one of the servants saw a jackal carrying Fairy off by the throat. Everybody shouted and ran, frightening the beast into dropping Fairy and running off. The little dog was picked up with her paws and throat badly torn, and apparently so dead that William told one of the men to bury her. But after the man carried her away

---

* William's favourite greyhound.

she showed signs of life, so her funeral was countermanded. She screamed and howled for two days, and as dogs who had been bitten by jackals generally went mad, William had her kept in a cage. After a week she began to recover, and William was able to make the final arrangements for the tiger hunt with his customary calm restored.

Now that Fanny had made up her mind that she must put up with the shooting part of the expedition, she could look forward to it. She felt ready for adventure. And to complete her felicity, a few days before she was due to leave, a profusion of letters arrived from England, together with a box of gowns for her and Emily. Lovely articles! True, Fanny thought the latest London fashions hideous, and remarkably unbecoming. But the gowns themselves were beautifully made, and both she and Emily were thankful for something new.

On the morning of February 13th Fanny and William, with their servants, set off from Barrackpore for the first stage of the journey to Rajmahal. They were in good spirits, for on the previous evening there had been a thunderstorm with pouring rain, the first that had fallen for five months. This would bring back cool weather for another month, besides laying the dust for their journey, which was no small consideration. Their tents and gear had already gone on; two sets of tents, one to live in on Monday, while the other would be carried on twelve miles or so, to be ready for them on Tuesday. In this way they expected to have shelter set up for them in a new place every day, with the minimum of trouble. They were to meet the rest of the party in a week or ten days; Mrs. Cockerell, it now turned out, was to be the only other lady besides Fanny.

Emily sent three of her own servants with them for a short part of the way. Her *jemadar* returned the following day, saying that the *chhota lady sahib* had sent her love, and said she had all she wanted. The *chhota lady sahib*, he reported, looked very comfortable in her palkee.

So Fanny was off. Emily never minded being alone, so long as George was not too far out of reach. But she suddenly realised that she was going to miss Fanny.

4

FANNY'S JOURNAL

[Extracts from letters to Eleanor Grosvenor]

Barrackpore, February 13th, 1837. William and I are here because it is fifteen miles on our road—that is a march and a half. Do you think we shall get safely back? I have my doubts, because the wild beasts in this country are real wild beasts, who will not listen to reason.

Bullea, Tuesday, February 14th. We left Barrackpore at four o'clock yesterday afternoon, went in the carriage to Pultah Gaut and there left our state behind us in the shape of guards, postillions and *syces*, and squatted down under the straw covering of a country boat—touching monuments of abdicated grandeur. On the other side of the Hooghly we found our palanquins. As I got into mine, I felt very much as if I were getting into my coffin. However, there was a comfortable bed made up in it.

The afternoon was beautiful, not the least hot. William, Jones and I were carried side by side with the doors of our palanquin open, and it was a much more cheerful and much less shaking mode of convey-ance than I had expected. When the sun set, though it was bright moonlight, the bearers who ran by the side lighted great torches and we got on quickly, every now and then having to get into a boat to cross some small river. . . .

We arrived at seven in the morning, having travelled at the rate of five miles an hour, which is fast for *dak* travelling. The tents are very comfortable. We find we have 260 people altogether in the camp. Half our followers bring their followers; we have twenty elephants, too. Jones, my English maid, travelled in a palanquin with us. Myra, the *ayah*, I found in a violent fit of anger because we were later than she expected, and she thought we must all have been drowned crossing a river.

I was lying very comfortably on a sofa, when they ran in to tell William there was a large aligater on the bank of a *jeel* close by the tents; so he took his gun and I went with him, and he shot it so as to wound it, and thus it took to the water. Upon which ten of the elephants were sent in to hunt it there, and it was very grand to see how eager they were, and to hear them scream whenever they found it. The chase lasted more than an hour, the elephants trying to trample down the aligater, and the aligater turning on them; till at last the *mahouts* threw themselves off into the water, and there were men, elephants and aligater all splashing about together. Then it was driven on shore, when William shot it—such an enormous beast.

Birkrampore, February 15th. We left Bullea at seven this morning. The vultures and jackals had left nothing but the bones of the aligater. This is the order of our match. William and I have [the] cash and double set of tents, and one for our drawing and dining room. There are, besides, Sepoys' tents, cooking tents, and a tent for the servants. Jones sleeps in my tent, Myra and *syce* in the verandah which goes round it. At night we put all our goods and chattels outside, under charge of the sentry. All the inferior servants sleep under trees, or make themselves little straw huts. After dinner we send on our dining tent, and two of our sleeping tents, and our cooks, baker and half the servants, so we find breakfast ready and tents pitched when we arrive the next morning at the new encamping ground. . . .

Spring is begun now, and the jungles look beautiful with the different shades of green, and the red cotton tree, which is one mass of crimson flowers and abounds everywhere. It has no leaves yet, only large blossoms—like a daphne multiplied the size of an elm.

My Mussulman *jemadar*, Ariffe, brought us a handful of wild duck he had shot, which he handsomely offered us for dinner, and which we as handsomely declined. That pompous old bore Dullhoo*

* The Hindu steward.

condescendingly accepted same, though he could not eat anything religiously which had died such a death by a Mussulman's hand. He cut all their throats after they were dead and so satisfied his conscience and his hunger, without inflicting any great harm on the dead ducks.

At four o'clock William took his gun and I my sketch book, and we got on our elephant, and went out after subjects. I found . . . a little temple and made a masterly sketch . . . while William went from one *jeel* to another murdering the innocent wild ducks. If he goes out of sight for a minute I begin to think it very shocking to be left all alone in the middle of Asia.

Pangotta, 16th. We did not set off till $\frac{1}{2}$ part of this morning, for we had only a march of six miles. The country perfectly hideous, flat uncultivated plains, nothing uneven but the road. However . . . there was a great improvement the last mile. A forest and a river and a really pretty village, the huts with verandahs and neatly thatched, and great signs of farming implements about.

The instant we come in sight the women cover up their faces and scuttle away as fast as they can. One of them having no other means of escape, scrambled over a high mud wall with her child sitting on her hip, the way they always carry children here. . . .

The weather is quite perfect—no fog, no dew, and the thermometer in this tent only seventy at the hottest time of the day. I feel exactly twice as strong as I did four days ago at Calcutta. William is out shooting snipe, and I have got up a case of oppression for him when he comes home. Ariffe, who speaks excellent English, has been telling me that some of the villagers have followed from the last station to complain that the elephant *jemadar* and the Sepoy *havildar* and my *kitmutgar*, who caters for us, took their fish, kids and eggs without paying for them, and beat one old man who had a natural distaste for parting with his property on these terms.

I hear a great deal of loud recrimination going on, and I suspect from the looks of the culprits that we have innocently performed the guilty act of eating a stolen dinner. William is just come home with some snipe and quails, so we shall have something to eat which we have honestly earned today.

We have had a regular trial; Ariffe and the villagers on one side, and the culprits on the other, who had nothing to say for themselves. So now we are to send on every day to the head man of the village to tell him not to let anybody have anything till it is paid for. As this constant change of air makes me very hungry, I shall go out with my own little purse and buy our own little dinner.

February 17th. We had a long march this morning, twelve miles . . . Will it shock you to know that though excessively like gypsies in other respects, we have something bordering on civilisation in our tents in the shape of a chess board and cards? We play at chess for an hour after luncheon while William smokes his hookah, and when it is too glaring even to *look* out of the tent. At cards for half-an-hour after dinner . . .

We are engaged in a very complicated system of gambling, and the grand result is to be a large ivory elephant which we are to have manufactured at Moorshadabad, *the* place for ivory carvings. It will simply be the death of me if William should win.

Berhampore, Sunday, February 19th. We are in a house again, and have a roof over our heads and walls round us. . . . A house is clearly a very inferior habitation to a tent—a very confined feel about it, and mosquitoes in full force. We have not had one in our tents. . . .

I went to the chapel this morning where Dr. Hill, a missionary, preached, and there was the presbyterian service. It was a very striking sermon, violently Methodistical. He preaches twice a day in the bazaars to the natives. The Europeans at the stations are very fond of him; they say he is a sincere religious enthusiast.

Mr. Forbes and Mr. and Mrs. Russell dined with us. The poor woman is just arrived, half broken-hearted at leaving four children at home in the care of strangers. She was to have left the fifth, but when the ship was at the port of sailing could not part with it, and smuggled it on board.

Moorshadabad—20th. We came on here yesterday afternoon. . . . The Nawab of Moorshadabad borders too much upon what we call here the political affairs of the country for me to ask many questions about him. But as far as I can make out from my own accurate observation, he is one of the Native princes living under our tender care and protection. The city of Moorshadabad and £10,000 a year we leave him in possession of, with Dr. Melville* settled close at hand to watch him how he spends his income. A considerable portion of it, we very much against his own consent have undertaken to spend for him,

* The political agent.

because we say he is a dissipated young man and would waste it if left to himself. So we have been building a palace for him, a magnificent modern-looking palace, which would make our king's new palace turn pale with envy.

A thousand workmen have been employed upon it for six years. One more year will see it finished, and of all the palaces I have seen, it strikes me as one of the most perfect—so beautiful outside, and such splendid rooms within. It is all to be paved with grey marble from China. The dining-room and the ballroom are each . . . 170 feet long. The immense heights of rooms here adds much to their beauty. They have brought out mirrors and large panes of glass for it from England, and eight hundred panes of glass were broke in the course of the voyage. £60,000 will pay the whole cost of the building.

The Nawab till last week never entered the doors, but stuck to his declaration that he did not want a new palace and would rather not live in it. However, last week he softened on the subject, and went over it and was delighted. He is to furnish it himself, and it is to be hoped will manage better than the Rajah of Lucknow, who brought over some fine statues and set them up standing on their heads.

The Nawab sent us a great quantity of fish, vegetables and fruit in baskets covered with scarlet cloth. Later in the day, so did the old Begum. *Her* fish were very far from fresh, but the servants were happy to eat it all.

Bamanier, 21st. We had a short march here of twelve miles—the first three through the city on an elephant. We passed a beautiful temple with a rival clay elephant as the idol, and, upon the whole, we on our elephant looked the most worshipful of the two.

Moorshadabad must have been a splendid city in its day; the river-side . . . bordered by mosques . . . the market-place a beautiful sight with four old gateways leading into it. The swarms of natives buying and selling seemed without end, and the bazaar around looked quite brilliant from their manufacture of silver fringe.

Ever since we set off, there have been such bright moonlight nights. This looks to me like a flourishing dwelling place for rising young tigers, and we are going out in the afternoon, as usual, after game, like two babes in the wood on an elephant. There is a pleasing sound of singing birds today, such as I never heard in Calcutta. I do not like the notion of going back to that great, hot, shut-up prison of a palace.

'I sketched a mosque'

Now we are in a scrape. We thought we were within twenty-six miles of the place of meeting, and have just got a messenger to tell us there has been a mistake about it, and that the rest of the party will be at Oudnulla, 56 miles off. . . . We have seen the elephant *jemadar*, who says he will contrive for us to go seventeen miles tomorrow. . . .

Comra, 22nd. Here's a heartrending situation. After seven miles on an elephant, and six in the tilbury over a road which made our progress very much like sailing in a ship on a short sea—within five miles of the place of encampment—we passed five men with our dining-table on their heads, two more with my sofa, two more with chairs. In the distance was the distracting sight of Sepoys guarding hackeries, the carts that carry our kitchen utensils. Our fates flashed upon us at once. There were our advanced supplies, and we were to find nothing but empty tents—no breakfast, no nothing. And so it is . . .

William is smoking a cigar in a state of placid contentment that is very irritating to see. What is more, he had got hold of the *thanadar* and together they are going to empty the village of its simple and innocent inhabitants and hackeries, that they may relieve our own servants tomorrow and enable us to push on twenty miles. The baker, a most exemplary man, has in a most supernatural manner produced some gingerbread nuts, everybody else in the camp having denied the possibility of getting a bite of bread.

It is ½ twelve and we have breakfasted. Our breakfast was enlivened by old Dullhoo bursting in, in a fury, such as I never saw equalled by man, but probably soon shall by a tiger. It appeared that a monster, who we have seen wandering about the camp, with, I may say, a remarkable absence of clothing, is Dullhoo's servant and cooks his dinner. He had desired the said monster should travel on an elephant with Ariffe and some of our servants. They had arrived without him, and he suspected that they had turned him off. He said that all the others being Mussulmen, look for each other, but that he being an Hindu, must have an Hindu to cook for him.

William humbly represented that all *his* servants walked, and that Dullhoo's would not cook the worse for walking, too. He was in much too great a fury to listen, and we still hear him roving about the camp scolding whoever comes near him.

February 23rd. We accomplished our twenty miles with great success this evening. We saw some unhappy *dak* travellers sitting under a tree by their palanquins, without any bearers to carry them on. It is sometimes necessary here to arrange ten days beforehand the relays of bearers that are wanted; if they choose to set a traveller down in the middle of a jungle, he has no redress. When we got up, we found the victims were Mr. and Mrs. Cockerell, a remarkably small couple with a remarkably small lap-dog. There they all three sat in apparently a state of placid contentment, he with a book in his hand and she holding an umbrella over her head, and nothing in the shape of a human habitation near. Our natural question was, "Where are your bearers?"

"Oh, heaven knows; all abroad over the country, I believe. If you happen to meet any, send them on to us."

We suggested their mounting the first of our elephants and coming on to our camp, but they did not dare leave their palanquins. Happily, before we were four miles from them, we met a set of bearers in full trot towards them; some other travellers had taken them on, and they were like tired post-horses.

Oudnulla, February 24th. Here we are, in the very jaws of the tigers. The first man we asked about them said he heard one roar at twelve o'clock last night—an hour that makes it peculiarly awful. There are hills all round us, and a beautiful old bridge opposite our tents. The rest of the party's tents are on the other side of it. Besides the Cockerells, there are Mr. Stopford, Mr. Holroyd, and a Mr. Bracken, who having once had his foot in a tiger's mouth, has been an amateur tiger-hunter ever since.

We have seen none of them yet. They went out hunting at four this morning, that wonderful little woman Mrs. Cockerell with them . . . they have found no tigers, but have brought home quantities of spotted deer and black partridges—the sort of savage animals I should prefer meeting. . . .

We had our first sight of the Ganges, which looks more like a small sea than a river. In the middle of the day the sun is burning hot, the thermometer 89 in the tents. In the morning the wind is really piercingly cold. The hunting people went through a change of more than 45 degrees in twelve hours. Tomorrow morning they are going [on] what they call a home beat over some very pretty hilly jungles, and I believe I shall go with them for a little while.

February 25th. I got up at six, put myself in Mrs. C.'s howdah, and made my own elephant follow that I might come home when I pleased. Jones and Ariffe were on that, and Jones observed with a tender reminiscence of Emily's maid, "To be sure, what would Wright say if she saw me going out tiger hunting."

The jungles are beautiful at this time of year; trees covered with blossoms of different colours, and creeper, the peacocks flying in every direction—their scream has a sound of home. Herds of spotted deer starting out at every step, and then the quantity of elephants beating about, and the line of shooters on theirs. While I was with them, we saw nothing worse than wild hogs, but I had not left them ten minutes before they found a tiger and wounded him. Instead of showing fight he ran away as fast as he could.

One rhinocerous has appeared in the distance. When he does charge an elephant it is tremendous. I set off to go home through the jungle we had beat, with nobody to defend me and the elephant against the tigers, if they should come, but Ariffe and his dagger, and nothing to offer them to eat but Jones. When the elephant suddenly stopped, threw up his trunk and screamed, if there had been any use in it I should have begun to scream, too. They say he certainly must have smelled a tiger. I must not try the trick again of coming home alone, but the real fact is I fear the sun the most of the two.

I am low about seeing no monkeys.

Ramahal, February 26th. We moved six miles today, and all the way through jungles literally overrun with wild roses. The gentlemen have with them each six rifles in their howdahs, and shoot at all the innocent wild beasts they meet. Just as I was disserting upon the exceeding beauty of one rose bush, a great wild hog rushed out of it and charged the elephant Mrs. C. and I were upon. The instant after, it had five balls through it—and then I settled that I had no taste for the shooting part of the expedition, and shall confine my genius to the picturesque, and there is more than enough space for it here.

I thought that hog's was a shocking case of murder.... The elephants set to work to trample it to death, and when at last it was dead, they insisted upon my looking at it. It seemed to be such a fine strong beast, so exactly fitted to its own jungles. I do not see our right to take our love of destruction there.

Rajmahal Hills, February 28th. Anything more thoroughly eastern or prettier than the country we have passed through it is impossible to conceive ... the Ganges on one side and hilly jungle on the other, with

magnificent palm trees and bamboos rising from it. The rose trees
are white with roses growing higher than our heads. . . .

The others are shooting their way here. I had settled myself in my
tent to writing a letter, when some of the servants ran in and pointed
to what I thought an otter swimming; which otter rose out of the
water and turned out to be a small part of an aligater's head, the tail
being at a considerable distance. So very pleasant—it will be poking
in its head in a minute and reading this. I am very fond of aligaters—

'Elephants are the best beasts to see much of'

I say that to please it. And in this, my utmost need, I am deprived of
Ariffe, the only man in the camp who could speak English reason to it.
I have handsomely lent him to William because he can load a gun.
By way of making me quite comfortable, when I sent for my *ayah* to
tell her to stop the men who were in the *jeel* getting water, as I had
a particular dislike to see an aligater eat a man, she answered:

"Yes, Ladysheep, plenty aligater. Three more."

There actually are three lying on the opposite bank. Not make-
believe beasts at all, but eighteen or twenty feet along. I have nothing
but Mrs. Cockerell's little lap-dog to offer them in exchange for
myself.

Those men will be the death of me. They are all in the water again, in spite of all a William-trained *kitmutgar* can say to prevent them. Now they are putting a trough to stand upon, and I am better. The others are come back now, and twenty-seven elephants have swam the *jeel*, so that will settle the aligaters for the present.

'*They killed their first tiger*'

March 1st. I have been out from six till $\frac{1}{2}$ nine. . . . Our safety consists in being in the thick of the shooters, who have no time to think about us, but would naturally shoot any animal that would attack us, because it is the object they are after. Very soon the elephant we were on and two others near gave a roar, and an immense rhinocerous started up within a yard of us. All those near shot, and all declared it was hit, but if it were bore it very philosophically. While we were chasing that, our elephant still was snorting. Then we found a young rhinocerous was left, not much larger than a great pig. They wanted to take him alive, but he showed much more fight than the mother—charged a line of sixteen elephants and made them roar and turn round, for they hate a small live thing. The *mahouts* threw themselves off, to bind it with cords, but though they caught it three times, at last it fairly got the better of them and escaped to the thick jungles.

Ten minutes after, we found another old rhinocerous, probably the respected father, a very magnificent looking beast. The chase after him was beautiful. All the elephants get so eager and press on as hard as they can. He made his escape, too, which I was not as sorry for as I ought to have been, for the half-hour's chase was just as grand to see. After that I left them to come home across what was called a safe bit of country, and in that same bit, within a quarter of a mile of the camp, they killed their first tiger ten minutes after I left them. Mrs. C. came home smaller and fresher and better dressed than ever, quite delighted, and only wishing it had showed more fight.

March 2nd. Last night, just as I was going to bed, they came and told me a rajah had brought a spotted deer, two peacocks and a pot of honey. As they were jungle productions I was not to refuse them. I sent my salaams, wondering what on earth I should do with the peacocks, but he made such a point of making his salaam to the *lady sahib,* I went out in a pink flannel dressing-gown, which I hope he thinks an approved English mode of dress. There he was, in a gold kincob dress and turban, with his servants holding torches and the peacocks and the deer, which turns out the greatest of pets, follows me about, and lies by me on the sofa like a little dog.

March 4th. We moved three miles today among some fresh hills, very pretty and thoroughly English. . . .

Some of the servants met a tiger this morning, but it walked on, never minding. They found, too, the half-eaten body of a man. The gentlemen were out again this afternoon. There are some lovely sketches about, but William says it is not safe to go. However, Mrs. C. and I went a little way on an elephant, and did nothing more frightful than put up a jungle cat, which is a little larger than our cats. It ran through the camp, and as it bounds and looks like a little tiger, they all began screaming out, "Tiger!" Upon which Jones and Myra barricaded themselves in my tent. One very clever man called out: "No tiger," upon which they called louder than ever: "Young rhinocerous!" and Jones and Myra added an extra chair to their barricades.

March 5th. It is Sunday, and I staid at home thinking I was going to read prayers; but the Hindu religion is so much more vociferous than mine, I can do nothing. It is one of their festivals, and many hundreds are passing to wash in a stream near here, to offer plantains and kids. What with their singing and screaming and tom-toms and the bleating of kids, I don't think I ever heard such a noise before. Of course Dullhoo said he must go, and instead of offering a kid has brought one back. So have half the servants in the camp—sacred little kids that are not to be eaten. But it is dinner-time, and a suspicious lull is come over them.

March 6th. I saw Dullhoo rush up to Jones with a stick today when she came out of my tent, and thought he had gone mad; but there was a large scorpion on her cloak as big as the top of a tea-cup, which had settled itself there in the night. She had a narrow escape, for their sting is horrible, and if it were the same to everybody I had rather not have scorpions in my tent at night.

My little deer is such a treasure. He travels in my howdah, and I hope he hides his face when they shoot any of his connections. He has his own spoon, tea-cup and saucer, and is very particular about the grass and young leaves he makes his servants pick for him. He trots after me from one tent to another in a most majestic manner. . . .

We have changed our route, and the consequence is George may be recalled and he and Emily set sail, and I not know of it, for I shall get no letter for ten days. They have heard of tigers three marches off, "real good tigers," Mrs. C. says, "worth going after, for I understand they have eaten quantities of human creatures."

William and I strolled about on an elephant this afternoon, and beautiful it was . . . wild rose trees and reed grass on high ground, and the hills in the distance. I sketched a mosque where there is the head of a dead saint which is inhabited by a live one; the servants say that two tigers come every day and sweep it clean with their tails.

March 7th. We came eight miles today. I came with the shooters the first five miles, and saw them beat through jungles which are evidently remarkable for the peaceful character of its brute inhabitants. I say nothing, but if I were given to shooting, I would shoot deer and peacocks without having fifty elephants to help me. . . .

The natives burn the jungles at this time of year, and of an evening the flames on the hills are very grand. This morning at one part of the road the jungle was burning on each side, and we had to make a circuit to get past, the bearers singing a sort of melancholy chorus all the time: "Jeldee, Jeldee, kubbadar"—"Make haste, make haste, have a care."

The tall palm trees rising out of the flames and smoke looked like a scene on the stage, but the heat was so great, I was glad when we had passed. . . . How unlike to any life one has dreamed of before, this tent life is. When we go up the country at the end of the year, with all our pomp about us, it will not be half as amusing; but if we get back without any calamities from tigers or jungle fevers, this journey will have been a most successful experiment. I have twice the strength I had when I left Calcutta. As to William, if he gets twenty miles deeper into the jungle, I do not believe it will be possible for him to be caught up and led back again to his military secretaryship. He will go off as one of the elephants did last night.

March 8th. We have moved seven miles. They shot deer and partridges all the way. We passed the remains of an old fort today. The hills near it are a stronghold of the Thugs, the people who religiously strangle their fellow-creatures. One confessed the other day after a long life of Thuggism that he had assisted at the deaths of seven hundred.

There is but one step from the jungle to our tents, and a jackal just now put his head out within three yards of me, which promises well for the security of the night.

March 9th. We are staying here, excessively baffled by the tigers. They saw one large one yesterday afternoon, but in such thick jungle the elephants could not make their way after him. . . . There was something grand in the way all the elephants set off stamping and screaming, and follow up the traces of a tiger in jungles where it seems a sin and a shame to fancy a tiger could be—soft grass, with clumps of rose bushes white with roses, and thousands of butterflies hovering over them.

Elephants are the best beasts to see much of—I cannot say the respect I have for them. Though not naturally witty I suspect they have much more common-sense than we have. When the sun is hot they throw dust on their backs if they cannot get grass, and when that gets heated they brush it off with their trunks and throw on fresh.

March 10th. I went off on a bold expedition of my own this morning. I had a hankering after those Thug ruins, which are only three miles off. There is a sort of semblance of a road to them over the hills where an elephant can go, so arming myself with Jones and Dullhoo, both equally efficient, I suspect, in case of danger, I set off, trusting to William's assertions that the tigers would not attack an elephant nor the Thugs strangle a woman. 'Murray' is the Hindustani word for carcase, and it gives them all the greatest pleasure to find one because they instantly assume it must be the remains of a tiger's dinner. By way of making me quite happy, William affectionately added:

"I'm sure I shall be very sorry if anything does happen to you, but at the same time it will be a melancholy consolation to find your half-eaten Murray."

We went through an awful pass where the banks were higher than one's head, so if a tiger had sprung, it would have sprung into our howdah.

Teliagurry. While I was sketching today, the man carrying the letters passed us, who for six shillings a month goes full trot every day twenty-five miles through this tiger country at all hours, with nothing but a large stick to help himself with, and professing his full belief that the tigers eat human creatures by the dozen. I was so proud of not being eaten, I went through a gateway and found a remarkably eligible ruin a little further on, and the remains of an old mosque.

March 15th. We are out of the hills . . . we moved today four miles to a hideous open plain with nothing but white ants' nests to break it, and a burning sun beating on the tents, and so the thermometer being nearly ninety, I am a lee-tle hot. . . . We have long been away from any post, and it is a whole fortnight since I have had any tidings of George and Emily. He was growing very despotic when I left home; he may have committed any atrocity during our absence—he has probably cut off the heads of all the aid-de-camps.

Gorroburreeba, March 16th. That is a nice simple village name, so I give it you and as I lie on my sofa on one side of the tent . . . The villagers come out in crowds to look at us, never having seen a European woman, I take out my sketch book and look full at them and pretend to sketch them, and they cover up their faces and run away as if a shot were fired among them—a very simple method of dispersing them.

Gornobureeba — March 16th That is a fine simple village
name), so I give it you & as I lie on my sofa
on one side of the tent, that is the view
presented to me on the other. Though the mornings
& evenings are still fresh & very unlike the same
articles in Calcutta — it is growing very hot
in the middle of the day — & I believe
all the camp sleep except me — William
has been in that attitude for the last

'. . . that is the view presented to me'

March 23rd. We are at what was Gour today, the remains being exceedingly small and diminishing every year, for it is in the possession of natives who had no respect for antiquity. . . . There are heaps of monkeys about here, and in their manners they assume a tone of careless superiority towards us which is rather humiliating. I wonder whether they really are the cleverer animal of the two.

We found an enormous skeleton of a snake—Ariffe said a boa-constrictor and that it was thirty feet long. I trust that none of his relations are alive, because we shall hardly have room for them in our tents. In these remote parts where there are only monkeys to comment upon it, William and I have taken to going about on an elephant in a very *dégagée* manner; nothing but a large stuffed crimson cushion on its back, without the howdah. Upon this we sit, very much as if we were in an Irish jaunting car. The animal goes twice as fast, and as smoothly. It is the common native way of being carried on them; but we think Dullhoo looks severe about it, as if he thought it undignified.

All our camp keep well. The few cases of illness we have had, I treated with great medical skill. The natives always send the most moving petitions for medicine the instant they are ill, but seldom swallow it unless they like the taste. Being told of that fact, I made Jones see them swallow it, and I suspect have heard much less of illness in consequence. When the moon got up last night we set off upon an elephant after a gateway that we rashly passed in the morning . . . so beautiful a bit of ruin I never yet saw. The arch is such an enormous height, and immense trees seem to grow out of the walls. . . .

These people must have been so very magnificent in what they did before we Europeans came here with our bad, money-making ways. We have made it impossible for them to do more, and have let all they accomplished go to ruin. All our excuse is that we do not oppress the natives so much as they oppress each other, a fact about which I have my suspicions. . . .

Surreet, March 24th. This is the last place we camp at upon this side of the Ganges. The chief of the Brahmins in this part of the world sent word he was coming to make his salaam, a fact which Dullhoo evidently considered of immense importance. Accordingly, in the evening, he did come in a *tonjon* with an umbrella held over his head, and a set of ragged servants after him. He and William and I sate gravely down on three chairs in front of the tents, and then he offered me a bag of rupees, which I was to touch, not take; but the touch was to show I would take them if I wanted them. As it happened, I did want them, very much, for we cannot get any notes changed. However, the high integrity of my nature prevailed, and with an air of benign condescension I only put my hands upon them.

He left some sweetmeats for the servants, the division of which kept the whole camp in a wrangle for three whole hours. We heard Dullhoo more than usually disputateous and tiresome about his share of a cake made of sugar.

Comra, March 25th. We are a mile beyond our last encampment, close by the factory of an indigo-planter—or, as the natives call him in their language, 'a blue fellow'. Some of these planters live all the year round without ever seeing another European. One who came to speak to William the other day really seemed to have forgotten how to speak English. Now and then, with one good season and good speculation, they make immense sums of money.

The nearer we get to Calcutta, the more this shocking old furnace heats up. From one to four, the outer air is really quite scorching, and as in the tents it is impossible to shut the air out, I am reduced to wishing myself between stone walls again. The thermometer is at 95 at this moment. I keep writing on because if I were to think how hot I am, I should die of it. William very cleverly goes to sleep while the sun is doing its worst, and we have eight months of this hot season to come. My spirit quails when I think of it.

Moorshadabad, March 27th. Again we have a house over our heads, and this time I do not despise it. To have the outward air shut out and punkahs pulled after the broiling of the last four days makes us feel positively chilly. . . .

I have been to see the oddest building I ever saw—the size of a small village. It must be substantial because it is old, but it all looks as if it were made out of talc and tinsel. The tombs of some of the Nawab's ancestors are there. I sketched one in an arch of an enormous gallery that goes round an octagon building, where there is another tomb that looks, upon a large scale, like the sort of thing I once used to fabricate out of foil and tinsel, to look pretty in a baby house.*

We are returning in country boats called 'budgerows', and the prospect is a hot one, but less appalling than travelling *dak* day and

* Doll's house.

79

night, or a twelve-days' march. There are only two rooms in each of our 'budgerows'—Jones sleeps on the sofa in my sitting-room. William's boat is smaller and lighter than mine, and if he chooses to go on at once to Calcutta without waiting for me, I cannot stop him. However, the cooking boat sticks close to me, and he will hardly leave that. We have a goat upon which he and the deer and I are all dependent for milk. I hope we shall have no storm, for this river is like a small sea, and would make nothing of swallowing up these small boats.

March 29th. We landed last night, for the boatmen anchor when it grows dark. We would not let them be near a village, for that ensures a noisy night; but we had our dinner table put out upon a very handsome sandbank. It looked so odd when we were walking at a little distance, to see a table with silver plate and candlesticks. The insects did not plague us in the least, and we played at écarté with great success, with nobody but the pariah dogs to look on.

It is lucky that the boats we pass are picturesque and no two alike, for there has been nothing else to look at; the shores are all sand without a human habitation. We are getting on so fast, we ought to-morrow to be in deep water enough for a steamer.

March 31st. A Missionary came to ask for a passage on board the steamer to Calcutta. William and I were taken by his look, and asked him to dinner. He had been living for seventeen years in the Rajah of Burdwan's city—the only European there—who allows him to have as many schools and make as many converts as he can. He seemed satisfied with what he had done in both ways.

He seemed clever and sensible, and said if ever there was a country where Missionaries are needed, this is it. Every year, at the time the crops are sown, a certain number of human creatures are sacrificed and their limbs spread about the land—sometimes they are literally cut up alive. Three weeks ago, the European Resident there rescued twenty-eight; some of them had been bought as children, and brought up for the purpose. Eight girls he had sent down to the orphan school here—they would have been sacrificed this spring. Some of the future victims are allowed to marry, but their families as well as themselves are sacrificed in time.

All this is a new discovery, and Government will take what measures they can that are safe, to stop such horrors.   But all such customs can only be done away with by degrees.

Barrackpore, April 1st.   We landed this morning, and found George and Emily here to meet us, and both looking particularly well.   In this country to have been away for near two months without one trouble or fright of any kind, is a blessing to be thankful for.   Certainly this expedition has quite answered to me in point of pleasure.   Then I am rather proud of having seen a tiger killed, because, except for Mrs. Cockerell, there is not another woman in India who has, I believe.

The park looks very nice indeed just now; the grass and trees are such a beautiful green at this time of the year, and we shall be alone for the next three days.   I am persuaded that if the beasts we have left were a little tamer, and the people we are going to were a little wilder, the improvement would be remarkable.

On the banks of the Ganges

5

PRELUDE TO A JOURNEY

WITH Fanny away, Emily declared that she was quite over-worked. Besides answering letters from home, she wrote at least every other day to Fanny or William. But as this was the kind of employment she liked best, she did not take her own grumbling very seriously.

A large package of mail from home had made her very happy. Fanny's and William's shares had immediately been dispatched after them, and Emily was gratified by an extra large number of letters for herself. It was not only the family connections who wrote; her friends remembered her passion for hearing about everything that was happening.

Theresa and Pamela could always be depended upon, but her political friends did not forget her. They sent news of what was happening in Parliament, to supplement the scant items in the Indian papers.

Charles Greville found time in his busy life to send her the kind of letters she valued very highly. Discreet, kindly, surveying the scene with shrewd, objective eyes, Greville was writing the Journals which were to be the best quarry for future historians of the period.

To Emily, he allowed himself an occasional pungent comment. There was a split in the Whig camp, and though he was not surprised at this, with so many men of strong and obstinate opinions among them, he expected they would be sensible enough to reconcile their differences in order to stand firm against their common enemy, the Tories.

Emily read this kind of news with mixed feelings. She was as anti-Tory as ever she had been, and would have hated a change of government. Yet, if there *were* a change, and George were recalled . . . With a pang and a sigh she pushed away the enticing thought. Mr. Greville held out no such threat—or hope. She read through his long letters attentively, taking in the implications behind the accounts he gave of the moves which monarchs and politicians were making on the chess-board of Europe.

Charles Greville's acquaintance with diplomatists in the Courts on the Continent gave him the advantage of obtaining his information

WILLIAM, SMOKING HIS HOOKAH. From Fanny Eden's Journals

Draw here have go a on board the flat — & that is the other flat & the steamer that has it —. The ball

FLAT (RIVER BARGE) ON THE GANGES.   BISON AND CART
From Fanny Eden's Journals

at first hand. He had met Prince Esterházy at dinner, and the Austrian Ambassador had told him of his attempts to bring about a reasonable attitude between the Powers now glaring at each other across the map. England was watching France and Russia. Palmerston was showing a prickly front to Louis Philippe over events in Spain. As for Russia —the English Foreign Minister epitomised the growing detestation and fear of that empire, rolling slowly but purposefully towards the East.

All Europe wanted a limit set to the tremendous ambitions of Russia; but England, in particular, had a vital stake in the game— India. And Palmerston, brusque in manner and with an undisciplined tongue, did not hesitate to call Russia names, and to shake his country's fist in the face of a possible aggressor.

Prince Esterházy had talked with the Emperor of Russia in Prague, and with Louis Philippe in Paris. England's prejudices, Louis Philippe told Esterházy, were unreasonably violent. Surely there was nothing to fear if the northern Powers stood together? If only Palmerston were more diplomatic, and less swayed by his own passions, negotiations would not be so difficult.

At the other side of the world, Emily Eden studied the map of India and thought of the journey up the country which her brother had planned to make, starting the following October. He intended to travel to Simla, and then go on to a meeting with the Maharajah Ranjit Singh, in order to discuss with him what should be done about Afghanistan. The trade mission to Kabul had not been a success. Dost Muhammad was uninterested in commercial treaties. What he wanted more than anything else was Peshawar back from the Sikhs. The Governor-General had already impressed upon him that the British could not interfere in the affair. Besides, Ranjit was an ally, and an important one. It was out of the question on any count.

Now came the news that Dost Muhammad had turned to Russia for comfort—and possible help. It was important that the Governor-General should see Ranjit Singh personally, and decide what was to be done next.

There was another place on the map which interested Emily immensely, besides the Sikh kingdom of Ranjit Singh. All the letters which reached her quickly from home were invariably stamped 'to the care of Mr. Waghorn, Cairo.' Lieutenant Thomas Waghorn of the Royal Navy had been sent by the home government to Egypt, to see what possibilities there were of communication between England and India by way of Suez.

'Waghorn, I see, is not [now] at Cairo,' Emily wrote to Charles Greville. 'If I thought he were there I should, in defiance of the authorities, address this to the care of *dear* Mr. Waghorn!' The possibility of letters going by the overland route as a matter of course, and taking only two months to arrive instead of five or six, was a prospect to cherish.

Meanwhile, she must try to give her friends some kind of picture of her life by answering in detail questions which Theresa had been asking. 'My intellect and memory are both impaired, and my imagination baked utterly hard,' she warned Theresa. But here, for what they were worth, were her answers.

Did she find amongst her European acquaintances any pleasing or accomplished women? Not one. Not the sixth part of one. There was nobody she preferred to any other body whom she could think of setting out to visit. The Calcutta ladies read no new books, they took not the slightest interest in home politics; everything was melted down into being purely local.

Yes, it was a gossiping society. They sneered at each other's dress and looks, and picked up small stories about each other from the *ayahs*. It was a downright offence to tell one woman that another looked well. It was not often easy to commit that crime with any regard to truth. But still, there were degrees of yellow, and the deep orange woman who had had many fevers did not like the pale primrose creature with the constitution of a horse, who had not had more than a couple of agues. In her secret soul Emily thought the new arrivals, with their good colouring, looked fresh and cheerful; but gossip immediately decreed that they were coarse and vulgar. Was it a moral society? Yes, said Emily, it was a very moral society. Every man was employed in his office all day, and in the evening drove with his wife. It was out of the question for one to attend an evening party without the other; if Mr. Jones was ill, everybody knew that Mrs. Jones could not go out, so she was not expected.

'Looking at India dispassionately and without exaggerating its grievances for fun,' added Emily, 'I really think I hate it more now than at first. I try to make out for you stories and amusement from the pomp and circumstance of the life, and I can fancy you saying, "Oh, they talk so much about that, they must like it." But it is because there is nothing else to frame a cheerful letter on. I think the climate is a constant and increasing evil, inasmuch as it becomes every day more difficult to occupy myself.'

She looked forward to Fanny's letters from camp. Fanny, at least, was enjoying herself; she said so constantly. Emily wrote in reply nearly every day. She usually began her letter during the time when they would have normally been sitting together, and she found herself looking forward to telling her sister of the day's happenings.

The hot weather was beginning again. The *hotter* weather. Emily was finding it difficult to sleep well. One particular night turned out to be a horror of noise and accident; a hot wind blew up and raged like a hurricane, blowing away the mosquito netting from its supports over her bed. The mosquitoes made the most of their opportunities, and Emily scarcely got any rest. The following day she retired to her sitting-room after luncheon, and decided she would try to get an hour or two's sleep on the sofa. She took off her sash, loosened her gown, took up a French novel, and settled herself comfortably with Chance at her feet and a pet mouse-deer, which she had adopted, curled up at her elbow.

Soon she was asleep, but not for long. The servants came tumbling in, saying that the Lord Sahib and the Lord Padre were approaching. Almost at once George entered, attempting to look as if he went to church twice every Sunday. He was followed by the Bishop, Archdeacon, and a brace of chaplains. Chance immediately began to bark a protest.

Emily did her best. She shook herself straight, gently kicked Chance, tried to give Balzac's *Fleurs des Pois* a botanical air, sat carelessly down on the mouse-deer, and began to converse with considerable freedom. She was slightly checked by seeing her sash, in graceful serpentine folds, reposing under the Bishop's chair, and she quietly tried to fish it out with her foot. She was also aware of undone hooks and eyes at the back of her gown. Fortunately the Bishop was not too observant. He had been twenty days in a steamer coming down from Allahabad, and was nearly baked; he was too full of his own sufferings to notice anything.

Emily liked him. She had heard that he was sometimes very odd in his sermons, particularly if he saw that his hearers were inattentive. "You won't come to church. Some of you say it is too hot," he had been known to remark, wiping his face as he stood in the pulpit. "To be sure it is hot. I myself feel like a boiled cabbage, but here I am, preaching away."

A few days later she had more visitors in her sitting-room; this time a crowd of native petitioners who took up all the floor space. Captain MacGregor had turned off one of the servants for being absent three weeks without leave, and the man had now come, with a train of fellow-servants to beg for reinstatement. He had also brought his old mother to cry for him. It was all very interesting and very difficult. Emily did not wish to interfere with what the aides-de-camp considered their duty, but it was almost impossible to withstand this mass pleading and crying. The culprit knelt with his turban disordered, looking as if he were going to be hanged; and his ancient mother was huddled in her dirty veil, hideous except for tiny, beautifully shaped feet. Emily had a great mind to ask her for them; she looked such a dry old thing that she might easily have unscrewed them and taken them off. They would have been invaluable, Emily thought, to Chantrey, the sculptor.

The wailing increased, and Emily gave in, promising to speak to Captain MacGregor. She knew that one reason why servants were attached to Government House was because they were not beaten. She had always been horrified and disgusted to hear some of her callers let out from time to time that they were in the habit of beating these timid, weak creatures. Few of the natives seemed to know that they could have redress from a magistrate; she hoped they were beginning to find out.

The days now seemed very long. Emily was thankful when March neared its end, and she had a letter from Fanny saying they would soon be back now. Emily had been experimenting with modelling, as a change from sketching, and she had finished a little group of Fairy with her new puppies, as a present for William on his return.

* * * * *

The *Muharram* fell in the middle of April, and the Governor-General and his party went up to Barrackpore for the week-end with hardly any servants, for they all asked for holidays during the week of this sacred Muslim festival.

William, too, would have welcomed a good reason for not going to Barrackpore. He did not like the journey. If he came by steamer, said William, it refused to paddle; if he came by road, the horse fell down in the carriage shafts. Nature itself was obviously opposed to his going to Barrackpore. He had only two resources left; either to go on an elephant and pay the fine which was levied on all private individuals riding an elephant through the streets, or else to look about Calcutta for a gigantic *ayah,* who would carry him backwards and forwards on her hip in the manner in which *ayahs* carried children.

April, in spite of the heat, was a month to remember. There were packages upon packages of letters from home. Out of order, of course; it was quite usual to get letters dated August before those dated June. But what did that matter? Robert's letters had come by the overland mail in two months and a week; Eleanor Grosvenor's by sailing vessel in six months.

'You cannot think how we rummage about the letters,' Emily wrote to Robert, 'and pick out a stitch here and put a patch there, and bring dates and hints together, and make out a story of life for you all.'

Then there was a cuckoo in the park at Barrackpore. At this time of year, the birds affected a little singing; incoherent and confused, but still, the attempt was commendable and spring-like. Fanny and Emily heard one who kept saying "Cuck", but he couldn't say "Coo". However it was good of him to speak any English at all.

April was also celebrated by two Calcutta ladies who thought that sinful pursuits, such as theatrical performances, must be exposed, in spite of the patronage of the Governor-General's sisters. The European Orphan Asylum being badly in need of funds, the privates of the Cameronian Regiment acted a play—remarkably well, it was generally conceded. The proceeds were offered to the Asylum, and gratefully accepted by the ladies of the committee. Emily and Fanny, as patrons, added their signatures to the letter of thanks sent to the privates of the Cameronian Regiment. Two of the ladies on the committee, however, disapproved of the whole affair. They drew up a resolution to the effect that no establishment could expect the blessing of Providence that received contributions earned in this unchristian manner. If the orphans—a remarkably naughty set of spoiled girls, Emily considered —knew such subscriptions were received, it would hurt their feelings and their principles.

Emily and Fanny were vexed as well as amused. George, who now entered the fray, was simply vexed. He drew up a protest against the virtuous ladies' protest, which Emily and Fanny signed and sent off to the committee. Then they all had a pleasant evening's entertainment of two little French vaudevilles, uncommonly well acted by the company of French players, who were still in town. Nothing further was heard from the minority on the committee.

Early in May a ship brought more mail, and a box of books—a really satisfactory profusion. Here were riches. Besides a quantity of novels, there were the latest numbers of *Boz* and *Pickwick*, much to their delight; both Fanny and Emily had a particular affection for *Pickwick*.

May was the best month for Barrackpore. The park was at its greenest, and Emily's private garden was bright with scarlet and yellow, pink and blue. Everything exotic and flaunting grew in this climate; flowers which, at home, would have been the size of a crown piece here grew to the size of a dinner-plate. The menagerie was flourishing, too, though there were mishaps. The young tiger had taken a young fancy for a young child, and was shut up in consequence; the little bear gave a little claw at a little officer, and had to be shut up likewise. A large white monkey, which *was* shut up, got out, walked into the coachman's bungalow, and bit a little boy's ear. The 'rhinocerouses', through their fence being unmended, roamed about the park, and a respectable elderly gentleman, given to dining out at the cantonments, had been twice nearly frightened into fits.

A new interest for the two sisters at Barrackpore was a school for native children which George had built at the end of the park. He had engaged a clever native schoolmaster who had, in two months, taught the small Barrackporeans to read English and to answer questions in English remarkably well. When Fanny and Emily went for a drive by moonlight, they were generally accosted by small boys from the village who ran after the carriage calling out, "Good morning, sir!"

The sisters had by now become sufficiently Indianised to notice every means by which they could thwart the hot season. Last year had been an unpleasant period of being broken in; this year they practised what they had learnt. There was, to begin with, the question of draughts. With the thermometer at eighty-seven degrees in the rooms at Government House, Fanny and Emily had discovered an accidental draught in the marble hall, where the wind came down one of the corridors, cooled by the tatties. They both took to sitting there without a punkah—until Major Byrne, discovering them, said it was very unwholesome. Lady William Bentinck had never sat there. Emily assured him that that must have been because Lady William had never had the luck to discover this particular draught. Whereupon Major Byrne sent Dr. Drummond to say how prejudicial it must be. Dr. Drummond found it so pleasant that he drew up an arm-chair and thought it much the best place in the house.

Fanny and Emily were beginning to discover that Major Byrne was a remarkably sly old fox. He managed everybody, they observed, in a pleasant way, buttering and smoothing, and trimming his sails according to his company. Emily's dislike of him crystalised when she detected him in a piece of foxishness which she knew would wreck what comfort she could get out of her Indian way of life. George's chief native servant went to his own house in Dacca to get rid of a fever and did not return. Emily asked Byrne to write to the servant, but no answer came. She then told him to make arrangements for a new head servant, as there was not one among the other twenty in George's corridor who spoke English.

One morning Emily followed after Byrne to George's room to settle this important matter. She found him actually proposing to the Governor-General to take Emily's own *jemadar*. That jewel of a man! The only one who spoke English perfectly, and was her stay and support! As she entered the room, George said: "Here is Miss Eden, but you might just as well propose to her to cut the nose off her face as to give me that man."

Emily was quite prepared to give George her *jemadar* to take up the country, if he could be of use to her brother; but she did not like Byrne's behind-back methods. When he turned to her and suggested that it would be quite easy to train another servant to wait on her, she cut him short.

"Oh, dear, no!" she said. "I will not have any of your horrid strangers, who will steal all my goods, and take no care of Chance, and put too much wine in the seltzer-water. I will have my *chobdar* for the new *jemadar*."

This was too much for Byrne. A *chobdar* was inferior to a *jemadar*. "No, I think not," he said. "He is not of the proper caste—not authority enough. And he cannot wait at table."

"Then I will have one of my own *kitmutgars*."

"No, they do not speak English. I have one or two men in my eye whom I have always wished to put on the Government House establishment. They speak good English and you can teach them to be good servants. It is a great advantage to all succeeding Governors-General to find this sort of man in the house."

Emily had the greatest difficulty in preserving her calm manner. She did not in the least care for the comfort of future Governors-General, whoever they might be. Major Byrne was already eyeing the establishment from that point of view; he was in charge of the household of the prevailing head of state. The perfect official. He had won a tactical victory, but in the end he had to hold his hand.

George asked him to write to the Resident at Dacca, to find out what had happened to the missing head-servant; and so the matter rested.

Slowly the summer wore itself through. Social engagements were down to the minimum, because of the extreme heat. George would have been unable to attend functions, in any case, for the sessions of his Council were growing longer and more frequent.

The Governor-General had to come to some decision about Afghanistan: a definite decision. So far he had tried all peaceful ways to bring about an alliance with Afghanistan. But there was now a Russian agent at Kabul, reputedly on the best of terms with Dost Muhammad.

William Macnaghten, the Governor-General's Political Secretary, was a Russophobe, who did not trust an Afghan ruler known to be friends with the Tsar. It might be necessary, Macnaghten urged Lord Auckland, to take steps to depose Dost Muhammad and put someone more amenable on the throne. There was Shah Shuja. *He* had a valid claim to Afghanistan; his father had been the king, so he was the true heir. Shah Shuja had lived twenty years in exile, it was true, but Macnaghten was sure that he would be only too willing to be restored to his kingdom. Ranjit Singh would help. Ranjit and Dost Muhammad were old and bitter enemies; it would not be difficult to rouse the Sikhs against the Afghans, their traditional foes. Macnaghten himself undertook to go to see Shah Shuja, then to rejoin the Governor-General's camp in time for the state visit to Ranjit, with the Tripartite Treaty in his pocket.

The Governor-General had not come to India expecting to make war. But his dispatches from the Board of Control were clear. The rampart was to be built. In a dispatch sent by Hobhouse in 1836, the Governor-General had been told plainly that he must act firmly and decisively if diplomatic measures with Dost Muhammad failed. He was told he must 'counteract the progress of Russian influence in a quarter from which, from its proximity to our English possessions, could not fail, if it were once established, to act injuriously on the system of our Indian alliances, and possibly to interfere with the tranquillity of our own territory.' The mode of dealing with this exceedingly important matter was left in the Governor-General's hands. If interference in Afghan affairs was considered to be necessary, then Lord Auckland was to act as he thought best.

The Governor-General listened to those of his Ministers who agreed with Macnaghten's plan, and to the others who argued against it. The strict policy of both his predecessors had been to leave the native states alone, and to keep out of any entanglement with countries beyond the frontiers of India. Lord Auckland's entire instinct was for non-interference. He would make further attempts to establish a workable relationship with Dost Muhammad. But he reluctantly agreed that he must also consider a defensive war as a possibility. A regiment of 7,000 or 8,000 strong would accompany him on the journey north, and an army under Sir Willoughby Cotton would gather on the banks of the Indus.

The preparations for the great journey went on. The Governor-General intended to make many halts, so that he could meet the native rulers of the states through which he would be passing. It was clear to Emily and Fanny that George had no intention of sparing himself on his 'progress'. He had grown very grey, they noticed. Now over fifty, he had become even more reserved in manner than he had been in England. Mild and sardonic by turns, he relaxed only when he was alone with his sisters. For them he had no need to assume a diplomatic mask, or to be careful in speech and demeanour.

'I could not be away from George, and think of him alone in this country, for any earthly consideration,' Emily wrote to their eldest sister. 'He could not have existed here alone, and, for want of other colleagues, I can see constantly that it is a great comfort to him to have me to talk over his bothers with.'

The day fixed for their departure was October 21st. On the Thursday beforehand, Emily and Fanny received two hundred morning visitors in two hours. The rest of the week was taken up with going to a wedding; attending a play at the theatre, whose roof could not stand the weight of punkahs; hearing the details of packing seventy-two camel trunks and trying to keep Wright and Jones from losing their entire wits; and persuading Major Byrne that pets were even more essential to the Misses Eden than servants.

Besides Gazelle, Fanny had acquired a tame lemur. William brought it in to her one day, observing cheerfully: "It's just the sort of animal you will like in your tent. You may let it loose there, and it will scramble like a cat and a monkey together."

Such a combination of horrors, Fanny thought at first. But the lemur came to her with little black hands that looked almost human, and she liked him immediately. To her relief, he and Gazelle got on to good terms very quickly; they regarded each other coolly, but without distaste. Major Byrne simply had to accept the fact that she was taking a lemur and a pet deer on the journey, and provision must be made for them.

On the morning of the 21st they all rose at five o'clock, and came down to coffee to find the hall full of officials and local notables. The Ministers in Council were all there—even Mr. Macaulay, who was not famous for polite attentions.

Emily and Fanny got away as soon as possible under the escort of one of the aides, Emily stepping aside at the door to tell Wright not to fuss so over the bandboxes and carpet-bags.

There were troops at the landing-place, and a band playing marches. Carriages and riders kept moving up behind the soldiers, and the acquaintances Emily and Fanny had made in Calcutta fluttered in between, waving handkerchiefs under their parasols and above top hats. George arrived with William and a flock of aides-de-camp, and his sisters watched as he inspected the guard of honour. He was not so shy as he used to be at these ceremonies, they thought, though a long walk through troops presenting arms must be a trying experience enough.

He reached the place where they were waiting, offered his arm to Emily, made a gesture of general good-bye to the crowds, and boarded the vessel standing by for them. Fanny followed on William's arm. The guns fired, the gentlemen on the landing-stage waved their hats, the soldiers saluted. Then the boat moved off, and they left Calcutta.

'*My little deer is such a treasure*'

6

AN EMERALD PEACOCK UNDER
A DIAMOND TREE

THEY were in a 'flat': the special kind of barge fitted only with bedrooms and sitting-rooms, which was a very comfortable invention because the noisy and active business of life was carried out on the steamer which towed them. There was nobody on board the 'flat' except themselves, the two aides-de-camp, Dr. Drummond, and, of course, their pet animals. Fanny had christened the lemur Rolla, and he and Gazelle soon took to life on the water with the same unconcern that their companion, Chance, showed for all changes in this Indian existence.

The other 'flat', towed by a second steamer, was much more crowded, and promised to be interesting. The Colvins were there, and Mr. and Mrs. Torrens—the latter a handsome woman and a wonderful player upon the harp. It was a talent, Fanny considered, wasted in India, for the heat and damp cracked the strings and eventually the sounding-board. The wonder was that they did not all crack from the heat and damp. There were moments when Fanny began to feel that they *were* all a little cracked. . . .

The Macnaghtens were also on this second 'flat'. Fanny liked Mr. Macnaghten, and tried not to mind the fact that, as he was the Government Secretary, any little trifle that it might please their black brethren to bestow on them would be taken away by him with great celerity.

Captain Hawkins was in charge of the commissariat. He was the man who was to kill enough sheep and boil enough vegetables every day to feed the ten thousand people—the regiment and followers—who composed the camp. Mrs. Hawkins was always written about in the newspapers as 'the beautiful Mrs. H. in an appropriate costume' when she went to fancy balls.

Then there was General Casement, who had been in India an unimaginable number of years. He was a gentlemanlike old man, with a wife in England who spent all his money. The vessels had not been four days out from Calcutta before it became clear that General Casement did not like children, children's Persian cats, or *ayahs*. During a state visit one evening to the Governor-General's 'flat' there were mysterious allusions to the apple jelly they had had at breakfast on the other barge, innuendoes which were hastily nipped in the bud by Mrs. Macnaghten, who thought such domestic details inappropriate in the Governor-General's hearing.

The first stage of the river journey was through dreary country, the Sundarbans—a sort of salt-water creek bordered by jungles and devoted to tigers and fevers. It was a scene of desolation. No birds flew about; there was no grain to eat. They saw only one native boat, which appeared to have been there since the Deluge. Occasionally there was a bamboo stuck up with a bush tied to it, to mark the cheerful fact that there a tiger carried off a man.

Fanny liked the life aboard the 'flat'. Except during the very sunny hours of the day, she could sit out on deck; she found she possessed more vitality to write and draw than she had had for weeks. Gazelle usually sat at her feet. William hinted that Gazelle was now the very image of a young donkey—a libel which the deer and Fanny alike ignored with dignity. Emily had settled down to spend most of her time reading; she had brought all the parts of *Pickwick* with her. Hitherto she had read them piecemeal, in whatever order they had reached her; now she assembled them into a coherent book, and began to read it through from the first chapter. That Winkle and the horse that would not go on! That dear Mr. Pickwick, trotting about all day with a horse he could not get rid of! Emily sat in a shady part of the deck and laughed and laughed—until she found herself weeping, remembering that Mr. Pickwick's Kentish countryside had once been her own.

A week after leaving Calcutta, they stopped at Surdiah for the steamers to take on coals and sheep. Two of the Company's young 'writers' were waiting to pay them a visit: Mr. Graham and Mr. Lushington, whom they had already met in Calcutta. The cadets in the Company's service began with the rank of 'writers', or clerks.

It did not take Emily and Fanny long to realise that these men, not long out of their teens, had come to detest the life they had chosen. Mr. Lushington, brought up in Naples and Paris, loved society and the novels of Victor Hugo. He was stationed in a place where there were scarcely half-a-dozen Europeans besides himself and Graham. Their days were always the same; listening to squabbles between natives concerning a few strips of land or a handful of rupees, riding in an uninhabited jungle for exercise, reading a little, and going to bed.

There was no social life. Of the three married ladies in the station, one lady had low spirits and did not wish to entertain, the second had weak eyes and wore an enormous hat; the third suffered from bad health, had had to have her head shaved, and wore a brown silk cushion with a cap pinned on top of it because she could not get a wig.

Why the young men did not go melancholy mad, Fanny could not imagine. Some, she knew, did return to Calcutta in a nervous state; others took to the life, and grew dreamy and stupified. The indigo planters were in worse case; some of them really forgot how to speak English.

After Surdiah, the country slowly improved. By October 30th they had got to Rajmahal and their first sight of the hills. They had come two hundred miles from Calcutta, and it had taken them ten days. George sighed for the Salisbury 'Highflyer' and a good road-side inn. Rajmahal provided some picturesque ruins for sketching. But the real charm and beauty of the place were in a great fat *babu*, standing with two bearers behind him carrying the post-office packet. There were dispatches for George and over a dozen English letters for Fanny and Emily. Such letters! Everybody writing about that delightful invention, the young Queen, and the enthusiasm she was exciting. Fanny could hardly wait to reply to one long letter that was full of the most satisfying detail.

'All everybody says about our young Queen is excessively interesting,' she wrote that night. 'It must have been such a strange feel to her at first, as if she were acting a play upon a great scale; and she seems to be having a great success in her part. I can imagine the Duchess of Kent must be very proud of the success of her work.'

But Emily, for her part, felt that there was something mysterious in the Duchess not being with the Queen during all the pageants which were taking place in London to show the new monarch to her people. Why was the Duchess of Kent being kept in the background? There was probably a simple explanation, but still, Emily felt she would like to know what mother and daughter said to each other when they met in private.

They reached Monghyr two days later, a curious old town with a fort; and after passing an island covered with pelicans, landed for the day—their boat surrounded by tiny vessels full of birds and bird-cages, work-boxes of inlaid wood, straw bonnets and buffalo-horn necklaces.

It was a Hindu festival, and the banks of the river flowered into a gorgeous kaleidoscope of colours. Crowds of natives clustered at the water's edge, carrying baskets of fruit, which they dipped into the river with deep salaams, asking a blessing from the holy Ganges.

Fanny and Emily had grown so used to natives walking about near-naked, that it was strange to see people wrapped round in *chaddar* of every variety of hue. Even the little children wore holiday dress, their brown faces peeping out from bright orange or pink drapery, edged with scarlet.

'I wish you would have one little brown baby for a change,' Emily wrote to Pamela Campbell. 'They are so much prettier than white children.'

Behind the crowds, they could see old mosques and temples and natives' houses, and the boats of rich men in front with gilded sterns, and painted peacocks at the prow. They were indeed in the India of travellers' tales—strange, picturesque, ablaze with every colour of the rainbow.

It was November 5th, 1837, and they were come to Patna, half a world away from the squibs and crackers of apple-faced small boys stamping round bonfires in the crisp winter air of home.

      ★   ★   ★   ★   ★

'I think that little iron is coming well out of the fire,' wrote Emily on her first evening in Patna.

Fanny, too, had been keeping a noticing eye on the one young lady in the party, Mrs. Colvin's niece, Miss Sneyd. Would Mr. Beadon declare himself soon, or was diffidence still making him dumb? Fanny was sure that the right quantity of affection was there.

Both Emily and Fanny retained their incorrigible fondness for matchmaking. Mr. Beadon, a remarkably eligible young 'writer' whom they had meant to propose to Miss Sneyd in Calcutta, had arrived in Patna from his station some way off. They remembered him as an exceedingly shy young man. He was still shy, but he showed unmistakable signs of distracted attention when Mrs. Colvin's niece was anywhere near. Promising, thought Fanny.

They were well entertained at Patna. It was a large station, with at least twenty English residents. A regiment had been brought from Dinapore to receive his lordship, and lined the way to the house where the Governor-General and his sisters were to stay. Their host was Mr. Trotter, the opium agent for the district; a widower with a quiet manner and a dry sense of humour which appealed to Fanny. His house was furnished in good taste, and he did what he could to make them comfortable. But when she was undressing, Fanny heard her *ayah* exclaiming over the hardness of the bed. Fanny was resigned to hard beds. She believed that in India generally they stuffed the mattresses with deal boards, studded with brass nails.

Patna meant the renewal of ceremonial and official appearances. Invitations to a ball had already reached them from Brigadier Richards and the officers at the station at Dinapore, five miles up the river. Fanny foresaw that this was the beginning of a constant course of dancing they would have to go through until they reached the Himalayas, and the horrid thing was, they had but one *young* dancing lady with them—Miss Sneyd.

Emily and Fanny received all the ladies of the station, breakfasted with thirty people and luncheoned with as many more. George gave audiences from ten to three o'clock, and then held a durbar for the native nobles, who came in great state.

'One rajah is here with a solid gold howdah on his elephant,' Fanny wrote home. 'Another with a silver one. If you could but see George at this moment as I see him from my room. There he is, sitting with Mr. Macnaghten as interpreter, the native he is talking to preparing to have the attar of roses poured over his hands. All our servants and all his own stand behind him, some with their great silver sticks, others with their peacock's feather *chowries*, others with their gold-embroidered punkahs. A cloud of puzzled aide-de-camps flit about, and William is superintending the dressing of two old rajahs who have had their dresses of honour given to them—one mass of gold stuff, turban, vest and tunic.'

The most interesting visitor was General Ventura, an Italian soldier who, with the Frenchman, General Allard, had been in the service of Ranjit Singh for twenty years, training Ranjit's army. General Ventura had with difficulty obtained leave from Ranjit to go to Europe for eighteen months, but he had been obliged to leave an eight-year-old daughter behind him as a hostage, which made him miserable.

George visited an opium manufactory with Mr. Trotter. There was opium to the value of well over a million pounds in the store-houses, and Mr. Trotter said that they washed every workman who came out. Even the little boys who worked among the opium contrived to roll about in it, for the washing of a little boy well rolled in opium was worth four *annas*, or sixpence, in the bazaar, if he could escape to it.

Emily and Fanny took a drive with William to a large granary famed for its echo, and found there a group of other visitors, including Mr. Beadon, who had brought his flute. He played on this instrument, the echo repeating the notes; and there, listening entranced, was Miss Sneyd.

George and his aides and Secretaries went on to Dinapore by the 'flat' early the following day, and Emily and Fanny followed later, by road. It was not easy to transport Gazelle, who, with great pertinacity, kicked every native servant who offered to lead him. In the end he was tucked into a palanquin carriage with Wright and Jones, being rather larger than the ponies who pulled it.

The ball at Dinapore was a great success. Mr. Beadon danced three times with Miss Sneyd, which was considered equal to a proposal and a half. Mr. Trotter himself came to Emily and Fanny to say: "The little affair is going on remarkably well—he is dancing with her again." Then came the satisfactory climax. Before the evening was over, Mr. Beadon proposed. Emily and Fanny were pleased and proud to have married off their only young lady. Mr. Beadon was a nephew of Lord Heytesbury's, and though not yet of age, a promising cadet in the Company's service. Miss Sneyd was very young, too; hardly pretty, but ladylike. As one of a very large family, she had been sent out to her uncle and aunt to be a companion to their children. Her marriage was generally approved, and already it had been decided that

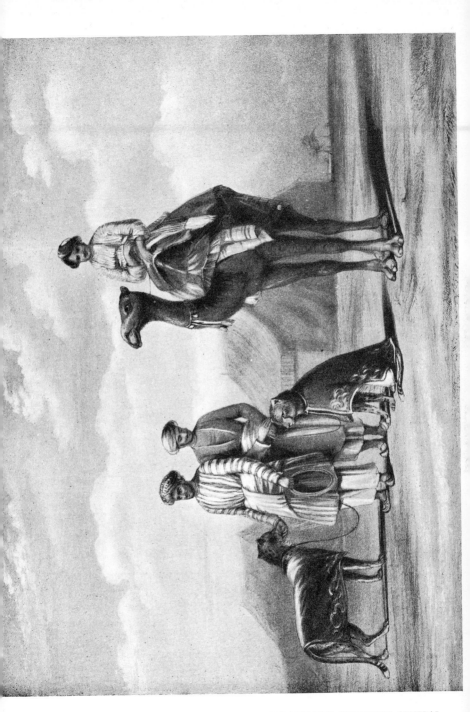

CHEETAHS SENT BY THE KING OF OUDE TO ACCOMPANY THE GOVERNOR-GENERAL
From a drawing by Emily Eden

THE MAHARAJAH SHER SINGH (*above*) AND THE MAHARAJAH RANJIT SINGH (*below*)
From drawings by Emily Eden

when they stopped at Allahabad three weeks hence, the wedding would take place.

Yes, it was a great ball; the Governor-General's sisters really enjoyed it. There was a large supper afterwards, and George made a speech—the first of a long series he would have to make all up the country. They did not get back to the 'flat' until one o'clock, and the monster of a captain began sweeping the decks at five.

There was a review of troops in the morning, and another great dinner, and another ball, and a supper. Emily and Fanny were tired out, but they stayed as long as there was actually no danger of their falling asleep from exhaustion. Patna and Dinapore had received them so cordially that they must bear with a little fatigue. Some ladies had come sixty miles; they would have something to look back upon for weeks.

The local rajahs had been invited, and came in splendid dresses and magnificent jewels. Most of them had never been at an English ball before, and doubtless thought the ladies who danced were utterly good for nothing. Still, they seemed rather pleased to see so much vice.

Emily and Fanny had never beheld such gems as the rajahs wore. In Calcutta the native nobles were too poor to have really valuable ornaments. In this part of the country their necklaces alone were worth a fortune. A native jeweller came on board with a collection which dazzled the sisters into silence. There was an emerald peacock under a diamond tree, with diamond pears hanging from its mouth. A *supèche*, the ornament which the rajahs wore in their turbans, was also fashioned in the shape of a peacock—this time made of diamonds, holding in its beak a rope of enormous pearls which passed through an emerald the size of a dove's egg. The tassel of the ornament had a cap of immense diamonds from which hung short strings of flawless pearls, ending in more diamonds.

What a pity it cost seventy thousand rupees, sighed Fanny.

*   *   *   *   *

They said good-bye to the hospitable station, and the 'flats' began to move once more in the wake of the steamers. But they had not left Dinapore far behind when they saw a huge crowd of natives at a village on the river bank, and were told there was a horse fair in progress.

George decided to stop and see it, causing Mr. Macnaghten and Mr. Torrens nearly to faint away on their decks. Such an unprompted piece of amusement was not in the day's programme. They were sure the Governor-General would be murdered; he really must not go.

The Governor-General merely said he *would* go. He took Emily and Fanny with him, but no official followers. His personal body-guard went first, asking the people to make a lane through the fair, and George walked after them, with his sisters following in *tonjauns*.

Fanny and Emily were delighted by the brilliant dresses of the women, some of whom wore bracelets from the wrist to the shoulder, and tinkled as they moved. The bazaars were full of trinkets and pretty shawls and cottons; it was stimulating just to look at the dazzling colours. Emily went round sightseeing until she was tired—for once, she had almost as much energy as Fanny. They both returned to the 'flat' in good spirits, leaving George to look once more at the horses.

They would have liked to tell the Secretaries that they had left the Governor-General on one of the merry-go-rounds, but it was not a subject that admitted of levity. Mr. Macnaghten said stiffly that the Governor-General should never appear in public without a regiment, and that there was no precedent for his going to Ballia fair. Emily told him that they had made it a precedent, and that it would be Mr. Macnaghten's duty to take the next Governor-General, be he ever so old and gouty, to this identical fair.

The following day, at Ghazipur, they gave another shock to Mr. Macnaghten's constitution by going unattended into a church on their way back from a visit to Lord Cornwallis's tomb. When they got into camp proper, Fanny reflected, they would have to reform and behave themselves. Meanwhile, it was pleasant to slip away occasion-ally from the cloud of peacock's feathers, silver sticks and golden umbrellas under which they were always moving.

At Ghazipur they were taken—officially—to an opium factory. It was refined barbarism, Fanny thought, for they had been receiving visits all morning, and they must dress later for a great dinner, which was to be followed by a ball. Fanny knew she would hardly be able to keep awake.

The dinner was delightful, in spite of half-hour intervals between the courses. One of Emily's neighbours turned out to be from Kent, and his conversation brought back visions of country balls and cricket matches. And he knew Eden Farm and Penge Common! Fanny and Emily liked him very much. At the dinner-table there was also some talk of the Bishop, who had been going about everywhere, preaching to have steeples added to the churches. Considering there was not half enough money to keep them in repair, thought Fanny, he might have excused the steeples.

There was a ball afterwards, as usual; and it was a remarkable ball, owing to the extraordinary plainness of the ladies there. One was pointed out with great pride: "That's our only unmarried lady." That fact, indeed, was the only thing not remarkable about her. Her tawny complexion was set off by a narrow strawberry-pink gown, she had the sort of drawn-up features which allowed a view of the back of the skull, and an embroidered bag, cavorting in time with her feet, hung over her arm while she danced. Then there was a lady whose gown was two inches shorter than her petticoat, *bounding* through every quadrille. Emily was fascinated to learn that the three grown-up young men dancing round her were her sons, that she was an exemplary mother, had been a widow many years and a grand-mother many more, and that she never missed a ball.

The next stop on their journey was Benares. There they were to leave the river and join the main camp. Seen from the water, Benares was a beautiful city, all Fanny expected a native city to be. It was too early to land, so they sailed the whole length of it and back again. There was the most perfect mob of temples, minarets and mosques rising one above the other to an immense height. Benares was a sacred city, and the *ghauts* were covered with natives dipping their hands in the holy waters of the Ganges, or making salaams to the colossal white figures of Vishnu lying on the steps.

The camp was four miles from the city, and they found carriages waiting to take them there. The baggage from the two 'flats' and the steamers was soon being transferred to the backs of camels and elephants, and into hackeries—the bullock-carts which were indispens-able to the journey, but which they were to find maddeningly slow. Emily and Fanny drove off, escorted by their own guards and two of the aides-de-camp—the living images, Fanny thought, of Rosencrantz and Guildenstern. When they reached the cantonments the guns began firing, and as they drove through the long lines of troops, following George, the bands all took up 'God save the Queen'. They at last arrived at the encampment in a transport of loyalty to their monarch and themselves.

Their tents were dull and grand compared to the small, cosy affairs Fanny had been used to on the Rajmahal expedition. She, Emily and George each had a large tent which was divided into bedroom, dressing room and sitting-room. A fourth tent was the general reception room, and all were connected by covered passages which were, Fanny thought, probably full of *dacoits*. There was a further screen of red canvas, eight feet high. Not an elephant, or camel, or cooking fire was visible. 'I shall take my pen-knife tomorrow and cut a great hole through my canvas screen, which will be a heartrending scene for Byrne and Macnaghten,' she wrote home. 'But nothing shall induce me to let them make a Government House of this. One comfort is, William's tent is outside the compound, and I shall get my sketching and a little cheerfulness there.'

The following day they went through the city. The streets were

Silver chariot

too narrow for carriages, so they all got upon elephants—Dr. Drummond, Rosencrantz, Guildenstern, everybody. As they rode along, they could have touched the women sitting in the upper stories of the houses on each side of them. Women covered in silver ornaments stared, peering out of little holes of windows; and in the bazaars below, merchants with long white beards sat cross-legged at their stalls, so close together that the ground looked like a mass of heads.

Presently the street grew too narrow for elephants, and they all got into *tonjauns*. The Governor-General's was of solid silver, shaped like a great shell. George himself looked impressive in his cocked hat and gold-laced coat. He had been persuaded by the united earnest exhortations of the aides-de-camp, instigated by Mr. Macnaghten and supported by William, to ride on his elephant alone; a woman by his side would have detracted from his dignity. Fanny thought he looked quite happy and natural in his solitary state.

'I often wonder whether it really can be G., the original, simple, quiet one,' Emily wrote home that night. But he did it very well, though she knew he disliked most of the ceremonies—particularly embracing the rajahs.

Emily and Fanny were on the other state elephant, with crimson velvet umbrellas held over them; and they were also peacock-feathered and silver-sticked according to rule. Emily had a large emerald ring, full of flaws, which the Company had provided as her present to the old Ranee, whom they were to visit. Fanny wore a long gold chain round her neck for the same purpose. It was etiquette to give something they had on, and these were the kind of handsome gifts which the Honourable Company provided by the hand of Mr. Macnaghten.

Their destination was the Rajah's palace, which was at the end of one of the narrowest of the streets. The Rajah's eldest son received George at the outer gateway, where they embraced. He then led the way through the courtyard into the palace. Emily and Fanny followed George into a small room, and were each given a sofa to sit on. The Rajah pointed to a gold curtain and said that his mother, the Ranee, was behind. George immediately hoped through Macnaghten that she was in good health, and Macnaghten, in the most solemn manner answered:

"The Ranee, my lord, says that it is utterly impossible for her to express how inconceivably well she feels since your lordship has entered her dwelling."

Fanny was fascinated, as always, by the extreme gravity and emphasis with which Mr. Macnaghten translated every word that passed, never moving a muscle of his naturally immovable countenance. She had never seen a man more born for the business.

The Rajah took Fanny and Emily by the hand and led them behind the curtain. The other ladies from the camp had been following the Governor-General's part of the procession, and several of them now appeared behind the two sisters. One of them, who understood Hindustani, was asked to act as interpreter.

The Ranee was a little old woman with enormous eyes. She was dressed in a pair of tight white trousers, and a tight net jacket draped with muslin. She shook their hands warmly, asked which was the elder, begged them to remember her and to write to her, and put diamond rings on their fingers and silver tissue necklaces round their throats. Emily and Fanny gave their presents, and she poured attar of roses over their hands and they took leave. Mr. Macnaghten promised to assure George in her name that she was feeling as a locust in the presence of an elephant. He also took the sisters' diamond rings the instant they were clear of the door, which made Fanny feel like a locust, too—but a denuded one.

The following day the party was again entertained by the Rajah, this time at Ramnagar, his country-house by the side of the river. Here he had prepared the most extravagantly lavish fête Emily and Fanny had yet seen. He sent his boats to convey them across the water; boats which were contrived to look like gigantic peacocks swimming. On board one was a solid silver chair with a canopy, for George, together with a red-embroidered tent for his 'women' behind it. Two inferior silver chairs had been placed on another boat for the Governor-General's sisters, but they risked shocking the Rajah, and placed themselves in the red tent, leaving the second boat to the other ladies of the party, and lowering George's prestige by their presence in his.

On the other side of the river, elephants were waiting. George was lifted up into a golden howdah on the first one, and Emily and Fanny mounted elephants on either side. Fanny had a particular dislike of being alone on an elephant, and held on tightly, hoping that the howdah would not turn over. They rode for several miles, with crowds of natives calling "Wah! Wah! Hi, Lord Sahib!" and running on each side. At last, as it grew dark, they turned towards the palace.

It was a wonderful sight. The great mass of the palace buildings and the village which clustered round it were illuminated by thousands upon thousands of small lamps; windows, doorways, houses, temples stood out in fiery outline. The elephants passed through the gateway into the courtyard beyond, which was a crowded scene of torches, spearmen, drums and people. Tall guards sat on camels, holding torches aloft, the oil held in deep cups of silver.

For a few moments the sisters could hardly take in the scene. It was like a melodrama magnified by a solar telescope. Emily half expected the actress, Ellen Tree, to appear, snatch up a stage baby and cry: "My boy, my boy, my rescued Agib!" or words to that effect.

The Rajah's servants spread a path of scarlet and gold *kincob* from the door to the end of the hall, and as Emily walked on it she mourned to herself that this stuff was a pound a yard in the bazaars; she had been trying to make up her mind for a week to afford enough of it for a dressing-gown. And here she was *treading* on it.

The visit took the normal course of being entertained by nautch-girls dancing, and visiting the Rajah's female relations in their quarters. The young Ranees were shy and stood back, but the older ones amused themselves by pouring so much attar of roses over the English ladies that Emily's silk gown was ruined—not the last time this was to happen.

They came away very tired, and starving hungry, for they had not been offered any refreshment. Emily determined that she would always wear washable muslin for these visits in future, and Fanny wondered what would be the best way of carrying a little food done up in a pocket handkerchief.

*   *   ʌ   ʌ   ʌ

They made their first march on November 23rd, and proceeded as far as Mohan Ke Sarai.   The day began very early; the bugle sounded at half-past five, and they set off as the clock struck six.   This, they found, was to turn out a very comfortable rule, for they escaped the terrible dust by striking camp while the dew was still on the ground. George, who lived in a state of concentrated impatience during short marches, settled to allow the main camp to go for the eight miles they were due to cover that day, while he and Fanny, together with Rosencrantz and Guildenstern, made a detour of thirty miles in the palanquin carriage to see Chunar, which was an old fort high on a rock.

Emily, Major Byrne and William trotted off on their elephants with the ten thousand or so people of the camp, and arranged to meet the sightseeing party at Mohan Ke Sarai at the end of the day.   Emily had decided that she would have enough inevitable sightseeing to do without travelling an extra thirty miles when she need not.   Fanny was always ready to see fresh sights, and generally took her sketch-book. She was not in the least self-conscious about her lack of conventional drawing talent; she liked illustrating her letters, and so long as she was able to give her family and friends some idea of the scenes through which she was passing, she knew that they would forgive deficiencies in execution.

Chunar turned out to be unexpectedly beautiful.   All of a sudden, without any particular reason, a whole ridge of hills came into view, with Chunar planted on an immense rock rising from the river—a fort full of ancient buildings.   Fanny and her companions were carried to the top, to look at the view, and she could not think how a prospect of such variety could have arranged itself in that flat country.

They went to breakfast later with a Captain and Mrs. Stuart, who gave them porridge and oatcakes. Then Mrs. Stuart took Fanny to a room where was nothing but a sofa and pillows, eau-de-Cologne and lavender water. She said she was sure Fanny would like to go to sleep, and so left her. Fanny was grateful for her tact.

The party reached Mohan by way of Sultanpore, and spent their first night in camp. The following morning they learnt of robberies which had taken place throughout the camp during the night, in spite of the vigilance of the guards. Mrs. Torrens had awakened to see a man on his hands and knees creeping through the tent. Mr. Colvin related that when he and his wife had been encamped on this same spot the previous year, they had lost everything, including the clothes Mrs. Colvin had left out to wear in the morning. Mr. Colvin had had to sew her up in a blanket and drive her back to Benares for fresh things.

Emily and Fanny had not lost anything, but there were other irritations. Several servants had been dismissed for bad behaviour two days previously. Now they appeared, with all the relations they could find, and lay down and cried at Emily's feet. She knew that she could not countermand Captain MacGregor's orders, yet who could withstand such genuine penitence?

Her *jemadar* interpreted for them, tears rolling down his cheeks.

"They have followed lordship and ladyship great way from their own homes," he said. "They made one fault, one very bad one. But God Almighty even forgive everybody once, else what become of us all?"

Emily could not help thinking of the 'seventy times seven'. If, indeed, men were forgiven but once, what would become of mankind?

She had no power to reinstate the servants, whose offence had been against their own people and therefore a very serious one. She gave them enough money to take them back to Calcutta, and was wretched because she could do no more.

When the camp broke up, Fanny and William remained behind for half an hour to see the cavalcade. Five minutes after George and Emily had left, every tent was down. Within another ten minutes, the procession had begun moving. It was an astonishing sight. Camels with their loads, strings of elephants carrying tents, bearers leading dogs, who all wore little red coats against the chill of the early morning. Chance's servant stalked along with a shawl draped over his livery, Chance's small black nose peeping from under the folds.

Then came palanquins and *tonjauns* innumerable. Mrs. Colvin in a temper, in hers, with Mr. Colvin riding by the side. Mr. Wimberley, the chaplain, driving his large family in a carriage; General Casement riding by Mrs. Hawkins's palanquin, and Mrs. Macnaghten very grand in a smart carriage, with Macnaghten ambling on a pony before. The hackeries followed, heaped high with beds, sofas and chairs. And troops and yet more troops. soldiers marching and officers riding. Then came *faquirs* beating drums, with swarms of camp followers filling up every space as far as the eye could roam. So that was what they had behind them every morning. Fanny liked to have a picture in her mind.

They pitched camp for two days, the following day being Sunday, which was always to be a halt. The great durbar tent was set up as a church, and on Sunday morning Mr. Wimberley read the lessons and preached a good sermon. Fanny reflected that if he kept up this standard, the whole party would be all very good by the time they reached Simla.

She had grown fond of the Wimberley family. They attracted misfortunes as a magnet attracts needles, and they were poorly off. But they had in good measure the traditional Scottish quality of doggedness, and she admired the way Mrs. Wimberley tried to make a home in the most unpromising circumstances. Marching in this fashion did not give her much of a chance. "Just as I have got a few things aboot me, they are all whisked away on the back of a cammil," she said resignedly to Fanny one day. Not having a double set of household gear, what she did possess was always on the road, being taken on to the next camping place.

The very same evening on which these words had been uttered, Fanny and William sat outside Fanny's tent watching with amusement the gyrations of a vicious camel. The animal at last contrived to throw its load, which proved, to Fanny's horror, to be the Wimberley's entire stock of crockery.

On Monday morning they moved off once more, bound for Mirzapur. Fanny hoped that Major Byrne was too busy to notice that Gazelle was travelling like a Christian, being carried in a specially-made howdah-like affair which had been fitted into a bullock-cart. Gazelle was becoming a problem. While they were at Benares, he had been exercised every day, being led between a goat and a kid, for whom he had manifested some slight affection. But he had ended by kicking them, and they had butted him; so he had had to have his own

Mirzapur

special conveyance for the journey. The lemur travelled with Myra, and was a pattern of good behaviour.

The Rajah of Benares was riding behind the camp with his followers, a courtesy escort as far as the border of the Rajah's dominions. There would be a formal audience of leave-taking at the frontier, and the usual offerings. "In return for which he will be generously presented with something worth three-and-sixpence," thought Fanny.

She was riding horseback that day, and enjoying it. It was enjoyable sleeping in a tent, too, and Fanny was somewhat impatient with George for grumbling so constantly about his. He had christened it Foully Palace. Emily had named her tent Misery Hall. Fanny told them both that she thought them odd to be so determined to dislike what they must put up with. For her part, she would continue to be pleased with the open-air life they were leading, for as long as possible. George laughed, and continued to grumble.

They had made a detour to Mirzapur before going on to Allahabad. George and William, with the aides-de-camp, went off to see the jail and the carpet manufactories, while Emily and Fanny sat sketching by the river, where there was a mass of temples, all richly carved. When George returned, they were all taken to partake of a late breakfast at the home of the magistrate. Thirty people had been invited to meet them—all gentlemen. The magistrate's wife was the only lady on the station. She took Emily and Fanny to a rest room after the meal, settled them on sofas, and sat down herself, talking all the time. She was evidently so glad to see two other women that she could not cease. The more they told her they had got up at five that morning and were almost asleep, the more she said no wonder, and talked on. In the end she fairly talked them into the broad sun, and they turned with relief to sightseeing.

William drove Fanny in a buggy, the only local kind of conveyance, to the centre of the city, where she stayed sketching while Emily and George visited ancient buildings. The carving in stone on the native houses was beautiful in its minuteness; it looked as if it had been cut out with small scissors.

They rejoined the camp at Ghoopir Gunj, where the Governor-General gave a great durbar for the Rajah of Benares to take leave. A white cloth carpet had been laid down for the Rajah to walk on without his shoes, but he wore very long pantaloons and entered the durbar tent *in* his shoes. Mr. Macnaghten and Mr. Torrens only discovered this at the end of the durbar, when the Rajah had received all his presents. They both turned pale with horror, and when he was well away from the Governor-General they rated him for discourtesy. He told them he had had no idea that he was doing anything unusual, but they continued to upbraid him.

Major Byrne strongly upheld the Secretaries. William was amused. Fanny thought it all a pack of trash: grown men behaving in such a fashion! Emily said nothing, but she was grimly pleased when Byrne tied himself into a knot a few days later, over an invitation which reached them from Allahabad.

They were near that town, and the order of visits which they must make had long been settled. They heard now that the Baiza Bai, a dowager queen of the Gwalior country was anxious for a visit from them, for reasons of prestige. Major Byrne said that neither the Governor-General nor his sisters should go near her, as she was suspected of intrigue. Polite letters of refusal were accordingly sent to the dowager queen. The Baiza Bai was persistent. She sent ambassadors and letters and presents, until in the end Byrne himself went to see her, to put an end to her importunities. He was either talked over, or else was ashamed of always putting a spoke in everybody's wheel, for he came back with his confidence shaken. Emily very nearly told him what she privately thought of him: he was a Spoke himself—an animated, walking and talking Spoke; and now he was finding out what it was like to be pulled up himself.

He asked the Governor-General to pay the dowager a visit, after all. But he could not get out of his lordship's head what he had earlier put into it with such force. George now refused to go. He would send his sisters instead. Just the very thing *Spoke* had wanted to prevent! Emily watched him complacently, and said that she and her sister would certainly add the Baiza Bai to the Allahabad list.

They crossed the river at the confluence of the Ganges and the Jumna. The operation took two days, and Emily and Fanny sat in the doorway of a tent and watched the continuous movement and bustle for hours at a time. The river was full of low, flat-bottomed boats which ferried to and fro, carrying laden camels and carts—eight hundred and fifty camels there were. Then several hundred horses, quietly behaved, and their attendants. One hundred and forty elephants swam across, the *mahouts* standing on their heads, the tent walls rolled up behind on the elephants' backs and bobbing just above water level. After that there followed the bodyguard and the escorting regiment, together with the hundreds of camp followers.

Ten thousand people, said Fanny. Nearer twelve thousand by now, said Emily. And news had come of a state of famine in Agra, through which they were to pass. It would be impossible to take their great party through that stricken country. They had heard often enough of these terrible disasters of nature, when the rains failed. Now they had come very near to the scene of one of the worst famines within the memory of their servants. Some dreadful tales were filtering through. Women were selling their children for next to nothing. There was a rumour which sharpened the picture of the ghastly hunger in the famine district; it was said that the Hindus were killing and eating their sacred bullocks. They must have been at their very last gasp before they would do that.

Fanny and Emily had little heart for the balls and suppers which lay ahead when they thought of Agra.

⋆   ⋆   ⋆   ⋆   ⋆

'I am at Allahabad, Theresa—"More fool I; when I was at home I was in a better place," as dear Shakespeare, who knew all about Allahabad, as well as everything else, observed with his accustomed readiness.'

Thus Emily to Theresa Lister, writing on December 1st, 1837.

Their tents were pitched in the Fort, and they were to stay for nine days. Emily still hated her tent, and George still hated his. They both inclined to a house with passages, doors, windows, walls that could be leaned against, and much furniture. It irritated Emily afresh every night to see her belongings taken out of her tent and put in a special place under the gaze of sentinels, because of the ever-present danger of robbers.

But the weather pleased her. It was now the cold season, and the mornings were really cold, so that they had to put on wraps. The sun came ranting up later, and there was a general moulting of fur shoes and merino wraps, and shawls, and an outcry for muslin; but as soon as it grew dark they needed cloaks and boas and all sorts of comforts again. Those cold hours of the day were very English and very pleasant.

Fanny thought that Allahabad had a flat, Calcutta look about it, with the same crowd of smartly turned-out people driving in the cool hours, and going to parties in the evening. She and Emily received before dinner, attired in silk gowns which Wright and Jones had extracted from the metal-lined trunks. But they were aware of not being patterns of fashion to their guests.

The station ladies turned out to be talkative, tight-sleeved, and well-dressed to the last degree. They surged into the great durbar tent, which had been allowed to suck up all the chairs and sofas from Emily's and Fanny's private tents, and was accordingly very hot and overstuffed with furniture and fashionable females.

Mrs. Macnaghten said that Allahabad was a nice, sociable-seeming place, and that she would have liked to stay there for two months. Neither Emily nor Fanny would have wept if she could have been granted her wish.

Then they forgot the station ladies and everything else. A heap of letters arrived on the third day of their stay, and they were each afflicted with the old, familiar heartache and homesickness. The letters which had come overland were dated October—October, 1837 —only two months from England! Fanny could so far think herself at home as to take an interest in the elections which had earlier been held there, and to agree with Emily that the Whigs might have done better, though taking the defects of both sides, things seemed to be much as they were in the home government.

December 6th was another red-letter day. They married the Beadons. The bridegroom having arrived, there was no occasion to wait, and Fanny and Emily began with zest to make preparations for the wedding. The durbar tent was fitted up as a chapel and decorated. Mr. Wimberley had made a petition for a proper reading-desk, for, as he observed to George, though the camp medicine-chest, covered over, looked quite well, it was not quite regular. Still, he continued to use it in that fashion. He was, however, difficult in the matter of an altar. He treated with scorn Emily's idea to improvise an altar out of chairs and cover them with the state housings of an elephant, which were scarlet and embroidered all over with gold. But Emily had her way, and made a fine altar with four arm-chairs for railings, and some carpets and velvet cushions in front.

It was quite picturesque, but they were obliged to warn Mr. Beadon that neither he nor Miss Sneyd were to faint *towards* the altar, because it would then all come down with a crash. The bride cried less than Emily had expected, but indeed her spirits were very much kept up by a beautiful shawl which the Governor-General gave her.

Fanny found something ludicrous and heartrending in the business. It seemed such a great deal to make these two poor young creatures pronounce such solemn promises in a tent. And there were no bridesmaids. She felt too old and weather-beaten to proffer herself. Then, they would have no proper wedding journey. They were to have gone straight off on a fortnight's voyage on a 'budgerow', but no free vessel could in the end be found. A kind-hearted magistrate had lent them a house for two days, and they would set off, travelling *dak*, night and day in palanquins; and no servants to help them, for they could not afford any—and twenty-one years of India before them.

It was a great mercy, Fanny thought, that there were different ways of being happy in the world. The prospect of twenty-one years in this enormous, baking country might have made some people want to sit down and die. She considered herself fortunate to have only six years lopped off her English life; and she knew that she was glad to see what India was like, and would later be more than glad to *have* seen it.

There was a great wedding dinner, and Fanny and Emily felt that they had all started the young Beadons off in life as well as possible.

The following morning George held a durbar, and his sisters received another batch of ladies. In the afternoon there was the visit to the Baiza Bai. As it was not to be a political visit, Fanny and Emily, with great promptitude, told Mr. Macnaghten how sorry they were that they could not take Mrs. Macnaghten, as, of course, it would be out of the question. They themselves wondered why this should be so, and, they suspected, Macnaghten wondered the same. But it sounded plausible, and they went without her. Mrs. Macnaghten always insisted on acting as interpreter when she got the opportunity, but Fanny and Emily had discovered that she put the most extraordinary statements into their mouths.

The Baiza Bai sent a granddaughter to fetch them in a gold and scarlet litter, but Emily and Fanny were already in their own carriage. The princess therefore remained in the litter and was carried by their side, while William Osborne and three of the aides-de-camp rode in a carriage behind. The princess's show of state was a parody of the official panoply in which the Governor-General travelled. Six of the *ayahs* ran by the palanquin, and a body of Mahratta horsewomen, blazing with jewels, rode behind. Fanny noticed that their nose-rings, which were fringed with large pearls, hurt the riders so much that they presently took them out. The princess's uncle was perched on an elephant which had been painted bright green and blue. With this odd-looking escort, Fanny and Emily were brought to the palace of the Baiza Bai.

The visit followed familiar lines. The Begum was a grand-looking old lady who paid them extravagant compliments, presented them with emerald and diamond necklaces, pearl and emerald bracelets, rings, shawls and gauzes. She was quite aware that all gifts were handed over to the Company, and through an interpreter tried to persuade her guests to accept these offerings for themselves, saying that she would send presents of less value to the Company.

Emily laughed, and used all her tact to explain to the Begum that this was not possible. However, she and Fanny agreed to accept rings of small value, in return for the presents they themselves had brought. Emily's ring was of seed pearls made in the shape of a mitre. When they got back to the tents, William put it on Chance's tail, where it looked so fine that Major Byrne would be sure to overlook it.

*   *   *   *   *

'We are rather oppressed just now by a lady, Mrs. Parkes, who insists upon belonging to our camp,' Fanny wrote to Eleanor Grosvenor. 'She has entirely succeeded in proving that the Governor-General's power is but a name. She has a husband who always goes mad in the cold season, so she says it is due to herself to leave him and travel about. She has been a beauty, and has remains of it, and is abundantly fat and lively. At Benares, where we fell in with her, she informed us she was an independent woman and was going to travel to Simla by herself—which sounded very independent indeed. Then she applied to Captain Codrington, who manages the ground, to let her pitch her tent among ours. Now, the surroundings of the Governor-General's street of tents is such that we allude to it in a kind of concentrated voice, and of course that [permission] was refused. The magistrate of one station always travels on with us to the next. To each of these magistrates she has severally attached herself, every successive one declaring they will have nothing to do with her. Upon which George observes with much complacency, "Now we have got rid of our Mrs. Parkes"—and the next morning there she is, on the march, her fresh victim driving her in a tilbury, and her tent pitched close to his. William knew her a little when he was in India before, and she plies him with constant notes and small presents. We are longing for the day when we shall find him conducting her on the march.'

Fanny and Emily had long known the astounding Mrs. Parkes*—it was difficult for any European *not* to know Mrs. Parkes—and they had as long tried to keep her at a reasonable distance. They appreciated her qualities, but they had a feeling that she might make the climate appear to be more oppressive than it actually was. Fanny Parkes's energy was a byword.

The wife of a Collector of Customs, she had been in India a good many years and had travelled about the country with her husband on his various postings. He was a mild, conscientious official; his wife had twice as much vitality as her skin could comfortably hold, and an unslakeable thirst for information. She kept a journal which she packed with details of everyday India life: she seemed to miss nothing. Food, *faquirs*, clothes, animals, family feuds, buildings, scenery, superstitious practices, amusements, customs, servants, furniture— everything interested her, and everything went in. One could not mention any event or crisis without Mrs. Parkes opening her notebooks and quoting the appropriate Indian proverb or wise saying.

The passing years had done nothing to lessen her overpowering exuberance. It was not surprising that her husband had decided to go discreetly mad every cold season in order to recuperate.

Fanny Parkes was now in her forties, and was as obstinate, thick-skinned and courageous as ever. In her early years in the country she had learnt Hindustani and Persian, and had been content to devote her energies to acquiring every kind of knowledge about native life that

* Probably 'Parks', but Fanny's spelling is retained here.

came her way. She was useful as an interpreter to people newly come to the country. Now she considered that her long experience of India and her knowledge of native customs entitled her to offer her services to the Governor-General and his sisters, and no amount of polite side-stepping of these offers had any effect. Mrs. Parkes was determined to be of use to Lord Auckland and the Miss Edens, and there she was, in the camp.

A much more welcome companion was expected at any point between Allahabad and Simla. George had some months before received a letter from William, Prince of Orange, saying that his son, the young Prince Henry, was on his way to Java and later wished to visit India. Would the Governor-General receive him and afford him facilities for seeing some of the country?

The Prince arrived at the camp in the middle of December, having travelled up from Calcutta with his aide-de-camp, Captain Ariens. He was a fair, quiet-looking boy, very shy and silent, and Emily and Fanny wondered how they were going to entertain him, for he spoke little English, and did not appear to share William's enthusiasm for hunting. The King of Oudh, whose country they were now in, had sent his cheetahs to give the Governor-General's party some sport. He also sent his cooks to serve the Governor-General during the months which it would take the camp to cross his territories. Some of the dishes which they made were very good, though strongly spiced and perfumed. They had a habit of gilding and silvering their rice which made it look exotic but did not add to its digestibility. St. Cloup, George's own chef, was furious at having these new colleagues thrust upon him, and snubbed them on every occasion. The Oudh head cook took no notice of this reception; he was determined to please the *bara lady sahib* and the *chhota lady sahib*. He sent in twelve dishes every day at breakfast, and stood by with his satellites to see that these were eaten. It was unfortunate that Fanny had a small appetite at the best of times. George tasted everything handsomely, and the old *khansama* always insisted that Fanny should take some from each dish, and chuckled behind his long white beard in the most inhuman manner when he saw her sufferings.

The young Holland was invaluable during the Oudh cook visitation. He had turned out, on closer acquaintance, to be a heavy, ingenuous boy, always happy when he was eating. But the deep and complete happiness which he enjoyed when he was eating rice which looked like silver were beyond words to express. Fanny and Emily could only wonder that even a boy of seventeen could put so much food away. Captain Ariens was a pleasant man who spoke good English, but he could not turn the prince into a conversationalist. The young man's best effort came when he had to mount an elephant, which made a slight movement as he was about to climb into the howdah. "Oh, do tell it to set still!" he implored Emily, who was standing by.

When they were actually on the march, he travelled by Emily's side in her carriage, for nothing would persuade him that it was safe

Line of beaters

to mount a horse in that country; and Captain Ariens put on an old nurse's frightened look for her baby whenever such a thing was proposed. But for all the boy's timidity, it was impossible not to like him, he was so good-natured and easy to please.

The enormous camp moved on from place to place, covering a few miles every day. The weather was cool, so Fanny and Emily could go off sketching ruins and mosques in the day, while the gentlemen of the party, sometimes accompanied by officers of the escorting regiment, went off hunting.

      ★   ★   ★   ★   ★

Maharajpur, their next halt, was, Fanny thought, the finest country for dust it would be possible to imagine. The sands on the track came halfway up the wheels of the carriages at times, and the whole progress became a series of jolts. It was a relief to get to Cawnpore, at long last. Fanny was sadly disappointed with this station, too. Of all the ugly India stations she had yet seen, this was the ugliest. It was dead flat, with not a single blade of even brown grass to be seen; nothing but loose brown dust which rose in clouds on the slightest provocation.

The Governor-General made a state entry. Emily and Prince Henry kept to their carriage, but Fanny rode in boldly on a white Arab, following George and his staff. The guns roared out a salute, but the Arab did not even rear. Fanny was able to ride composedly along the lines of cavalry drawn up for George's inspection—thus maintaining, she hoped, a reputation for military ardour.

George held a levee an hour after their arrival, and Emily and Fanny had their reception the same evening. Cawnpore was one of those large stations where there was no chance of getting through all their duties if they lost an hour. The people looked red and coarse, Fanny thought. None of them had that delicate yellow tinge so much admired in Bengal. Ah, well, that came, no doubt, of living in a cold climate.

It was deliciously cold. There were thick carpets down in the tents now, and stoves were lighted morning and evening. The largest tent was pitched for dancing, the floor beaten flat, and the band arranged. George and his sisters dined with the leading people of the place, and between two and three hundred more turned up for the ball.

Here was something else which Prince Henry liked, besides eating; he liked dancing. Fanny told him that three of the ladies he danced with were of high rank and perfectly beautiful, and she hoped he believed her.

The following day George held a durbar for the King of Oudh's son, the 'Heir-Apparent', as Macnaghten solemnly designated him. The old king himself was too infirm to come, and his heir was arriving for an audience instead. This Nawab was to be treated with a good deal of ceremony, Macnaghten insisted. Oudh was of great political importance. So four aides-de-camp went to the Nawab's tents to hope he was pretty well—if three only had gone, Fanny remarked, he would have been very ill, no doubt. Then, at seven o'clock the next morning, four set off again on elephants, to invite the Nawab formally.

At eight o'clock he was seen approaching, his train of elephants magnificently decked with gold and jewels.

William and Mr. Colvin set off to meet him a mile from the camp, while George got up and began to dress.

'I went to George's room,' Fanny wrote home, 'and found him putting on his very *goldest* coat, star and ribbon, and cocked hat, and in a frenzy of indignation at having to set off on an elephant—that figure, at that hour in the morning, Byrne watching him like a cat watching a mouse. . . .'

George met the Nawab at the entrance to the encampment.

'When the Prince of Oudh got off his elephant, George had to embrace him three times,' Fanny wrote. 'We shook hands with him. I nearly made a snatch at the great emerald he wore on his thumb. He wore a turban of jewels and gold cloth, an aigrette of diamonds with two great emerald pears hanging from it—his vest and tunic absorbing a quantity of jewels, too. He had two sons with him, very fair looking boys, and a little rouged.'

The Nawab and George sat next to each other, flanked by Colonel Lowe, Resident of Lucknow, on one side, and Macnaghten in green spectacles on the other side, as interpreter. Emily and Fanny, with Prince Henry, sat opposite, and there were fifty other people, mainly from the *entourage* and from local Cawnpore society.

Prince Henry grew excited at the magnificence of the breakfast, wondering how such things were contrived in the middle of the desert —as he was pleased to call the flourishing station of Cawnpore.

Then Macnaghten handed Fanny a huge plate of buttered rolls, and said, to her dismay: "The Heir-Apparent expresses the delight it will give him if you will honour him by eating these."

Fanny looked at the Heir-Apparent's sword and dagger and immediately began.

Macnaghten next presented a hookah from the Heir-Apparent to George, who detested hookahs but who was obliged to smoke this one. The considerate old *khansama* put nothing but hot water into it, and George tried to make the right bubbling noises, without much success. To see him and the Heir-Apparent puffing in each other's faces was some compensation to Fanny for the rolls.

★   ★   ★   ★   ★

It was Christmas Day, 1837; their third Christmas Day away from home.

119

'My dearest,' Fanny wrote to Eleanor Grosvenor, 'does it not strike you that we are little better than a set of banished men and women? However, we shall all meet again, some day, I hope, but I am growing very old.'

She was thirty-six, and did not often give way like this in her letters. Characteristically, she at once went on to another subject.

'They have sent word that a rajah wants to look at my lemur, and there it is, surrounded by spearmen. What a crisis! Gazelle is always excellent, but he is growing enormous, and I expect him some day to murder all the native servants in a body. The parrot is out of spirits with the cold, Chance not generally civil, and Fop and Fairy, William's favourite greyhounds, devoted to their domestic duties.'

The servants had hung garlands at the doors of their tents, and though Emily knew it was very wrong of her, she recoiled when they assembled and wished her a happy Christmas in their own vernacular. And though Mr. Wimberley performed the Christmas service very well in the great tent, she found it unnatural to kneel just where the Prince of Oudh and his turbaned attendants had been sitting at the durbar two days before.

'There was nobody except G. with whom I felt any real communion of heart and feelings,' she wrote to Pamela Campbell.

The Prince of Oudh returned the Governor-General's hospitality by an enormous breakfast in his own tents. He asked the whole station. Emily sat by George, still oppressed by her sense of isolation from everyone else. She looked at the official presents on the carpet spread out before them.

'Trays of shawls I am hardened about, but I have been seriously ill of a diamond and emerald fever,' she told Pamela.

Fanny sat beside her sister, her mind on the letter she would write to Eleanor describing the glittering scene. She was finding it more difficult this year than last to keep her loneliness from bursting out into letters home. Christmas was the family festival she loved most; it always brought her so close to the others. But here she sat, gazing at diamonds and pearls, like a scene in a child's story-book.

Diamonds and pearls. Fanny concentrated her attention on the gifts which the Heir-Apparent had brought. There were two diamond combs, mounted in European fashion, for her and Emily; gifts which would distress Major Byrne, who would not be able to give them to any Begum in return, as Indian ladies did not wear combs. There

'There was much to sketch'

were pearl and emerald necklaces, and diamond ear-rings with emerald drops, all without flaws. How could she hope to describe them all? The deep green of the true emerald, the fire in the diamonds, the glow of the pearls. She had grown philosophical about jewels, but their wonderful beauty always held her eyes entranced.

Cawnpore seemed to be a city of jewels. Oudh was the greatest independent kingdom next to Ranjit Singh's dominions, and the native princes were very wealthy, their riches being shown forth in precious stones. In the chief room of one of the King's country palaces, which they were taken to see the following day, the throne had pillars studded with rubies, the fringes round the canopies being made of pearls and emeralds.

The city was crowded with mosques and palaces. The King's garden palace was built entirely of inlaid marble, with fountains playing in all the rooms, the gardens full of flowers, orange trees covered with ripe oranges, and parroquets flying about in flocks.

They had become accustomed to luxurious show. What they were to remember Cawnpore by was the Thug prison. Captain Patten, who was in charge of these peculiar murderers, invited the Governor-General's party to go and see a regular Thug exhibition which would show them how the Thugs dispatched their victims. The gentlemen of the party went; their description of the business was enough for Emily and Fanny.

Thuggee had been going on in India for hundreds of years. The Thugs were a murderous society who considered it a necessity of their religion to strangle travellers. Lord William Bentinck had begun decisive action against the Thugs. He put William Sleeman, an energetic political officer, in charge of the operations. Sleeman and his assistants had an extraordinarily difficult task, as there were thousands of Thugs and it was difficult to bring their crimes home to them in such a way as to make their conviction certain. They worshipped the goddess Bhawani, the goddess of destruction, and believed that they had a divine mission in killing, as in that way they were helping to maintain a balance in the population of the world. Their method was to ingratiate themselves with a traveller, eat with him, make jovial fun, and then, at a given moment, overpower him and quickly strangle him with a sacred piece of cloth. Within a few minutes the victim's body would be stripped and buried, leaving no trace.

★　　★　　★　　★　　★

The young Dutch prince left the party at Cawnpore; he and Captain Ariens went on to Delhi.   The camp resumed the journey on January 2nd, and within two days they were on the edge of the famine district. There had been no rain in the area for a year and a half.   The cattle had all died, and the people were dying or had gone away.   The crops were withered up; the rich natives who had grain in their granaries would not sell it, from the fear of a greater scarcity the following year.

Fanny and Emily were miserable at all the starvation they saw about them.   They knew there were funds at Cawnpore and the smaller civil stations for giving food to those who wanted it, but many died upon the road to the town.   Fanny was thankful they had received such large supplies from the King of Oudh, for they were able to give away a great deal.   Every evening, all who came to the tents were fed with rice.   Some scarcely looked human; it was difficult to prevent them from tearing the rice from each other.   The children in particular were dreadful sights, with the bones showing through their skins. The women looked as if they had been buried, together with their infants.

'I am sure there is no sort of violent atrocity I should not commit for food, with a starving baby,' Emily wrote home.   'I should not stop to think of the rights or wrongs of the case.'

The following morning, as Emily walked with George down to the stables, she found a miserable baby who flew like a possessed atom at the cup of milk she held out.   Rosina found the mother, who said she had had no food to give it for a month.   Dr. Drummond declared that the baby could not live, it was so diseased with starvation, but Emily decided to try what could be done for it, and told Rosina to bring it to the tent.   A little food four times a day worked wonders; the mother followed the camp, and the baby remained alive.

They rested for a few days at Fatehgarh, then went on to the Ganges, which they crossed on a bridge of boats.   Fanny and Emily hoped that they would lose Mrs. Parkes, for Mr. Rose, the magistrate, had been told by Captain Codrington to conceal where the latter's tent was to be pitched.   He was very much worn out attending to Mrs. Parkes.   William had had a note complaining that her little Irish harp was stolen and where was she to go for redress?   William, for once, had been at a loss for a reply.   He, too, would be glad to see the back of Mrs. Parkes.

Captain Codrington's forethought appeared to have been successful, for there was no sign of the lady in the camp during that afternoon.

They had peaceful thoughts during dinner. George suggested a walk afterwards, and Fanny went with him, as Emily was tired. It was a pleasant, cold evening; they enjoyed their walk. Then they came upon a little tent just outside the line of sentinels. George wondered aloud whose it was, and about twenty voices answered that it was the *bibi* Parkes's. This was a heavy blow.

She did not attempt to intrude upon them in their private quarters, but she was always *there*.

'I am sure you will be pleased to know that yesterday, as we were returning from seeing some ruins,' Fanny wrote home, 'George said, "Here come MacIntosh and Colvin on an elephant. How fat Colvin grows." Colvin turned into Mrs. Parkes in a man's hat and riding habit. She had met Captain MacIntosh, and as far as we can make out, climbed up the elephant's tail into his howdah when least expected. She will certainly be the death of us all.'

George held a durbar, and a troop of irregular horse joined the camp. Some of them walked in for orders when Fanny was sitting with William. They went straight up to her and offered their sheathed swords. Fanny was puzzled to know what to do with them, being, as she told William, totally unused to fighting with three swords at once. However, she majestically touched each sword—at which evolution William looked relieved.

Fanny had an eye for swords since seeing the native one which had been presented to Major Sutherland, an officer who had joined them. The sheath of his sword was the prettiest thing that was ever composed: a mass of large turquoises and small diamonds. If ever there should be a Mrs. S., thought Fanny, she would probably wear it herself. Fanny could not think where all the precious stones came from in this country. She looked about at every fresh encampment, but could never pick up any.

They reached Rohilkhand by the middle of January. The country was so different, they might have been in another world. The crops were green and flourishing, and the race of people they now met were like giants compared with the short Bengalees in the Governor-General's train. They wore a great quantity of shawl drapery, and fine turbans, and were altogether most imposing looking. The picturesque figures of the irregular horse supplied Fanny and Emily with many models for sketching; their dresses and saddle-cloths were covered with silver embroidery, their plumed turbans tipped with gold. They looked splendid, tilting with their long spears, fighting with single-stick, or charging at full gallop at tent pegs, which they carried off at the end of their spears. One of them sent the Governor-General's sisters nosegays every morning, which fact, coupled with their embroidered dresses, determined Fanny that when she took the field she would command a troup of irregular horse.

Bareilly was the next encampment. There they lost Mrs. Parkes. One unhappy day she actually camped in the lines, which threw the military authorities into an agony of fuss. Captain Codrington went to her and civilly insinuated she must not do that, and had better follow the regiment. To which she replied that if she did not go with the camp she would not follow at all. No answer was made to this and Mrs. Parkes departed in a state of fume.

Fanny could not even smile when she heard the news. She was worried about her lemur, Rolla, who practically lived on fruit. Some Persian merchants they met provided six apples, and a philanthropic magistrate sent a few guavas. When these had been carefully doled out and eaten, Rolla was reduced to plantains. Then an admirer sent him a box of pears, which had travelled a vast distance and were probably meant for somebody's dinner-party. Rolla instantly accepted them, and made Gazelle a present of the plantains.

William lounged in a chair outside Fanny's tent one evening, smoking a hookah and suffering under what he called a fit of the Bareillys. Fanny sat sketching him, and while she drew, she pointed out that he and George had no right to grumble about anything, because they were paid for what they did. It was she and Emily, the great unpaid, who were to be pitied; yet they kept their faces the natural shape, while William and George let theirs grow twice the length of human faces, if they should be the least bored. William agreed, and continued to grumble.

It was tempting to grumble with him. Fanny was weary to be at Simla, where there would be hills, and trees, and flowers, and a respite from this continual jolting on from day to day. She knew that there would also be a vast amount of entertaining to be done at Simla, but she and Emily were well inured to being polite to fresh faces by now.

All along the route they had travelled they had met young English-men who had often come great distances to pay their respects. Emily and Fanny could now realise—as they had never done to the same extent in Calcutta—in what a terrible solitude these faithful servants of the Company lived. Sometimes they did not hear a European voice for three months. Did they know what lay before them, these hopeful young men, when they came out to India to try their fortunes?

Tired as the sisters were, they never showed a trace of fatigue when any 'writer' rode into camp, no matter how inconvenient the hour. Emily assembled her books and Fanny her pets, and they talked, and entertained, and listened, and discussed with a friendliness and freedom which they had seldom felt in the drawing-rooms of Calcutta.

'*Rolled-up tent walls*'

★　　★　　★　　★　　★

There, at last, were the hills; a whole range of hills in view. They could see a dark blue line on the horizon, and a second white mass behind, looking quite pink at sunrise. It was a lovely sight after a thousand miles of uninterrupted plains. The very air smelt of mountains. There was a freshness in it which they had almost forgotten could exist in any air. It was very cold in the early mornings too; the thermometer was now at thirty-three when they started out at six o'clock, soon after dawn.

They were at a place which sounded to Emily like Kamovrowda-movrow; she had no idea how it was written. Fanny prudently waited until they reached their next stage, Moradabad, before entering up her journal.

The marching was now heavy, for the road was only a track of deep sand with great holes in it made by the hackeries, which had gone on the day before. There was a river to cross, which always meant a tedious wait; and the sand on the other side was just as bad as the sand they had left. One of the carts got stuck as usual; and, as usual, Mr. Wimberley and his innocent family were found at the hind wheel of their own carriage, and had in the end to borrow an elephant to drag it out, to the elephant's disgust.

Fanny rode her Arab close to George and William, and as George pursued his impetuous way through a deep ford, her riding habit got very wet by the splashings from their horses. She could not get out of the way because there was a dangerous cataract behind her of aides-de-camp, Secretaries, guards, camels, irregular horse, and a few thousand more human beings.

Emily, who had remained in her carriage, did not stay in it for long. Two horses kicked themselves out of their traces and she had to take to a baggage elephant, which jolted her so much that she felt she was composed of very small pieces loosely held together. In the end she got down and rested by a fire of dried grass, which the *syces* and bearers had made for themselves. She longed very much for an inn, or an English waiter, or anybody or anything from home. But otherwise it was amusing to see the camp roll by—the *babus* in their palanquins, Mr. Colvin's children in a bullock-carriage, Major Byrne's clerks riding like sacks on rough ponies, with their hats on over their night-caps; and then the artillery, with the horses all kicking.

They were in the Rajah of Rampore's territories, and George held the usual durbar and returned the Rajah's visit the following day. Then the camp moved on again, through the wearisome dust.

Captain Codrington always went on ahead to look for a stopping-place, taking with him a sergeant who sent back reports on the road. 'rst mile, ruff and dusty,' wrote the sergeant. '2nd, 3rd and 4th mile, rugged and sandy.' This was the sort of bulletin which carried desolation to Mr. Wimberley's heart, and made his family weep. In the morning he was to be seen in the dim light before sunrise walking before his palanquin carriage, pointing out to the coachman where the ruts were least deep; then getting on his grey pony to amble a little way.

Another touching sight on the road was old General Casement, walking up and down by his tilbury with a half-frozen look, watching for a distant sign of Mrs. Hawkins's palanquin, that he might persuade her to let him drive her for the remainder of the way.

The travelling grew worse and worse. Emily told William Osborne that she was so tired of being jolted, she would walk. William said he would hop; he had tried everything else.

The domestic side of the camp went on in spite of all difficulties. Mrs. Hawkins continued to flirt genteelly with the aides-de-camp in general and General Casement in particular. Mrs. Colvin excused herself as often as possible from society as she was now preparing for further maternal duties. Mrs. Torrens was being baffled in her attempts to teach her bright three-year-old son his Bible, and came to consult Emily about it. She had had to give up the Creation, she said, because her small son would always have it that the first man's name was Jack. She had tried the story of Samuel, which she thought would amuse him, and it had gone very well, in spite of a few yawns. Then, when she had asked, "What did Samuel say when the Lord called him for the third time?" the answer had been, "I'm a-coming, I'm a-coming, so don't tease I any more"—and Mrs. Torrens wondered whether she should go on with Bible lessons.

The village of Amroha was the next halt. Fanny was always anxious to see anything of local interest, and she persuaded William to go with her to a mosque a quarter of a mile away. Emily, thinking that a walk would do George good, fetched him from his tent and they followed the other two. Neither George nor their nephew was grateful. William wanted to know why he had been dragged through all that sand, and George said he was more bored than ever, and would go back to his tent. He still hated his tent, he added, and he wished he were back in Government House in Calcutta.

George was not bored; he was wretched with worry. He had sent Captain Burnes to Kabul to try to persuade Dost Muhammad to make an alliance, but Burnes had met with no success. There was disquieting news of the Persians; a Persian army had begun to besiege Herat on the day the Governor-General's camp had left Benares. Events were taking a new turn. If Herat fell, the way to India would stand wide open through Afghanistan.

How slow this journey was. George was growing increasingly irritable at being able to move only a few miles a day. Rumour and counter-rumour were constantly trickling into the camp. Even the servants were alert to hear the latest news from the north-west. Russian emissaries, it was said, were being received by Dost Muhammad Khan at Kabul. The Persians were at the walls of Herat—with the Russians behind them. There were Russian spies everywhere.

Russia—Russian intentions—Russian spies. The further north they travelled, the more the bogey took shape. Emily and Fanny listened to the rumours and went on with their sketching. There were always ruins and mosques and gateways to draw, or natives with unusual turbans. One day there were two pilgrims who were willing to pose. One of them refused to take money, but the other, a Brahmin, said he would apply it to a holy purpose, and carried off both shares.

*   *   *   *   *

By the beginning of February they were at Meerut. It was considered one of the best stations in India, and an awful phalanx of parties had been arranged. In the seven days they were to stay there, they were to attend three great dinners, three balls with suppers to follow, and one amateur play.

Emily disliked the place at sight. To her it was a quantity of bleak barracks and bungalows spread over four miles of plain. Fanny noticed that the gardens were full of flowers; she thought the houses pretty, and was of the opinion that if people happened to like each other, there were a greater number here to like.

William's old regiment, the 16th Lancers, was at Meerut. Hardly any of the men who had first come out with the regiment were left. Fanny and Emily went one evening to visit the European burial ground, which was near the camp, and noted the melancholy fact that few of those buried there seemed to have reached the age of fifty; most had been in their twenties and thirties.

Fanny had now to face a distressing parting. While she was up in the hills, she was to leave Gazelle with a Captain Champneys, who was living at Meerut. The danger from leopards and wild dogs in the hills was too great for a pet animal to be taken there. The deer had grown very much attached to Fanny, and she knew she would miss him very much. But he had become an anxiety, too, for he took dislikes to some of the native servants and she feared that he might run his horns through them. Captain Champneys had provided a large park for the deer to run in, and she knew Gazelle would be well looked after.

The overland post came while they were at Meerut. There were dispatches and letters for George, but not many for Fanny or Emily, which made them wonder despairingly whether their friends were going to give up writing to them. Robert, however, had sent plenty of newspapers, with accounts of the young Queen's visits to Guildhall and Covent Garden. There was also the political news of five months before, but it all seemed very far away.

The Meerut dinners and balls were much more real, looming over them every day. Balls, they had long discovered, were the same everywhere in India. The first one in Meerut, however, was distinguished by the presence of Mrs. Parkes. How she had got there nobody knew. Large, determined, vigorous, and cheerful, she danced and talked and supped with her usual enjoyment, before disappearing from the scene once more.

The suppers, Fanny thought, were improving as the party travelled northwards. She suspected that the roast lamb which was offered began life as innocent young kid; still, it was good. Her chief pleasure was in the abundance and variety of the vegetables which now appeared, especially the fruit. There were oranges and pomegranates and grapes, besides imported pears and apples, which arrived wrapped up in cotton and tasted rather like turnips.

The amateurs of the 16th Lancers put on the play *Rob Roy* for their entertainment. The character which the programme called 'Die Vernon' was acted by a very tall lancer with an immense flaxen wig, long ringlets hanging over his shoulders, short sleeves, and—as Meerut did not furnish gloves—large white arms with very red hands. Except in Calcutta, such a thing as an actress did not exist at military stations, so the lancer took most of the feminine leads. Emily was told that Juliet and Desdemona were his best parts.

They left Meerut on February 16th and at the end of three marches, were in Delhi.

7

DELHI

ELHI was one of the few sights which equalled Emily's expectations. Fanny thought that it was the grandest sight she had ever beheld. As they rode over the bridge from the camp, and got their first view of the city, it seemed to them one of the finest and most solid scenes of Eastern magnificence. Such gateways—and the enormous palace with its buttresses and battlements, and its miles of dark red stone walls! Endless mosques rose high above the other buildings, and everywhere the streets were full of people dressed in bright colours.

Fanny could not take her eyes away from the great mosque on the banks of the Jumna. It was built of red granite and white marble, with flights of marble steps leading up to the entrance. The domes were of marble; wherever she looked, marble gleamed above the red stone. Never before had she felt such awe of what man could do.

On the day after their arrival, Emily and Fanny set out to visit the King in his palace. George did not go with them. A point of etiquette had arisen over a meeting between the Governor-General and the King. The Secretaries insisted that it was the King's place to pay the first courtesy visit to the Governor-General's camp. The King thought otherwise. A compromise was made. The Governor-General's sisters would pay the first visit—ostensibly to see the interior of the palace.

They found the King sitting in the garden with a single servant behind him keeping off the flies. Around him were agate fountains, where the lowest servants seemed to cook and sleep if they wished. Everywhere they could see melancholy remains of former magnificence; marble halls which had once been inlaid with precious stones, but which now showed only the holes where these had been. The only remaining jewels were in the hall of audience, where they were shown the original Arabic inscription from which was taken Tom Moore's line: '*If there's bliss on earth it is this, it is this.*'

The following day they travelled ten miles out of Delhi to see the Kutb, the pillar of a royal tomb renowned for its striking beauty. Fanny had had an idea that all pillars would more or less resemble the Monument in London. But this pillar was breath-taking. It was built of red granite, carved round with triangular flutings, and incised

Delhi

all over with sentences from the Koran; each letter a yard high, inter-
laced and ornamented with carved flowers and garlands. Nobody
knew how many hundreds of years old it was, but it looked as if it
had just been finished—soaring upwards out of a wilderness of ruins,
carved gateways and marble tombs.

Not far away was one of the huge native wells, where men called
'jumpers' made spectacular jumps from the wall of the well into the
water, seventy feet below. Fanny went, not very willingly, to see
these feats, but she had to admit that they gave her the greatest thrill
she had ever felt. The jumpers did not turn over in the air; they went
down quite perpendicularly, the soles of their shoes touching the water
first. As one followed the other and ran up the steps of the well and
stood dripping on the edge, ready to jump again, Fanny—though
expecting to see them dashed to pieces—was held by a sort of fascina-
tion into watching them again.

Fanny and Emily did not think the European part of the community
at Delhi distinguished in any particular way, except perhaps that the
female part of it were addicted to black-thread mittens of their own
making, with large brassy-looking bracelets on them.

The Resident and local officials got up a supper and review for the
party; in the latter, blowing up mines and a dummy fort. And not
only the fort but Mrs. Parkes, for as the smoke blew off she was
discovered riding away. 'If she were not so fat,' Fanny wrote to
Eleanor, 'I would say she was something supernatural. My spirit is
broke about her. We shall find her settled in our home at Simla, and
shall not have the strength to turn her out.'

The Heir-Apparent of Delhi had been coaxed or threatened into
waiting upon the Governor-General, and a durbar was arranged. But
when it came to the appointed time, the prince took to his bed, and
sent for thirteen doctors to say he was too ill to come. However,
he changed his mind again and came, much to the satisfaction of
Macnaghten and Byrne, who were always worried when matters
did not go according to due form.

The person Fanny and Emily liked best in Delhi was Colonel
Skinner, who commanded a troop called Skinner's Horse—a set of
fearless men in wild-looking dresses. He was a native Colonel, very
dark, and much better society, Fanny thought, than any of the white
colonels they had met. The son of a Scottish officer and a Rajput
lady, he had been born in India and was brought up a Muslim; there
were any number of Mrs. Skinners and heaps of black sons, Fanny

132

found.   He was, however, a very unusual Mussulman, as well as being a very unusual man.   In his youth, when he had lain wounded on the battlefield, he had vowed to build a mosque if he recovered.   When he had accumulated fortune enough to fulfil his vow, he decided to build a church as well as a mosque.   Fanny asked him why.

"Where there is God," he told her, "there is religion."

They finished up their stay in Delhi by going to a nautch at Colonel Skinner's house.   He had engaged high-caste Brahmins to act scenes from the life of Krishna; and there were also troupes of dancers and singers.   One fat little nautch-girl sang a passionate-sounding song directly at George, which was translated by Major Byrne as it went on and on.   It set out to prove that George's countenance was so resplendent it was impossible to look at it.   Fanny decided she must turn her head the other way in future.

They were two marches on the road from Delhi to Karnal when panic broke out among the servants.   There had been a great deal of pilfering in the camp; it was a bad part of the country, known to be a haunt of thieves.   Early one morning a thief was seen running off with one of the servants' cooking-pots, and on being pursued turned and stabbed the man dead.   Other servants with the advanced camp, which habitually went on with the second set of tents, were set upon and robbed.   Almost everybody in both camps had something stolen. Fanny was glad to hear that the exemplary troop of irregular horse would patrol the road ahead in future.

The first thing she saw the following morning was Mrs. Macnaghten wandering over the countryside on an elephant, looking for a box of papers which had been taken from her tent.   The papers were found; the thieves had evidently been bored with them.

The camp had grown larger since Delhi.   One of the Secretaries had taken charge of a little niece and two nephews who had lost their mother suddenly, and was taking them up to the hills.   There was also a small European girl who had evidently nobody but bearers to take charge of her, and was probably going up to school at Mussoorie. Parents who were too poor to send children home to England generally sent them to Mussoorie.

Emily was always shocked when she met children travelling alone in this fashion.   There was a little girl of nine and two younger brothers who had been travelling *dak* for three days, and had a week's journey yet before them.   They had not even their names written on a piece of paper, or a note to the magistrates of the district, but were just passed on from one set of bearers to another.

'It is an odd way of sending children to school,' Emily wrote to Pamela Campbell. 'I should like to see you packing off your three youngest boys for the chances of these half-naked savages taking them, and feeding them, and looking after them on the road, without even a servant to attend to them.'

At Karnal, where the camp next halted, they found a large flat plain with a church and a cantonment; also a few bonnets of no particular shape driving up and down a road of no particular determination. A few bored-looking young officers were riding one way, and a great many bored-looking old officers riding another.

George held a levee in the morning, and Emily and Fanny were 'At Home' in the evening. The officers of four regiments, with their wives and daughters, all came and danced; one of the senior matrons wearing a turban made, Emily was sure, of stamped tin moulded into two fans, from which descended a weeping feather over some full sleeves. The next day they did a very great ball and a very great dinner. Fanny never remembered such large joints of so many large beasts on one table. She was certain they were serving up a baked shoulder of elephant and calling it a shoulder of mutton. She lost her head at one stage of the dinner and asked her neighbour to give her some dessert. But it was only the second course they had reached, and she had a whole hour to eat through before reaching fruit and wine.

They had hoped to leave Karnal the following morning, but the servants petitioned to stay, for it was one of their great Muslim festivals, which they were bound to observe. George was, as ever, impatiently anxious to get on, but he knew he must give way in this, and the camp remained at Karnal for another day.

The *nazir*, George's chief servant—he who had gone to Dacca but had returned at Emily's behest—provided a camel, and the others provided sheep, which were easier to procure than kids. Emily and Fanny watched the servants assemble in an open tent; nearly three hundred of them, dressed in white, with their priest standing in the centre, reading aloud from a manuscript book. The other tent, where the animals were assembled for sacrifice, was happily further off.

It was at times like these that Fanny had a sickening feeling of being in a heathen land. When, at sunset, she heard voices from the mosques calling the people to prayer, or watched the noisy worship of some grinning idol in a temple, she felt how thin was the crust on which they walked in this alien country. Europeans had lived in India for over a hundred years, preaching the Gospel, but there were few converts. And from time to time terrible facts came out about human sacrifices.

Fanny could not bear to listen today to the chanting voices in the tent. She was feeling especially low in spirits, for she was going to lose the companionship of William for three weeks. He was off for a tiger-shoot with General Churchill and Colonel Arnold, who commanded his old regiment. They were bound for the deep jungle, where there was an abundance of tigers, and would meet the main camp either at Simla or at the foot of the hills.

Fanny did not like the sound of that deep jungle. If all the tigers in the world took to eating William up, he would find no means of sending her a letter to tell her of it.

There was, however, some small compensation for William's going. As Fanny and Emily were walking over to luncheon, there appeared a procession of tired coolies carrying boxes. *English* boxes, which had come plodding after them from Allahabad. They hoped that a consignment of bonnets would come out of the boxes—but no, there were books. Even better, for they had come to an end of their reading. There was Mrs. Gore's *Stokeshill Park*, and some French novels, and, above all, more of dear Charles Lamb's letters, which Emily had been sighing for, and which she began to read instantly. Such a nice book! She so liked the way he went on, revelling in a bad joke and making nonsense by the piece. And there were many good little bits of real feeling. Such a jewel of a man! She quite dreaded going on with the book, for fear of finishing it.

At the next halt, Saharanpur, the camp broke up into two parties. The Governor-General and his sisters were to travel through the Dhun, which was cooler than the plains. It was a route which would not admit of a large escort; they were taking with them only the Torrenses, the Macnaghtens, Dr. Drummond and two aides-de-camp, MacGregor and MacIntosh. And, of course, Major Byrne. A minimum of guards and servants would suffice for their needs; the rest of the camp were to pursue the straight road to Simla.

This division, it seemed to Fanny, seemed to agree with the happiness of everybody. Mrs. Macnaghten was happy because she was following the Governor-General's camp, which she felt was due to her rank. Mr. Torrens was happy because on the upper route he would be able to go after a tiger which he would be certain not to find. General

Casement was happy because he was in command of the other camp, which included Mrs. Hawkins. He could go at the pace which the ladies liked best—poor Mrs. Wimberley, the only other lady, never being allowed a choice on the subject.

Then Mrs. Colvin was happy because she had just become the mother of a boy, and Mrs. Codrington was happy because she expected to become the mother of a boy soon. The aides-de-camp were happy because there were no levees or durbars. And William was happy, Fanny hoped, because he would now be having a tiger on one side of him and a wild elephant on the other.

A letter from William had come, saying he had just got out of his palanquin and found his camp surrounded by monkeys, and his horses frightened out of their wits by them. Two of his servants were in a fever, and he with only a turnscrew to bleed them with. He was within three days' march of the tiger jungle, and the Rajah of Rampore, with thirty more elephants, were to join him. Fanny had heard about that rajah. He was a sporting character, but was a little apt to go out not particularly sober, so Fanny hoped that they would only load his gun with powder.

Wild bees' nest

*   *   *   *   *

The route was climbing steadily towards the high land. They stopped within five miles of Dhera, and encamped in a grove of trees. The scene was soon made home-like with a slight sprinkling of camels and elephants, and people cooking. It was not light enough to see the distant view. Near at hand, Rolla, the lemur, jumped from one mango tree to another, with flights of parroquets swooping round him. Chance, at Emily's side, took in the scene with his accustomed interest.

The next morning, the magnificence of the Himalayas burst upon them; a wonderful line of hills, with snowy mountains behind. One of them, Fanny had been told, was the highest mountain in the world. That made it doubly pleasant to look in its direction. The climate seemed to be perfect, too, after the plains. It was hot in the tents from the sun beating in, but at sundown it was cold and bracing, and they were glad of their fur shoes and cloaks.

The gentlemen of the party decided to go out hunting, and went after a tiger which they had heard was in the neighbourhood. They fell in with plenty of deer, and by their own confession shot exceptionally ill. In fact, the deer at last fairly drew up and looked at them and their elephants to see what they were made of. Macnaghten, in a very large pair of blue spectacles, took aim at everything and shot nothing in particular. They did not meet the tiger.

Rolla had a new dress. It was an exceedingly handsome dress, for a lemur; crimson velvet, bossed with real gold, and long sleeves which particularly suited his black hands. It had been made by the best tailor in the camp, and it suited him to perfection.

Fanny had grown fond of her old tailor. She had never been able to discover where he put his feet and legs when he was seated on the ground, but she liked to watch his skilful hands at work. One of the ladies in the camp asked her whether she allowed her tailor thread to work with. What else could he work with, Fanny wanted to know. The other said it was an extravagance all ladies did not give in to. But . . . "Poor creet-churs, in a house like yours they all get lifted up," concluded the lady with disapproval.

They were to have stayed at the pleasant camp in the grove for two days, but George, all of a sudden, when Emily and Fanny thought they had settled in to camp, suggested that they should march into Dhera itself—it being only five miles off and at the foot of the hills. It was an odd, Eastern despot kind of idea, decided Fanny crossly. They had never marched after dinner before. She really did think that His Excellency and other men in authority led very enviable lives. They were the first Europeans in India about whom such a thought had crossed her mind. George giving orders in that decided way! Dear Byrne thought over his camels and elephants and looked astounded.

However, all their little goods were sent off; their beds were almost taken from under them, and after dinner they themselves followed by torchlight.

Fanny's crossness soon disappeared. The country was delightful. They were presently encamped on the outskirts of Dhera, and the following morning quantities of flowers—English flowers of every description—were sent along to their tents by Colonel Young, who commanded a regiment of Gurkhas in Dhera.

Colonel Young soon followed in person, to pay his respects. They went with him to see his Gurkha regiment manœuvre, and Fanny and Emily watched with admiration. They were the most dwarfish race Fanny had ever seen; they looked like a set of children in their dark uniforms. But they could fight. Twenty-five years before, a few hundred of them in their hills had beaten the British troops, and had kept beating them for a whole year. Now they fought equally well for their one-time enemies. 'I should say they will fight less well now we have brought them down to our English drilling and nonsense,' Fanny wrote home.

She found them fascinating to watch; quite unlike the native troops she was used to. They looked so hardy and ready for anything. Colonel Young told her that a score of them fell in with a tiger on the road she herself had travelled the day before. The Gurkhas were on foot and had no guns, but they made a circle round the tiger, and when he charged on one side, they cut at him on the other side with their swords, and so killed him.

From Dhera to Mussoorie, the next stop for the camp, was a climb of seven thousand feet. The party accomplished it on the following day. The men got on ponies, and Emily and Fanny were carried in *jonpauns*, which looked like open sedan-chairs. Emily thought they might just as well have been called *tonjauns*, which were the same kind of conveyances, but swung about more, and—familiar simile—also looked like coffins. Fanny had had enough after three miles, and got on a pony. It was an excellent little animal, and climbed up the hills like a cat. Fanny had a rule not to be frightened at anything, but she found her nerves tightening as the pony climbed up the perpendicular path, which did not even have a handrail to keep her from rolling down some thousand feet of precipice at the side.

Every now and then somebody said in a cheerful tone: "It's astonishing how seldom accidents do happen. That's the hill where poor Major Burton and his pony rolled down and were killed on the spot.

But then a snake crossed the path—*that* always frightens a pony."
Fanny kept looking out for snakes.

They reached Colonel Young's bungalow at Mussoorie, where they
were to stay, in the late afternoon. It was cold, but not the least too
cold. The bungalow was a regular cottage, very comfortable with
its carpets, and fires burning in containers on the hearths. And the
views from the windows! Nothing could have been grander. The
tremendous line of the Himalayas held their eyes whatever else they
wished to look at. One of the children in the camp, pointing to the
snowy range which towered above all the others, said:

"We seem to have got upon steps which are leading up to
heaven."

The only people who disliked the mountains were the Bengalee
servants. They walked about with long sticks to save themselves in
case they should slip over the edge of the precipices. Ariffe, Fanny's
jemadar, who had never seen anything higher than a molehill in his
native Calcutta, was particularly fearful of moving; and Rosina,
Emily's *ayah*, scornfully repeated his wails:

"There was poor Ariffe. 'Oh, what me do next?' he say. 'Me
tumble if me move me stick, or me foot.'"

But George's servant, Mars, had more feeling. Emily met him
leading Ariffe up to the house, and when she asked the *jemadar* whether
he did not think the hills very beautiful, he replied with an expression
of nausea, "No, ladyship, very shocking." And Mars did not laugh,
but sympathetically helped him on.

Emily and Fanny would have been content to stay at Mussoorie
for months. Besides the grandeur of the distant views, there were
masses of deep red rhododendrons everywhere, and other English
flowers which reminded them of home. But they had to descend to
the plains once more and continue on their way to Simla. George
and the Secretaries had more important matters to think about than
English flowers.

They came down from Mussoorie on March 19th. Captain
MacGregor put an extra spurt into their departure. He came into
the bungalow a short time before they were due to go, looking pale
and breathless.

"I have just seen Mrs. Parkes!" he said. Here she was in Mussoorie,
and she sent her remembrances to Lord Auckland, and to the Miss
Edens, and was delighted to think she had fallen in with them again,
and hoped soon to make her way to Simla.

There was something very horrid and unearthly in all this, thought Fanny. Nobody had ever had a fat attendant spirit before.

The two sisters kept a close eye on their pets on the way down to the plains. There were stories of leopards rushing into houses and carrying off dogs from under the eyes of their mistresses. Fanny was now thankful that she had left Gazelle with Captain Champneys. Chance seemed gifted with almost human common-sense, and stayed close to his mistress. Still, they decided it might be a good idea to make him wear a suit of armour to defend himself against the leopards.

They came down from cold air to the heat of the plains, and Emily had a sharp attack of spasms that night. Dr. Drummond was, as usual, close at hand, but it was alarming to be seized so suddenly. When they came to the Jumna, they found that it was not fordable, owing to the heavy rain. At last they were able to cross by boat. There were only three boats available for the entire camp, and the road on the other side was too bad for a carriage. Emily had to be put on the back of an elephant, which nearly shook her to powder. Dr. Drummond had given her laudanum, and she gradually felt better. What made her far more miserable than her own pain and discomfort was the fact that Chance had fallen ill with inflammation of the chest. The surgeon of the bodyguard bled him, and Chance, too, made a slow recovery.

A letter came from William, saying that he had fallen in with some tigers, and had been stung by hornets. It was a typically Williamish letter, designed to make them laugh and prevent them from worrying about him. He wrote a fuller and more realistic account of his adventures to his aunt, Lady Buckinghamshire.

'We . . . got to a place where no-one had hunted for eleven years, and whence men and women were carried off perpetually by tigers. It was a large, dark ravine with a stream of water running through it and high trees over our heads. After beating along for an hour, we came to a spot where we found a woman half-eaten, and the remains of a man and a boy. I left the ravine and went 200 yards ahead, and got down into it again to wait for the others to beat up to me—heard a roar and found two tigers charging my elephant about 10 yards off. I killed one dead with one barrel and wounded the other, whom I followed to a bush above the bank of the ravine, where he lay growling and looking beautiful—and told my man to put my elephant a little closer.

'The bank gave way and down I went, elephant and all, on top of the tiger. I did not fall out of my howdah, but unluckily the bottom was boggy and my elephant stuck. I was civil to the tiger; he was within two yards, growling horribly and not moving. I did not venture to get another shot for five minutes, when the elephant extricated itself. Then my civility vanished and I fired at the brute, and in two seconds found it at my elephant's head. After half a minute's fight I shook it off and killed it.

'Later . . . we had six tigers on foot at the same moment. They all fought well and charged repeatedly, but we killed four. And then came the best part of the fun, for looking for the other two, we disturbed a nest of hornets, and all the elephants ran away—mine went for nine miles. I jumped off behind, and got upon one of the troopers' horses, and rode off as fast as I could, but got dreadfully stung and could not see for three days.

'There, I won't give you any more. Do not tell all this to my mother or she will be frightened to death. I will bring you a few tiger skins for a rug.'

Fanny remembered the Rajmahal tigers, and tried not to let her imagination get the better of her common-sense. Awful risks surrounded every one of them all the time; fevers, a bite from a pariah dog, an elephant running amok, a *dacoit's* dagger in the night.

She wished very much that William were back.

*   *   *   *   *

They reached Nahan by the end of March. Chance was quite better; his constitution had become dreadfully Indianised, but Emily hoped that several months of Simla air would restore him to his usual philosophical state of health. However, he was done for as an English dog; he was now just the sort of dog one saw at Cheltenham.

The Rajah of Nahan met them on the last stage, and escorted them to his palace, which was at the top of a hill, set amid pretty scenery. He was one of the best-looking Rajput chiefs Emily had met, and his palace was the nicest residence she had seen in India. If the Rajah fancied an English Ranee, she knew someone who would be happy to listen to his proposals.

The palace was an odd collection of small rooms, painted and gilded in curious patterns. There were no tables or chairs; indeed, the only piece of furniture in the house was an English barrel-organ. And in one of the rooms there was a full-grown tiger, tolerably tame, and a large iron pot full of milk for his dinner. Emily's interest in the Rajah of Nahan diminished.

They were now within a few days' march of Simla. George decided to hold a durbar for the native officers of his escorting regiment, and presented them with matchlocks and shawls. They were extremely pleased at these marks of appreciation, and said that his lordship was the first that had ever been so good to natives. George had had some argument with Mr. Macnaghten and Major Byrne about this action—which had originally been Emily's idea. They had had to give in. George was of the opinion, which he expressed strongly, that there was too much neglect of meritorious natives; he was surprised that they were so loyal in the face of the high-handed manner in which they had for many years been treated.

Emily and Fanny were of the same mind. They always found it painful to hear the way in which even some of the best Europeans spoke to the Rajput princes. After all, these men were still kings in the eyes of their own subjects, in spite of being conquered by the British. The sisters never forgot this; they were always careful to observe the proper courtesies to any natives.

Raipur—Pinjore—Barh—Sabathu. Up and up they were carried in their *jonpauns*, the villages stringing out behind them. They started at four o'clock in the morning, and jogged by torchlight up perpendicular paths, the baggage following after. Every camel trunk needed eight coolies to carry it, and they had several camel trunks of stores alone.

Up and up, too jolted and joggled to look about them; up and up the narrow, winding paths. And then, incredibly, they were at Simla.

Emily wrote to Pamela Campbell that same evening.

April 3, 1838. 'Well, it really is worth all the trouble. Such a beautiful place, and our house only wanting the good furniture and carpets we have brought to be perfect. Views only too lovely; deep valleys on the drawing-room side of the west, and the snowy range on the dining-room side . . . and the climate! No wonder I could not live down below! We never were allowed a scrap of air to breathe. Now I come back to the air again I remember all about it. It is a cool sort of stuff, refreshing, sweet, and apparently pleasant to the lungs. We have fires in every room, and the windows open; red rhododendron trees bloom in every direction, and beautiful walks like English shrubberies cut on all sides of the hills. Good! I see this is to be the best part of India.'

To complete their delight, it snowed the following week. Fanny and Emily had almost forgotten the touch of snow; it was sublime. They spent crowded days furnishing the house. Carpenters and blacksmiths were shaping curtain rods and rings, and Emily and Wright supervised the making of the curtains. They had not brought half enough chintz or glazed cotton; they had to use the local country stuffs to eke out the supply. Emily was quite proud of a set of curtains for the dining-room which she made by sewing together strips of red and white material from the local bazaar.

They had brought carpets and chandeliers and wall-shades, and soon they had made it all as comfortable as a middle-sized country-house.

There was a garden, including a kitchen part which George put into the care of Giles, his second manservant. Giles was delighted with the charge; it reminded him of his own cottage in England. He was soon coming in and saying importantly: "I hope we may have rain tonight, ma'am, so I may bring a few asparagus from my garden."

They settled down, and for the first time since they had come to India, the long sense of strain lightened a little. Fanny noticed the ceilings without punkahs, and people riding and walking in the sunshine; it made her feel like the same species of human being she had been in England. And the sublime weather! There was hardly a day when she did not think of the battering heat of Calcutta, and contrasted it with the delicious coolness of these hills.

Emily was almost happy. George had turned one of the rooms into an office, and worked there with his Secretaries. But he was not so

far away as he had seemed to be at Government House in Calcutta;
he did not have the same hedge of officials and aides constantly round
him. She could persuade him to come out with her here; he enjoyed
making a party with her and Fanny, and riding into the valleys to look
for wild tulips and lilies for the garden.

There was little enough cause for any kind of pleasure in the
Governor-General's mind. The future was growing dark. Burnes
was on his way back from Kabul, having left a hostile Dost Muhammad
who would listen to no proposals which did not include the return of
Peshawar. Burnes had left when he saw there was no use in remaining
longer—and behind him was a Russian emissary, an honoured guest
at the Dost's court. Russian volunteers were known to be with the
Persians before Herat. All Asia was waiting for the outcome; and the
English government was watchful.

The Governor-General had failed to raise the rampart which was to
protect India. Instead of being a solid block in that defensive barrier,
Afghanistan might well become a highway for a potential enemy.
Lord Auckland knew that the time had come for him to act decisively.
He sat down with Mr. Colvin and put the question before himself in a
long Minute. First he set out the events which led up to the present
situation. Then he proceeded to study the courses of action open to him.

He could allow events to go on, and, if Herat fell, risk a potential
enemy reaching the very borders of India. Or he could assist Dost
Muhammad, should Afghanistan stand in danger of being overrun—
and risk the Dost turning against the Sikhs, England's allies. Or he
could follow Macnaghten's plan of reinstating Shah Shuja, with the
aid of Ranjit Singh.

The first course pointed to danger for India; the second to danger
for an ally. If Ranjit would agree, there seemed no alternative but
to go forward, depose Dost Muhammad, and put Shah Shuja on the
throne of Afghanistan.

*   *   *   *   *

There was a blackbird singing in the garden. It was certainly very
pleasant, Emily thought, to be in a pretty place with a nice climate—
and a blackbird. Not that she would have hesitated to set off in an
instant, and go *dak* all over the hot plains and through the searing wind,
if she were told that she could sail home when she got to Calcutta.
But as nobody made her that offer, she could spend her time here
better than anywhere else. Like meat, she *kept* better in the cold.

William had a house next door; his garden adjoined theirs. Emily and Fanny expected trouble over an apricot tree which stood on the boundary. It would only have enough eating on it for one, and they knew their William. But that would have to be thrashed out when the fruit was ripe.

They began to receive Simla society as soon as the house was in order, but they found, to their relief, that not too many people came at a time. There were no carriage-roads in Simla, and the only form of conveyance was consequently the *jonpaun*. This made people think twice before stepping out to call more than was necessary; being joggled in a *jonpaun* was a different matter from rattling along in a carriage.

Emily and Fanny as usual, enjoyed unexpected visits from young cadets who came in from distant stations. Two of them called one day, and after the first polite exchanges, began to talk. They talked without ceasing; it was impossible to edge in a word. One of them had been eight years, and the other four years, in stations where they never saw a European. They said they were so delighted to find themselves again with people who understood English that they were afraid they had talked too much. It was difficult to dispute the fact, but Emily was glad to hear their unending flow; it evidently did them good to let themselves go. And it was amusing to watch their delight as they listened to the regimental band; they had not heard any European music for so long.

★   ★   ★   ★   ★

Mr. Macnaghten was going to Lahore. Now that the decision to act had been taken, the Governor-General's Political Secretary was to discuss the proposed new treaty with the Maharajah as soon as possible.

But everything had to be done with due form. At the end of April, 1838, a deputation of Sikh chiefs and envoys arrived from Ranjit Singh to wait on the Governor-General, bringing messages and gifts. Soon after their arrival, George held a durbar for them.

Major Byrne was in a dilemma. He was in charge of the regular durbar tent which they carried with them on the march. There had been times when the Governor-General's sisters had made remarks about his covering the ground of the tent with white cloths; remarks which Major Byrne had ignored. But there was to be no tent this time. In Simla the durbar was to be held in the house—and Miss Eden was mistress here.

Emily had foreseen this pleasing state of affairs. Byrne usually managed to make the durbar tent look like a drying ground at a laundress's. There would be a change at *this* durbar. Emily and Fanny took charge of the arrangements themselves, and paid no attention to Byrne. They threw open the folding doors between the principal rooms, and covered the floor with scarlet linen. No more drying grounds! This would form an excellent background for the deputation at the durbar.

There were six principal Sikh chiefs and forty envoys, all in splendid dresses. Even the *faquir* who had come with them had a gold dress embroidered in seed pearl showing beneath his coarse gown.

George sat on a gilt chair and listened for an hour to Major Byrne translating flowery nonsense. George hoped that the deputation had not suffered from the rains, which had come on heavily since their arrival. They replied that the canopy of friendship had interposed such a thick cloud that their tents had remained quite dry. Which was touching, as Emily knew that their tents had been so soaked through, they had been obliged to hire the only empty house in Simla. They then conveyed the Maharajah's message, which was to say that the roses had bloomed in the garden of friendship and the nightingales had sung in the bowers of affection sweeter than ever, since the two Powers had approached each other.

The *faquir*, who was Ranjit's chief confidant and adviser, at last got down to business and proceeded to make indirect enquiries as to the size of army his lordship was said to be bringing with him. His lordship asked questions in turn, equally indirect and equally unproductive of any useful reply. Amiable relations having been established in due form, the durbar ended.

The real negotiations, the firm details of their joint policy with regard to Afghanistan, would take place later—after Lord Auckland had sent a return deputation to Ranjit Singh. Meanwhile, the Sikh chiefs had to be entertained for the remainder of their stay.

Emily and Fanny decided that a grand dance was called for, and sent out invitations to Simla society. Most of these were coldly received. It soon came to their ears that the ladies of Simla would not come to a ball if the Sikh envoys were asked; they did not intend to dance before natives. Emily called on one of the leading lady residents of the station, and pointed out that she asked at least forty natives to every dance she gave in Calcutta, and she had no intention of changing this habit. The leading lady resident replied that she herself was in deep mourning, and she was, in any case, not a natural dancer. But she would come to the ball and dance every quadrille, just to show the others what she thought of their nonsense.

It may have been her example, or the ladies of Simla may have had second thoughts. They came to the ball in force: only three ladies were absent out of the whole station. The Sikhs were very quiet and well-behaved. Two of them had seen English dancing before, and were aware that the ladies were ladies, and not nautch-girls. Emily hoped they would explain that important fact to the others.

8

THE MAHARAJAH

'THE Supreme Government of India having determined upon sending a mission to the Court of Lahore, for the purpose of endeavouring to place our alliance with Runjeet Singh on a more secure and decided footing than had hitherto been the case, in May, 1838, the following gentlemen left Simla, in company with several of the Maharaja's chief officers, who had been sent to escort them to Adeenanuggur, where his Highness was then passing the hot weather: Mr. W. H. Macnaghten, Political Secretary to Government; Captain Wade, Political Agent at Loodhiana; Hon. Captain W. H. Osborne, Military Secretary to the Governor-General; Captain MacGregor, Aide-de-camp to the Governor-General; Dr. Drummond, Surgeon to the Governor-General.'

So wrote William for posterity, in a journal which was later sent home to England to find a publisher within a few months of William's return to Simla—in spite of his declaration in the preface that it had been written 'to beguile the tedium of camp life, and without the remotest intention of publication.' It was William's first essay into authorship, and he became surprisingly articulate.

'The author will be more than satisfied,' he proceeded, 'if, in the present state of the countries beyond our north-west frontier, this imperfect description of a few weeks spent in familiar intercourse with a ruler, who the peculiar position of his kingdom, as well as his own extraordinary character, have rendered an object of more than ordinary interest, should afford one moment's amusement to those who, blessed in the enjoyment of all the comforts of their native land, can little guess the shifts to which their less fortunate and exiled countrymen are reduced, to pass the tedious hours of a hot and sultry sky, on the burning plains of the East.'

His letters to his aunts at Simla dealt with subjects on a somewhat lower plane. The Mission was met at the frontier to Ranjit Singh's kingdom by troops of Kashmiri young ladies, and William later had an embarrassing few moments fending off his host's enquiries as to which one he had chosen for himself.

Mr. Macnaghten was in charge of the party, and his object was quite clear. He was there not merely to reciprocate the compliments of the

Maharajah, but to discuss in the plainest possible terms the existing state of political affairs in that quarter of the world.

'The recent attempt of the Persians at Herat,' wrote William for posterity, 'the ambiguous conduct of Dost Mahomed, and the suspicions which had been excited with respect to the proceedings and ulterior designs of Russia, rendered it of the greatest importance to cement the alliance with Runjeet Singh, and engage him to a firm and effective co-operation with us in the establishment of general tranquility, the resistance of foreign encroachment, and the extension of the benefits of commerce and the blessings of civilization.'

None knew better than Mr. Macnaghten how much time it would require to bring an Oriental ruler to talk in plain terms, and he expected the Mission to be away for several weeks at least.

They arrived, together with their escort of foot soldiers and a squadron of horse, at the banks of the Sutlej on May 19th. There they were met by two sirdars whom Ranjit had sent with a *zeafut*, a gift of welcome, of twelve hundred rupees. The next day they began their march to Adinanagur, where Ranjit was holding his court, and after four days of uncomfortable travel in intense heat they were met by Ranjit's grandson, Pertab Singh, a seven-year-old boy who soon showed an intelligence far beyond his years.

'His manners are in the highest degree attractive, polished, and gentlemanlike,' wrote William, 'and totally free from all the *mauvaise honte* and awkwardness so generally found in European children.'

Mr. Macnaghten was inclined to be stiff; according to all precedent and custom, Pertab's father, Sher Singh, should have been sent to meet them. But it was explained that Sher Singh had been a little overcome at a drinking party with the Maharajah the evening before, and was, in consequence, unable to travel.

Pertab Singh was splendidly dressed, armed with a small ornamented shield, sword and matchlock, all in miniature; and covered with jewels. His horse, originally white, had been dyed with henna to a deep scarlet, and he sat it like a small warrior.

William was charmed with him, as Emily and Fanny were to be later. He presented the boy with a gold watch-and-chain as a gift from the Governor-General, and Pertab at once made a graceful speech of thanks. "You may tell Lord Auckland that the British Government will always find a friend in the son of Sher Singh," he ended, and galloped off, his escort curvetting and caracoling round him in circles till he was out of sight.

The next morning's march brought them to Ranjit Singh's palace at Adinanagur. It was a collection of buildings set in a large garden with gardens and shrubs; a canal running through the centre kept it irrigated, and William found the cool green of the trees and grass refreshing to his parched eyes. Beyond the garden was a level plain, in the foreground of which was pitched a scarlet and gold-embroidered shawl-tent. Here, they were told, was where Ranjit retired to rest, sleeping in the open air, and guarded only by a few Sikh sepoys. His sword and shield were always laid by his pillow, and a saddled horse stood constantly ready in front of his tent. Ranjit liked to superintend his army personally. At sunrise he was generally to be found mounted either on horseback, or on an elephant, inspecting his troops or watching the practice of his artillery.

The Mission was soon encamped in the tents pitched for them on the banks of another canal, a few hundred yards from Ranjit's garden. The following morning, after a bathe in the canal and breakfast, they were moved to small thatched bungalows, each furnished with a comfortable native bedstead covered by embroidered quilts. Then the *faquir* whom they had already met in Simla came to inform them that the Maharajah would receive them at his durbar on the following morning.

The Governor-General's presents to Ranjit were unpacked and got ready for the interview; Lord Auckland's picture set in a star of fine diamonds and suspended from a string of large pearls, a pair of gold-mounted pistols, a sword in a golden scabbard, and two thoroughbred Cape horses. The Maharajah was known to be passionately fond of horses; this would be a more than acceptable gift. He was also very fond of strong drink. William had brought bottles of wine—and had added some whiskey and brandy, knowing Ranjit's habits.

Early the following morning two Sikhs in glittering silks and gold-chain armour arrived to escort Mr. Macnaghten and his companions to the durbar hall. Two battalions of infantry formed a guard of honour, there was a salute from a hundred guns, and another guard of honour came into sight, lining the three-hundred-yard gravel walk across the garden. These were *gucheras*, Ranjit's personal bodyguard. In their quilted jackets of silks in bright yellow, green and scarlet, they looked to William like borders of gaudy and gigantic tulips.

He and his companions were led into the hall of audience, and for a moment or two even Mr. Macnaghten was dazzled. The floor was covered with rich shawl carpets, and a gorgeous shawl canopy, embroidered with gold and precious stones and supported on golden pillars, covered three parts of the hall. The place was crowded with Ranjit's chiefs, mingled with natives from Kandahar and Afghanistan, all blazing with precious stones, and dressed and armed in every conceivable variety of colour and fashion. In the centre, at the end of the hall, sitting cross-legged on a golden chair, was the old Lion of Lahore himself.

He was an ugly old man with one seeing eye, the other a blank. His nature and his mode of life were written in his dissipated face: the fierce, ruthless ambitions, the sensual debaucheries, the drunkenness. But his one eye was shrewd and somehow impish as he looked at the Europeans, and his mouth showed humour. A striking figure against the glittering background of his court, he was dressed in plain white, wearing no ornaments but a single string of enormous pearls round the waist, and a great diamond set in a bracelet above his elbow. The eyes of all the party flew to this gem, flashing fire on the white sleeve.

The Koh-i-nur itself, the most famous diamond in the world—the Mountain of Light! William tried to measure its size with his eye. It looked to be an inch-and-a-half long and an inch wide. A gorgeous jewel, inspiring awe by the perfection of its beauty.

He knew its history, and he recalled it now. It had once adorned the peacock throne at Delhi. The Afghan Nadir Shah had conquered Delhi, and taken the diamond. Came a rival chieftain, Ahmed Shah, who had overcome Nadir, and plundered his treasure. The Mountain of Light had descended to Ahmed's son, Shah Shuja. Twenty-five years ago he had been driven out of his country, and had come to Lahore in his exile. The Ruler of the Punjab seemed a friend. But he turned out to be a greedy friend.

Ranjit coveted the Koh-i-nur the moment he saw it. He did not employ greater severity than appeared absolutely necessary to persuade the Shah to 'sell' him the jewel; after all, the Shah was his guest. He simply deprived Shah Shuja and his family of all nourishment for two days. Their firmness was found to be proof against hunger, and Ranjit changed his tactics. He nagged. He asked continually for the diamond, and went on asking for it with a persistence and tenacity which at last wore Shah Shuja down. The Koh-i-nur was given up.

Ranjit Singh sat in his gold chair and smilingly watched the Governor-General's Mission taking in the scene—and himself. Mr. Macnaghten began to translate greetings from the Governor-General, and signed to an aide to bring forward the presents. Contrary to the usual custom of appearing to ignore gifts, Ranjit picked up the jewelled ornaments and examined them closely; he seemed to count every pearl and diamond before he passed them over to his treasurer. William had heard that the old man was grown avaricious, and now he saw that it was true.

The highbred horses were received with great satisfaction—and the wine and spirits brought an added glitter to Ranjit's bright eye. What did his lordship drink? Ranjit asked questions about George's personal habits, as he tried the hock and claret, and then the whiskey, which he had never tasted before. He turned to Mr. Macnaghten, his glass held high.

"Why does the Governor-General give himself the trouble of drinking seven or eight glasses of wine when one glass of whiskey would do the same quantity of work?" he asked.

As this was merely an audience of introduction, the chief object of the Mission was not touched upon. Their time was principally taken up with answering Ranjit's torrent of questions. He wanted to know the strength of the army which the Governor-General had brought with him, and he asked sharply intelligent questions about the British artillery. He had seen shrapnel shells used at manœuvres of British troops some years before, and one of his sirdars, who was a clever mechanic, had copied them. The shells were made of pewter, and William was impressed by the old man's ingenuity in adapting this new ammunition in his own way.

"You must come soon and see my troops on parade," he said to William, and brought the durbar to an end by embracing them all and half-smothering them in sandal-wood oil.

The Mission was treated to a display by one contingent of his troops on that same evening. At the nautch to which the Englishmen had been invited, a detachment of Amazons arrived with music and fireworks. With them was the far-famed Lotus. William had often heard of these fair warriors—and of the most beautiful of them, the Lotus. The establishment of the corps had been one of Ranjit's capricious whims, the result of a drinking bout. But he had not tired of the joke, and for several years now the corps had been an established part of his army.

When the Mission was seated in the garden for the evening's entertainment, a score of Amazons marched on before them, dressed in embroidered shawls and petticoats, and armed with bows and arrows. Several of them carried single-sticks, and at a word of command these girls began to wage a mimic combat. It was almost like a dance in a ballet, with its slow and graceful movements, the sticks clicking like castanets.

William easily distinguished the Lotus. Slightly built, with enormous eyes, she was a Kashmiri girl with whom Ranjit had fallen violently in love, and had been in the royal seraglio since the age of twelve. Ranjit had boasted of her fidelity to General Ventura, the Italian soldier who helped to train his army. One evening, in his cups, he challenged Ventura to seduce her. The challenge was accepted. The Italian did not find it difficult to charm the Lotus, who allowed herself to be transplanted from her royal lover's garden to the Italian's. Ranjit bore her desertion with equanimity, and in a short time she returned to him, saying she wished to be enrolled in his corps of Amazons.

William persuaded Macnaghten to arrange for the girl to talk to them after the nautch. The Lotus was friendly and communicative. She and her companions were materially well off, she told them; there were few who had not succeeded in getting grants of villages out of Ranjit. She herself was the owner of seven good villages, received at different times from Ranjit as marks of his favour.

There was a time, remembered William, when a rumour had spread through Lahore that the Maharajah was going to take back gifts of land. The report had been premature. Looking at the Lotus and her companions, William could easily believe that Ranjit would sooner face Dost Muhammad and his Afghans than one single determined individual of his Amazon bodyguard.

★   ★   ★   ★   ★

On the following day Ranjit sent word to say that he would receive the Mission that morning, for the purpose of hearing Lord Auckland's letter read. The real business of the visit was beginning. Mr. Macnaghten led the others after the sirdar who had been sent to fetch them, and presently they entered the palace. Ranjit was sitting, as usual, cross-legged in his gold chair—which William privately thought looked like a hip-bath. The compliments began.

Mr. Macnaghten knew when to slide into purpose. At the appropriate moment he opened Lord Auckland's letter and began to read it aloud. The Governor-General was explicit. His Highness the Maharajah Ranjit Singh was expected to act in concert with the British Government for the restoration of Shah Shuja-ul-mulk to the throne of Kabul. If the Maharajah preferred to take his own course and rely solely on his own military force, he was at perfect liberty to do so. If he should choose the other line, a British force would be ready to march and operate with the Sikh troops.

There was a murmur of disapproval from behind the royal hip-bath. Dian Singh, one of Ranjit's closest advisers, did not like the proposed agreement. Tall, strong, intelligent and ambitious, Dian Singh was Ranjit's Prime Minister, and he wanted no Europeans interfering in the Punjab. He had always been against any British connection, and showed his dislike of the Mission plainly now, in look and gesture. But he dared not make any remark, in the face of Ranjit's apparent cordiality and approval of Lord Auckland's proposals. Macnaghten took leave, and the Mission returned to their tents. William felt relieved that everything was going so well. It might not be many days before all minor arrangements would be settled, and then they could begin the return journey. Mr. Macnaghten said nothing.

The following day Ranjit sent for the English party to come and see the parade he had promised them. William, who had for long been a professional soldier, was keenly interested. Ranjit had two thousand men under arms, and some foot artillery. William thought them a very fine body of men, excellently disciplined, and good marchers. A useful force. How many troops had Ranjit got altogether? Ranjit parried by asking how many the Company had behind them. William, knowing that the old man knew, smilingly answered that they had about two hundred thousand.

"So I have been told. But you could not bring that number into the field at once, or at any one place?"

"It is unnecessary," said William. "Twenty, or at the most, thirty thousand British troops could march from one end of India to the other, and no power in the country could stop them."

"You are fine fellows. How many Frenchmen can an Englishman beat?"

"At school, in England, the boys are always taught to consider themselves equal to three Frenchmen," answered William.

"And how many Russians?"

"The French beat the Russians and we beat the French."

"If the Russians cross the Indus, what force could you bring against them?"

"Quite enough to drive them back, with your Highness for our ally."

"Wah! Wah! So we will," said Ranjit.

And there the subject paused. The days passed. The Maharajah entertained the Mission with more parades, more nautches, more entertainments. Nothing was said about a reply to Lord Auckland's letter.

Ranjit sent a sirdar to Dr. Drummond with a written abstract of his health; he consulted every medical man who could be persuaded to listen to him. He knew as well as they did that his continued excesses and debaucheries were fast sending him the way of all flesh, but he would not give up the pleasures of drink or the zenana. He demanded medicine from each new doctor. Dr. Drummond was quite aware of the state of affairs, and sent the Maharajah a harmless aperient. But he did not know that Ranjit forced some of his sirdars to swallow any new medicine in his presence, shutting them up afterwards to judge of its effects. One of Ranjit's favourite chiefs was directed to take the aperient and then sent home, with orders to report to his master the earliest possible intelligence of the state of his health on the following morning.

William, still with his eye on posterity, could not resist slipping that item into his journal. Writing privately to Fanny later in the week, he gave her further news of Dr. Drummond: 'All his medicines and instruments had been stolen during the night, including a stomach pump. This last was found, cut to pieces by the thieves. Such a blessing for Runjeet's courtiers! He would have been sure to see the article at some time; how the chiefs and rajahs would have been pumped!'

It was now June, and the thermometer had risen to a hundred degrees in the tents at night, and over a hundred during the day. Symptoms of cholera began to appear among the servants in camp. Dr. Drummond was appalled. If it turned into a real outbreak, he would be practically helpless without his medicine chest.

Mr. Macnaghten knew that it was useless to press Ranjit Singh for a definite answer to Lord Auckland's letter. The subtle old man had sent many messages to the Mission, questioning this point and that in the proposed treaty. It was necessary to send most of these queries to Simla and to wait for replies, a fact of which Ranjit was not unaware. He also saw to it that the Mission had information about the attitude of his own ministers towards them. Dian Singh and the other palace advisers were all against the English proposals. Ranjit told Macnaghten that it would take time to persuade them.

William decided to ask Ranjit for permission to go to Lahore for a few days; he had always wanted to see Lahore and Amritsar. When Ranjit rode over to the English camp to see the Company's artillery at practice, William accompanied him part of the way back and made the request. Ranjit at once agreed.

"I am going to Lahore myself," he said. "We shall have *burra tomacha*—great fun."

They left on June 8th, and almost at once William wondered why he had decided to move a limb oftener than necessary in that abominable heat. The next five days were intolerable. He was unable to eat or sleep, and was sure that he continued existence by suction alone. Three days later they reached Lahore, where they were met by Captain Alexander Burnes—the Governor-General's envoy to Kabul. Captain Burnes reported that he had left Dost Muhammad at Kabul with three thousand splendidly trained Afghan cavalry. Dost Muhammad, said Captain Burnes, was a clever, enterprising man.

The camp was set up in the Shalimar Gardens. William had his tent pitched in a large marble hall in the centre of the gardens, where the temperature was under a hundred in spite of a hot wind. The gardens themselves were beautiful; terraces of orange, pomegranate and mango trees, with paved stone walks, vines, and a hundred fountains throwing up fronds of water.

Now began the next stage of the delaying game which Ranjit knew so well how to play. On June 18th Mr. Macnaghten was told that the Maharajah was ready to sign the treaty. On the following day, the old Lion turned sulky and began to stipulate for all sorts of concessions which he knew could not be granted. Mr. Macnaghten, with no sign of impatience, promised to send a memorandum to Simla. But William was disgusted. He wanted to get back to his own people. He was a soldier, not a diplomatist, and this constant smooth-voiced parrying irked him. He took to sitting without clothes under the great fountain in the gardens every morning at daybreak, to soothe his growing irritation, and to refresh him a little against the torrid air of the day. Then the Sikh guard began to turn out regularly to present arms in the most soldierlike manner the moment he was seated under the water, and persisted in remaining at attention the whole time he was bathing. It was a matter of considerable difficulty to return the salute with the proper degree of dignity. So William sought to keep cool in other ways.

There was nothing else for the Mission to do but continue to wait for letters from Simla, and to try to prevent Ranjit from employing any more delaying tactics. William took every opportunity of watching the Maharajah's troops at their exercises. He soon found that only a small proportion of them were really well-trained by his own standards; and these were the soldiers who had been trained by Ranjit's French or Italian Generals. Ventura told him with exasperation that he could have made an efficient army if Ranjit would only pay his soldiers. But the old man's avarice was getting worse; he could not be persuaded into giving the men half the arrears due to them.

Yet they remained loyal to him. William reflected on the personality of this extraordinary old man. Cunning and distrustful himself, Ranjit had succeeded in inspiring his followers with a devoted attachment to his person. He could neither read nor write, but he had a quick talent for reading men's minds, and was equally adept at concealing his own. Without the benefit of any kind of education, he had by his own unaided intellect raised himself from the situation of a private individual to that of a despotic monarch over a turbulent and powerful nation.

His people obviously admired him; that was the secret of his power. He had a personal courage which had become legendary. A living legend, in India, had great power. Ranjit no longer possessed his old physical strength, but the force of his personality sustained his rule. He was a man to reckon with, and would be, until his shrunken little body was placed on the funeral pyre.

Towards the end of the month, news came that Mr. MacNeil, the Governor-General's envoy to the Persian camp, had left to return to India, and that Herat was in great danger. Twelve thousand Russians, it was said, were on the march through Persia to assist at its destruction. Ranjit was very much excited, and could talk of nothing else. What number of Russians did the Emperor of Russia keep in pay, he asked William. Were they good soldiers? Could the English beat them? William repeated that the French had often beaten them and that the English had beaten the French just as often.

"If they wished to invade India, what number of men could they bring across the Indus?" demanded Ranjit.

Fifty thousand would be the smallest number they would attempt an advance with, was William's reply. Probably a hundred thousand would be sent.

What would William do if the Russians were actually to attempt an invasion?

"Join your Highness with thirty thousand British troops, which, with seventy thousand of your Sikhs, would be quite sufficient to drive them back again."

Ranjit thought that would be *burra tomacha*. Especially if they had much money with them. William remarked that there would be little money to be got. Ranjit was puzzled. "Then there would be nothing but fighting—no plunder?"

None, said William. Ranjit looked sulky at that, and his interest in a possible Russian advance sensibly lessened.

Three days later a message came that the Maharajah had at last made up his mind to put his name to the treaty without further delay. With great relief the Mission began preparations for returning to Simla. The rains had set in, bringing out all the mosquitoes and reptiles which swarmed in the gardens. William was thankful to go. But etiquette demanded suitable leaving ceremonies, including the prospect of one which filled even William with apprehension: the Maharajah's own brand of drinking-party. Ranjit prided himself on a special wine, which was an extract of raisins mixed with a quantity of pearls ground to powder. As he always insisted on helping his guests himself, it was not easy to avoid excess without offending him.

By great good fortune, Ranjit was not well enough to indulge in the promised debauch, and William went for a farewell ride with him instead. As usual, Ranjit poured out questions. Was Lord Auckland married? Why not? Was William married? Why not?

"I can't afford it," said William.

"Are English wives very expensive? I wanted one myself some time ago, and wrote to Government about it, but they did not send me one."

The rains were growing heavier, and the Mission had to wait for the weather to clear a little before they could start. It was the middle of July before they were at last able to ask the Maharajah for leave to depart from his court. He gave a durbar in the hall of his palace, and William, Macnaghten, Dr. Drummond and the others put on formal dress and were conducted there.

The scene was as magnificent as the one which had greeted them on their arrival six weeks before. But this time there was something else added—an atmosphere, the obvious good-will and friendship of the Maharajah. He was sincerely genial towards William, in particular, and showed his favour by allowing him to see the Koh-i-nur diamond at close quarters.

The jewel was indeed a matchless treasure. Taking it in his hand, William noted that it was in the shape of an egg, set in a bracelet between diamonds of half its size. It was not often, thought William, a man held three million pounds in his palm. But one could not think long about its money value while gazing down at its brilliance, unmarred by any flaw. It was perfect.

The bracelet was again clasped on the Maharajah's arm; the time had come for departure. His presents to the officers of the Mission were brought in. William's were a string of pearls, a *chelenk* of diamonds, six pairs of shawls, diamond armlets, a sword, and a horse with gold and velvet accoutrements. The gifts to the others were smaller in proportion, but equally handsome.

Ranjit told William that he had put a carriage and horses at his disposal, embraced him, and retired. William and one of the officers took to the carriage with some misgiving; it was an ancient English family coach, with ropes for harness and horses which looked—and which proved to be—workshy. They were six hours doing the first ten miles, on roads which were under water—in some places up to the axletrees of the wheels. Both doors of the carriage parted company with their hinges, and William and his companion were more than thankful to reach the end of the first stage of their journey, and to get to Amritsar late in the day.

By midnight they were at the banks of the Ravee, which they crossed in an open boat against an immensely strong current. They arrived at Ludhiana the following morning, and after breakfast started for Simla, which they reached forty-eight hours later.

William was glad to be back, although he had enjoyed himself. He had actually become fond of the wily old Lion of the Punjab; it was difficult not to like that extraordinary character. It would have been pleasant to be able to keep at least one of the old man's gifts as a remembrance of their sojourn at his court. But—

'All these things were duly deposited in the coffers of the Honourable Company, much to our disgust, as well as to that of the Maharajah,' William wrote for posterity.

What he said on the subject to Fanny and Emily exceeded the bounds of official decorum.

9

A LIVING MAP OF EMERALDS

IT was like an English summer. A very hot English summer, of course, but still, one could call it 'summer' as a change from 'the hot season.' Giles had grown a fine crop of strawberries, which they had with ices as well as with sugar confections. The garden was a mass of pink and white roses; Emily worked with fork and trowel in the cool of the morning, and would have liked to return in the late afternoon, had there been no bejewelled rajahs or tight-sleeved Europeans to entertain.

She could have been happy, if she had been able to close her mind entirely in this strange land of emeralds and misery. There was famine in Agra. She remembered the children, as thin as sticks, whom she had seen at Cawnpore; she remembered skeletons of men and women tearing ravenously at the food she gave. What could one person do? The officials were helping wherever possible; she and Fanny were not able to interfere there. Famine on a scale which this vast continent produced was beyond human imagination.

When one of George's aides-de-camp decided to put on some plays for the benefit of the starving people of Agra, Emily had a wild moment of hysteria. Then her practical good sense established itself, and she set to work to get as much support for the performances as she could. There was soon a long list of subscribers, and things promised very well. The theatre at Simla was small, and it looked as if all the performances would be solidly attended. Then the actors fell out. One man took a fit of low spirits, another who acted women's parts well would not cut off his mustachio, and a third went off to shoot bears in the hills. The performances had to be cancelled.

The gentlemen of Simla having given up, the uncovenanted service said they wished to try.

'The uncovenanted service,' Emily wrote home, 'is just one of our choicest Indianisms, accompanied with our very worst Indian feelings. We say the words just as you talk of the "poor chimney-sweepers" or "those wretched scavengers"—the uncovenanted being, in fact, clerks in the public offices. Very well educated, quiet men, and [some] of them very highly paid. But as many of them are half-castes, we, with our pure Norman or Saxon blood, cannot really think contemptuously enough of them. . . . There were at least fifty of them in one camp, and I never saw better behaved people. Some had horses, some gigs, and some their nice little wives in nice little palkees. . . . And then, in the evening, we used to hear A and B disputing that they could not allow Mr. V and Mr. Z to sit down in their presence. Well! I daresay it is all right—or we are all equally wrong—for they are not allowed to enter Government House.'

Emily knew better than to attempt to take part in the arguments of European Simla where half-caste people were concerned. But she hoped her actions would speak louder than words. The uncovenanted clerks and their womenfolk took over the plays and the theatre. Emily lent them the Government House band. She and Fanny dressed in their best and went to see them play, taking George and some of the aides. The players acted remarkably well, and full houses resulted in a large sum for the famine fund.

Emily was glad when she could persuade George to relax from the strain of work and worry which were ageing him before her eyes. Since his arrival in the Upper Provinces, he had taken over the administration of the country, as the Lieutenant-Governor had re-signed. There was the usual clash of prejudice against his own ideas on education and social reform; George was familiar with arguments which had buzzed around his head in Calcutta. He listened quietly, and as quietly went on with his plans for enlarging the schools and establishing new ones.

There was also the impending war. Mr. Macnaghten had gone from Ranjit Singh's court to Ludhiana, to announce to Shah Shuja that the Shah's long exile was over, and he was to be restored to his throne at Kabul. The Shah had managed to raise a force of sorts—more for form than for use, was William's opinion—and it would soon be joined by a British contingent. Soon the Governor-General must set out to meet Ranjit at Ferozepore, to arrange for the Maharajah's part of the business. By the end of the year three armies would be marching on Afghanistan; Dost Muhammad would be sent packing, Shah Shuja restored, and a friendly buffer-state cemented into the rampart between Russia and India.

Meanwhile, Herat was still besieged, the Russians were egging on the Persians, and their agents were trying to do all the mischief they could on the frontier. Two Russian letters had been intercepted and sent to George. They were probably highly important, only un-luckily nobody in India could read them. The aides-de-camp spent hours making facsimile copies to send to Calcutta and Bombay, in the hope that some Armenian could be found who would be able to translate them. It would be amusing, Emily thought, if they turned out to be quite ordinary letters which some Caterina Iconoslavitch was sending to her Uncle Alexis.

The rains were now in full spate; throughout July and August they could only see the hills for a few minutes at a time. The unending downpour thinned out the usual round of social engagements, though they still had to give and be given dinners. A new and unpleasant distraction turned up in the shape of fleas. Emily and Fanny could not have imagined that these homely insects would be such an irritating provocation. William had actually been ill for two days for want of sleep from their attentions, and had to see Dr. Drummond. The more the house was cleaned, the worse the fleas seemed to get; they belonged to the soil, and even the garden was full of them. Emily was relieved to hear that the plague would cease in another month.

A few fine evenings indicated that the rains were breaking up. Emily and Fanny, with George and William, dropped in after dinner to the Commander-in-Chief's for tea and a rubber of whist. Emily liked whist, and decided it should be one of the small vices of her old age; though she did not anticipate dropping in at her London friends' houses with a train of torch-bearers and aides-de-camp, in full uniform, behind her.

William, having turned author, was making his journal into a book. He finished it in October, and gave it to Emily.

'There is a small parcel going to you,' Emily wrote to Charles Greville, 'a journal kept by William Osborne while he was at Runjeet Singh's court. . . . We think you will be just the man to edit it, and to cram it down the throat of an unwilling bookseller. . . . It is not to be published till George gives his consent, and as it gives an account of the Mission which formed the alliance, which is to end in the war—which may end we don't know how—and as William will indulge in levities respecting the Company highly unbecoming the Governor-General's Military Secretary, who is in receipt of £1500 a year from the said Company . . .'

Mr. Greville, she knew, would help William to find a publisher; and he could also be relied upon to talk about the book. Emily was pleased with William for having overcome his natural indolence, where mental discipline was concerned, sufficiently to set down a full account of the Mission's experiences. It would fill up a small historical niche,

PERTAB SINGH.   From a drawing by Emily Eden

'THAT IS A DROMEDARY.'   From Fanny Eden's Journals
A LIVING MAP OF EMERALDS.   From a drawing by Emily Eden

perhaps. And it would be pleasant to have *some* history written with irreverent asides.

Their plans for the state visit to Ranjit were taking shape. Emily dreaded the prospect of five months of living in tents, but she was curious to see the fabulous Ranjit. In any case, she had to go whether she liked it or not. She refused to make herself extra miserable by living through future discomforts before they were upon her, and spent her last few weeks working with Fanny for the fancy fair which the station got up annually for local charities.

There was a meeting of the Simla ladies to discuss who was to take the stalls, and Emily was respectfully asked to suggest a novelty of some kind. The only novelty she could offer was to enquire if the wives of the uncovenanted service should not be invited to send contributions to the stalls this year? This was rather a shock to the Simla ladies, and they said some of the wives were very black. Emily met this by the argument that the black would not come off on their fancy-work. The uncovenanted wives were invited to contribute.

It was while Emily was working for the fancy sale that quite suddenly, with an intolerable, aching longing, she wanted to go home. Homesickness was never far away, even when she forced herself to endure the slow-passing months. But one Saturday, as 1838 dragged leadenly on, she put down her needlework and went in to the garden, and wondered how she could remain in India any longer.

The rains had stopped; the air was so clear, it felt English and exhilarating. The near hills were blue and green and covered with flowers; they looked almost English, too. The double dahlia near her was in bloom; the one double dahlia in India, she was sure. There was honeysuckle, too, and lavender.

Emily went into the house and sat down to write to her eldest sister.

'I think of you, and Eden Farm, and Crouch Oak Lane, and the blue butterflies; and then the gravel-pit, and your reading *Corinne* to me. And then the later days of East Combe, and our parties there with George Villiers in his wonderful spirits, with all his wit, and all the charm about him. And all this because the air is English. I *should* like to go back to childhood and youth again. . . .'

*　　*　　*　　*　　*

It was nice, Fanny thought, to be in a tent again. True, when it rained it was a little inconvenient; ditches appeared wherever one stepped, and streams spouted through seams in the canvas. True, George and Emily wondered aloud why sane people came and marched about India, when they might by economy and taking in washing have a comfortable back attic with a fireplace and a boarded floor, somewhere in the neighbourhood of Manchester Square. But Fanny did not mind discomfort as much as they did, and in any case it was agreeable to be going towards fresh scenes.

Bearers cooking supper

She and Emily were the only two ladies in the camp. There had been an army order to leave behind 'all the women and other super-fluous baggage'. The husbands had taken the order very seriously, and had left the wives at Simla. Only Mrs. Macnaghten was with them, but she would leave them and return to the hills when she met her husband, who was now on his way from his mission to Shah Shuja.

The weather, when it was not raining, was beautiful. It was November, the cool season, and they were on the borders of the Vale of Kashmir. Fanny found plenty of subjects for her sketch-book, but she missed Gazelle. He was the only one who had really appreciated her sketching, and he had never laughed at her attempts at figure drawing, as William did. When she missed Gazelle more than usual, she consoled herself with the thought that he was not being eaten by tigers. And Rolla was a constant delight. He looked charming in a new pelisse and a lancer's cap with a gold tassel. When it was cold at night, she sent him to St. Cloup's cooking-tent to warm himself, and she always hoped anxiously that he would not be skinned and eaten by mistake.

The country was growing pretty. From Buddee to Nalighar there were little hills, and streams running. Fanny stopped to sketch a corner of the Rajah of Nalighar's palace, and met the Rajah himself— a melancholy old man, grieving for the loss of his best Mrs. Nalighar. She had been the only one he had really liked, he told Fanny, and she had died lately.

Fanny returned to the camp that day to find Emily in a state of excitement. A box had been sent after them—a box of bonnets. Emily was pleased. She had been expecting them for months; they had been sent off from London a year ago. She could hardly wait to have the tin ripped off the case and the treasures within brought out. How fresh-looking they were! The milliner's girl might just have stepped over with them from the shop at the corner. Emily meant to appear in the best creation, to give Ranjit Singh some idea of what was what in the matter of bonnets.

They were now nearing the place of meeting with the Sikh ruler and his court. The roads were very bad; they expected soon to come to two new roads which Ranjit had had made for them. Road-making was a foolish English custom, Ranjit said. Roads only served to show your enemies the best way into your country. Emily and Fanny were thankful that he had followed the foolish English custom in this instance, and had not stood by his principles.

The infernal jolting and shaking on the rocky roads had disturbed their normally well-disciplined tempers. The reception tent, which went with them, had the want of tact to hold twenty at dinner. Besides George's immediate *entourage*, the officers of three regiments had to be entertained in turn; four or five came to dinner every day.

'It must be obliquity on my part,' Fanny wrote home, 'but it strikes me that all those we have yet had are positive idiots. Of course, I only mean as far as conversation goes. I dare say they fight with the greatest genius. None of them can be made to speak at all.'

The preparations for the great pageant of meeting were now nearing a climax. Ranjit had sent six hundred gardeners forward to make a garden round his tent. Fanny did not know how they were to go one better than that in the department of horticulture.

On November 27th they were encamped upon an enormous plain three miles from the banks of the Sutlej; Ranjit Singh's tents were pitched on the opposite bank. The Commander-in-Chief was already in camp two miles away, with 'the army of the Indus, as we familiarly call the army which is to carry terror to the soul of Dost Mohamed, splashed generally about the plain,' as Fanny wrote to Eleanor.

The preliminary courtesies began. Karak Singh, Ranjit's heir, came to pay his respects to the Governor-General, while Mr. Macnaghten and William went on a visit of ceremony to Ranjit. He kept them there drinking his strong wine, and sent them back in a remarkable flow of spirits.

William had renewed a former acquaintance; the Lotus was with Ranjit's camp, and had been pleased to see him. She looked so pretty that William asked Macnaghten if it would be all right to give her the little bunch of pearl flowers which had been presented to him as a token gift of welcome. Macnaghten said it would amuse the Maharajah if William did; and so it turned out. But when they returned to their own camp, Major Byrne did not approve. Emily remarked tartly that he must not be so seriously uneasy at the dreadful loss to Government of the pearl bouquet; it could not be worth more than ten shillings.

Emily had not been well for some weeks. Her old enemy, the ague, had come upon her again as a result of the extreme changes of temperature in the day; wet and cold in the early morning, hot from breakfast onwards. Dr. Drummond insisted on her staying in her tent to rest as much as possible, and to leave all the necessary entertaining to Fanny.

But tomorrow she would have to appear, for Ranjit's first visit. She was encouraged to feel well by the arrival of a parcel of wonderful shawls, gowns and scarves to match. When General Allard had been in Calcutta, Emily and Fanny had commissioned him to get some shawls and gowns made for this state visit. He had sought out the most skilful weavers, and here were treasures that Emily and Fanny found almost impossible to describe in their letters.

'One gets to value shawls by their fineness, and we have seen nothing like these,' Emily told Pamela. 'They have been a year and a half in the making.'

'And now we must wear them, and George must pay for them,' wrote Fanny with great contentment to Eleanor.

* * * * *

He was exactly like an old mouse, with grey whiskers and one eye. Emily and Fanny had not quite known what to expect: Ranjit's reputation, together with William's descriptions, had conjured up a figure rather like a genie out of a fairy-tale. Now that he was here, sitting between them and George on a sofa in the great durbar tent, they tried to fit in all they had heard with this small, wizened, bearded gnome. He wore a plain red silk dress, without a single precious stone. He needed none. His one eye was the brightest Fanny had ever seen; it held her.

The tent was crowded with Ranjit's bejewelled followers and George's immediate staff, gleaming with gold braid and medals. George himself, stiffly uniformed and cockaded, gold-laced and gold-sworded, was an imposing figure. The first greetings over, the aides led the way to an inner tent. There was a rush after them, and soon the inner tent was packed. Emily wondered how she would be able to breathe after ten minutes.

Ranjit sat down on a chair near George, and immediately relaxed into his favourite posture—his legs tucked up under him, one foot nestling comfortably in his left hand. Off came that stocking and dropped to the ground. Major Byrne, standing by the Maharajah, was at once worried. Suppose his Highness got down and stood on the ground in his lordship's presence! With one foot bare! Major Byrne knew the intricacies of etiquette where properly shod native feet were concerned, but one stocking on and one stocking off presented him with a problem. After a few moments of agitated thought he moved close to the Maharajah's chair and contrived to edge it more firmly on to the ceremonial carpet which had been laid down.

At the end of half an hour of mutual compliments, George's gifts were brought in and laid before Ranjit. The most striking offering came first; a picture of Queen Victoria in her Coronation robes, which Emily had painted from various prints set out in newspapers and letters. Byrne had had it framed in solid gold, with corners of diamond-mounted shells; it looked handsome and costly. As the Commander-in-Chief presented it to Ranjit on a green and gold cushion, the English gentlemen present straightened themselves, and a salute of twenty-one guns was fired outside.

Ranjit took up the portrait and examined it with interest. Was Queen Victoria really like that? Was the dress correct for a state occasion? What were the orb and sceptre for? Major Byrne answered the questions in his usual precise manner, and Ranjit seemed satisfied. This was a most gratifying present, he said: he would hang up the picture outside his tent when he returned to his own camp, and would give it a hundred-gun salute.

The other gifts were then presented; shawls and jewels on trays, and the howitzer guns which had been specially cast, together with two hundred gunpowder shells. Ranjit was next invited outside the tent, to receive an elephant with gold trappings, and seven horses, equally bedizened.

The sisters were thankful that the durbar was at an end. The atmosphere in the tent had become overpowering; the heat outside seemed cool by comparison. Emily went to her own tent, feeling sick and giddy, and Fanny at once sent for Dr. Drummond. When he saw Emily, he was firm. Miss Eden must not go to any function that did not absolutely require her presence. Fanny was not surprised. She would have liked to receive the same orders from Dr. Drummond herself. When she read the dinner-list later that day, she, too, felt very ill. Forty-two excellent officers whose names she had never heard before, except that dear, brown, delightful Colonel Skinner— and she was sure he would not be placed next to her. Not a single woman. She went along to George's tent with the list, and pointed out how much better they would all eat and drink in her absence. But George was slow in taking in sensible suggestions of this kind, and Fanny had to resign herself to an evening of hard work.

The following day, William having gone with George and Mr. Macnaghten to visit Ranjit for a private conference, Fanny took a short walk outside the camp, attended by her tail of servants. She had her sketch-book with her, though there was little of a sketchable nature near; Fanny liked best to draw subjects which stayed still for an hour at a time. Old mosques, well rooted in the ground, were satisfactory subjects for drawing. But Fanny was always content simply to look, whether she could sketch objects or not. She stopped to watch the local people watering the roads, and thought it a leisurely method. A bullock brought water in large skins, and then men went and filled small skins from the large skin, squirting the water out a few drops at a time. Fanny had grown used to the scores of native servants who seemed so necessary to an average European household in India; but now she realised that everywhere in this land, men had a primitive conception of toil which kept them almost at the level of the beasts of the field.

"I can see Miss Martineau heading a chapter about it—labour cheaper than ants," she thought.

Two days later Ranjit gave a party in his own camp. Emily was unable to go; she was conserving her strength for the review of Ranjit's troops on the morrow—a show which she had been told she must not miss. Fanny set off with Sir Willoughby Cotton as escort, and a squadron of lancers to guard them—very grand and dusty. They had to cross the Sutlej, and were put upon elephants to go over the bridge of boats.

Ranjit's tents, made of shawls and embroidered cashmere, stood in a scarlet-lined enclosure filled with his chiefs, who were covered with jewels and armour.

Fanny was a little shy among them at first, but Hera Singh, Ranjit's favourite, and Sher Singh, Ranjit's natural son, talked courteously to her through an interpreter, and she was soon at ease. She was taken to a silver chair in a large tent, where George and William were already sitting with Ranjit. The tent was soon filled with his court, and the corps of Amazons half-circled round him to form a bodyguard. Ranjit called out an order, and a low, solid gold table was put down before the guests. Now came a procession of gold wine bottles and cups, then dishes of Sikh cookery; spiced balls of meat—very strong compositions, Fanny found these—and pomegranate seeds.

Fanny had heard much of Ranjit's special wine, and now she saw the liquid fire in action. It was his great delight to make people drink it, and watch the results. At first he was content with persuading George and Sir Willoughby Cotton to swallow it, then he began plying Fanny with a gold cupful. She got on very well for some time, pretending to drink it, and passing it back to his cup-bearer. Ranjit grew suspicious, took the cup from her, held it close to his one eye, looked well into the cup, shook his head, and gave it back to her again. The next time Fanny passed it to the cup-bearer, Ranjit intercepted it with a quick gesture, and put his finger into the cup to see how much was gone. Fanny asked the interpreter to explain to Ranjit that ladies did not drink so much in England. Upon which the Maharajah watched until George's head was turned the other way, and passed a cup to Fanny under his own arm, thinking that George was the tyrant who prevented her from drinking good wine.

Fireworks were going on all around them, and nautch-girls danced before them continuously. Ranjit sent for his great diamond, his Mountain of Light, the Koh-i-nur. Fanny looked at it long, knowing that she would never see the like again. Ranjit also showed her some wonderful emeralds; she hoped he had come by them honestly.

Later in the evening they brought him a tray, from which he took two diamond bracelets and a diamond ring, putting them on Fanny's hand. Next came a large string of pearls, which he tried to place round her neck but which got stuck on her bonnet; Fanny wore a bonnet because the Sikhs disapproved enough of women appearing in public at all, and would have thought worse of them if they were to appear with their heads uncovered.

That was the end of the visit. Fanny left the old grey man drinking when she came away, and was not left with the impression that the Sikhs led strictly moral lives.

She was not able to wear her diamonds and pearls for long; the efficient Byrne collected them as usual. They went into the Company's treasure chest, together with the pair of blue shawls and the gold bed, completely encrusted with rubies and emeralds, which had been Ranjit's presents to George.

George's social duties filled up almost the entire time between his conferences with Ranjit about the coming campaign. There were reviews of the troops of both armies, European and Sikh. It was now that Emily and Fanny saw Ranjit Singh as men spoke of him: the warrior, the conqueror. On horseback, he turned into another being. Energetic, tireless, commanding in spite of his slight stature, he rode up and down the British lines, examining them keenly, asking William questions, noting everything. He was anxious for the Englishman's opinion on his own army, and carefully listened to William's comments. William was impressed. He did not, himself, care for highly-jewelled soldiers, but his experienced eye took in the well-drilled marching and the disciplined lines of horsemen. Ventura and Allard had done well. True, they had been handicapped by Ranjit's avarice; one could never really rely on unpaid soldiers. But William was surprised that they were as well trained as this.

Fanny and Emily found it difficult to think of Ranjit's troops as a real army; it was more like an enormous theatrical pageant at Astley's. But the jewels at Astley's would have been tawdry imitations. Here they were real. Even the horses were hung with gems; Ranjit put some of his finest jewels on his horses. The sisters sat in a shawl tent one day, watching a review of the Maharajah's bodyguard. His own horses were led past first, the foremost one magnificent, the splendour of his housings and trappings surpassing anything they could have imagined. He was a living map of emeralds: glittering, gleaming in green and gold.

The Maharajah, sitting near them with George, noted their admiration with satisfaction, and begged George if he fancied any horse to take it as it stood. There was one with turquoise trappings which Fanny could have fancied herself, but George was already making a courteous refusal.

For the next three weeks it was clear that the Edens and the Singhs were going to be close friends. So much Fanny and Emily realised, for almost immediately Ranjit's family began to call on friendly visits to the camp, and to keep on calling. Karak Singh, the Heir-Apparent, was a bore; stupid, silent, a *nothing*, Emily thought. Fortunately he did not come often. Sher Singh, on the other hand, was a constant visitor. He was handsome and intelligent, and had excellent manners; and he was splendid to look at in his scarlet cashmere pelisse embroidered with gold, his turban covered in emeralds and pearls. A stimulating sight.

But he *would* come at dinner-time. Nobody asked him; he just came. Fanny told George that she found it impossible to eat and at the same time make the right kind of conversation through an interpreter; but George saw no reason why she should not learn to do two things at once. Sher Singh had an avowed taste for the English; he copied their customs as far as he could, dined off English plate, and used knives and forks.

It would not have been so bad if he had actually had dinner with them, but he only drank wine, and watched them eating. Emily and Fanny were in the end obliged to insinuate delicately through Major Wade that, though they hoped they would see him sometimes, they did not wish him to set aside his usual evening engagements in order to attend on them. But Sher Singh had no engagements which could compare with the honour of visiting the Governor-General's camp.

Then he took to bringing his small son, Pertab, and Emily and Fanny were immediately enchanted. William had told them of the grave little warrior of seven whom he had met at Ranjit's court, and now they met him themselves.

He was intelligent far beyond his seven years; he was more like a boy of ten or twelve. Slender, upright, he was a shining little figure in a gold cloth dress, with enormous emeralds hung about his neck. His old Sikh tutor stood behind him, with an interpreter at one side. Pertab was not in the least shy. He greeted the Governor-General's sisters with dignity, and after an exchange of compliments asked if he could have an English tutor; he very much wished to learn that tongue. The old Sikh, through the interpreter, prompted him with phrases about the garden of friendship, but Pertab took no notice. He wished to learn English, he repeated politely, and Emily decided she would do what she could for him while they were there.

The reviews, the nautches, the ceremonial visits, went on between the two camps. So did the conferences. Mr. Macnaghten, Torrens and Colvin visited Ranjit Singh every day, while William and the Commander-in-Chief conferred with Ranjit's principal officers. Soon the armies would be on the match towards Afghanistan. . . .

In the middle of December Ranjit sent an invitation to the Governor-General's camp which astonished them all. He asked if they would like to see Govin Ghur, the fort where he kept all his weapons, and most of his treasure. It was an accepted fact that whoever managed to take Govin Ghur after Ranjit's death would also take the Sikh kingdom, Heir-Apparent or no Heir-Apparent. Ranjit allowed no-one but his very closest advisers into the fort, and this mark of favour towards the Governor-General even astounded his own followers.

Fanny had heard of the treasures in the subterranean passages of Govin Ghur, and had often felt that she would like to take a hand-candlestick and have a good look at what he had down there. Half his tributes were paid in jewels, she knew. But she was not invited; nor was Emily. George told them on his return that Ranjit had taken him all over the fort, and had even allowed a number of English officers in to examine what weapons they wished to see in the great armoury. George and William were pleased for many reasons. This mark of favour indicated that Ranjit intended his alliance to be something solid and to be depended upon, and it also showed his Prime Minister and hostile sirdars that he was committed to firm friendship with the British.

Ranjit told George that he had consulted a sacred oracle about the alliance, and the oracle had declared for the British. He offered to take the party to the temple where the oracle resided. This was a great honour, because it was the only temple for which the Sikhs had any veneration.

There was some difficulty at first about the matter of George's removing his shoes before entering the temple. Mr. Macnaghten's temperature rose several degrees during the arguments about it. In the end, it was settled that it was impossible for the Governor-General to take off his shoes, except for the purpose of going to bed. All the Sikhs really cared about was that their sacred marble should not be defiled by shoes which had trod the common streets, so a compromise was made. George put on a pair of dark stockings over his boots, and Emily and Fanny drew off a pair of dressing-slippers—specially donned for the purpose—from their white satin shoes.

The temple stood in a small lake of holy water, with a marble bridge leading to it. It had a marble frieze up to man's height, inlaid with coloured flowers and birds. Above the frieze, the entire building was sheeted with gold—good, solid gold. Ranjit thought that Fanny was not sufficiently impressed by this, and took her hand and made her feel the yellow metal.

The inside of the building was more splendid still. Fanny had written so many accounts of jewelled magnificence to Eleanor Grosvenor that she had decided not to try Eleanor's patience with more diamonds for a long time to come. But the scene in this temple was so unreal, she felt she must write down that night every detail she could remember, so that in later years, when she re-read her letters with her friend, she would know it had actually happened, and had not been an Oriental dream.

'There was a large canopy, stiff with embroidery in pearls and emeralds. There was the oracle, with about twenty covers over it, and priests with long white beards sitting behind a low altar on which it is kept.

'A small cushion was put on the ground, on which Runjeet squatted, and pulled down George, Emily and me by him. It was very close sitting, and rather crampy. He evidently thought that women would want something to amuse their little trivial minds, and made signs for us to go up to the altar and look at the book. A fringe of very large pearls and emeralds about half a yard deep and a yard long is the first covering. Then the priests took off many more, and there was the book open. They all bowed to it, and I felt as if I was in the temple of Baal. Runjeet told George that in consequence of his coming to see that sacred place he should consider their friendship more firmly cemented. George made a most splashy answer about their united armies conquering the world. You will be pretty much taken aback, I guess, when they march over, hand in hand, and take Motcombe. . . .

I wish somebody could have sketched us all there, with the mixture of native and English officers round us, half kneeling, half squatting.'

When they came out of the temple, Ranjit took them on to a balcony of a nearby house. It was now dusk, and their entire surroundings were lit up by volcanoes of exploding fireworks, which illuminated the fish swimming in the sacred lake, and made the gold temple gleam like something out of a faery world.

They came down to Ranjit's more earthly kingdom at the nautch which he gave them the following evening. Emily and Fanny found these particular entertainments tiresome, and were rather alarmed when George said that he was growing fond of them. There was always a great deal of laughter among the Sikhs at some of Ranjit's questions, and Fanny suspected that Major Byrne did not always make a literal translation of some of the old reprobate's enquiries. Why wasn't George married, Ranjit wanted to know; it was very odd that the Governor-General had not one wife, while the Sikhs had each twenty-five. George said that in England they sometimes found one more than they could manage. Ranjit answered that if their women were troublesome they beat them. Fanny got Macnaghten to tell him that she wished he would not teach the Lord Sahib such a thing, which made Ranjit laugh violently.

The worst trial came at supper time. Ranjit tried to make the gentlemen drink too much, and Fanny and Emily eat too much. One of the Secretaries, who was living by doctor's orders on a diet of toast and water, contrived occasionally to empty his glass on the carpet, and Emily herself managed to deposit under her chair two broiled quails, an apple, a pear, a great lump of sweetmeat, and some pomegranate seeds which Ranjit had put into her hand with his dirty fingers. It was a great relief to get back to their own camp.

The sisters began to think with longing of Simla. The perpetual ceremonies and entertainments were becoming overpowering, and the concentrated dazzle of jewels was beginning to pall.

But the political part of the business was not yet finished. Mr. Macnaghten and the other Secretaries were still patiently drawing up plans with Ranjit and his unwilling advisers for the war on which they had embarked against Dost Muhammad. One could not hurry Ranjit Singh at the best of times. And now news came that he had fallen ill.

Dr. Drummond at once went to see him, and found him lying on a low bed, decidedly feverish. Dr. Drummond tried to give him some medicine, which Ranjit would not take. Instead, the old man sent his *faquir* to Mr. Wimberley to ask for a Persian translation of some of the sermons which Mr. Wimberley preached on Sundays; Ranjit was anxious to get some idea of the Lord Sahib's religion.

Mr. Macnaghten would have much preferred him to have taken Dr. Drummond's medicine. It had been evident for a long time that the Maharajah could not last very much longer; his death must always be expected. But if he died now, no-one knew how things would turn out over the proposed war. Mr. Macnaghten was strongly of the opinion that the war must go forward, and Kabul placed firmly in friendly hands. Shah Shuja was quite ready to sit on the throne from which Mr. Macnaghten intended to lift Dost Muhammad. It would indeed be inconvenient if Ranjit Singh were to die at this point, for the flames of his funeral pyre would not have died down before Karak Singh and Sher Singh would be at a tug-of-war for possession of the Punjab. And it was not they who had agreed to the British alliance; it was Ranjit.

'I am thinking of sending Runjeet some strengthening little messes,' Fanny wrote to Eleanor. 'We are, at this present writing, nothing better than hostages. Dian Singh will seize George, Kurruk Singh will seize William, Sher Singh, Emily and me. And when they march to fight for their kingdom, we shall each be put in front of their respective armies—so very possible and unpleasant. At the best, we shall have to make forced marches to the river, leaving all our baggage behind us—and I bought such a lovely agate cup just now. I shall never have the strength of mind to leave that behind.'

However, Ranjit did not get worse. George and Macnaghten were able to have a private interview with him to discuss the treaties, and Fanny and Emily set off to visit the principal Mrs. Ranjits, who nearly ruined Fanny's satin gown by smothering it with attar of roses. They were young wives, and almost like children—asking to hear Emily's repeater watch strike, and laughing heartily at her bonnet, which they obviously thought an odd form of headdress. Fanny and Emily felt like laughing in return at their enormous nose-rings, crescents of diamonds from which hung tassels of pearls and emerald drops. How they could bear such a weight on the nose!

There was plenty to sketch at Lahore, but the sisters found it tiresome always to be followed about by a great crowd, craning to see what they were drawing. Their servants were constantly asked how it was possible for two women to go about and show themselves in such an impudent way, and at last Myra, Fanny's *ayah*, told the crowd importantly that they were two powerful begums who could give themselves permission to do anything. That seemed to strike the Sikhs dumb, and there were no more questions.

The pleasantest place to sit sketching was in a thick grove of oranges and limes in the Shalimar Gardens. George settled to join them one afternoon, after his interview with Ranjit, and said he would go there with an aide-de-camp, and take a quiet walk while they were at their easels. Deluded creature! Inexperienced traveller! The instant he got on his elephant, bang went a gun. Sher Singh appeared, and a troop of Sikhs wheeled up and began playing 'God save the Queen' with every other bar left out, which made it rather a pretty air. His

'A city of mosques and palaces'

lordship dismounted in the gardens to be met by a train of devoted gardeners presenting baskets of fruit. Almost at once Karak Singh appeared, with the old *faquir*. As the brothers were not on speaking terms, Sher took George by one hand, and Karak held the other, and they walked along competing for his attention.

The lack of privacy was becoming irritating. Sher Singh still appeared nearly every evening at dinner-time. The only alleviation was that he often brought Pertab, who was as gay and lively as a bird. The first words of English he had learnt were: 'Chance, sit up,' which endeared him to Emily even more than before.

Soon it was Christmas again. It was difficult to believe in Christmas in this place, despite the calendar. Only when Fanny and Emily were actually sitting in the great tent listening to Mr. Wimberley could they bring themselves to realise that another twelvemonth was gone, that it was almost 1839, and that only three years remained of their exile.

* * * * *

176

They were leaving Lahore at last. Ranjit Singh had recovered sufficiently to sign all the necessary papers connected with the treaty, and Mr. Macnaghten expected the Governor-General to begin his journey back to Simla by the end of the first week in January.

Ranjit asked Emily and Fanny if they would like to make pictures of his favourite horses before they left, and sent round five of the finest in the stud, with all their jewels upon them. Fanny decided then and there that if ever George were allowed to plunder this kingdom, she would go straight to the stables and the horses' trinket boxes.

She now saw the emerald-decked animal at close quarters. There were necklaces round its neck and between its ears. In front of the saddle hung two enormous emeralds, two inches square, carved all over and set in gold frames, like little looking-glasses. The crupper was all emeralds, and there were stud ropes of twisted gold. The next horse was simply attired in diamonds and turquoises, and there was one with trappings of coral and pearl. It was a pity that they could not be painted in these precious stones ground down to powder; ordinary colours could give no idea of their glow and brilliance, thought the sisters.

The entire camp now awaited the day of departure with impatience. It was raining hard, and many of the tents were pitched on the old bed of a river. Fanny had a cold—most people had colds. There had been sneezing and coughing ever since Ferozepore, and everybody paddled about in overshoes, shivering. Emily and Fanny were carried over to the dinner tent in a palanquin, and then on to the tent which they used as a sitting-room, where a fire in a container had been brought in. They usually found Rolla sitting in the best arm-chair as near as possible to the fire, holding his hands spread out to the flames in a way which would have burnt any Christian's, for Rolla, too, had a cold.

On New Year's Eve they went to take leave of Ranjit. The old man embraced them, and gave them his leaving presents; his picture set in diamonds and pearls, for George, together with a sword, match-lock and belt, all much bejewelled; and a pair of shawls embroidered in seed-pearl for the Governor-General's sisters. George gave him, in return, a bunch of grapes made of emeralds, and a diamond ring which almost covered Ranjit's little finger—a gift which excited the old man and pleased him to a surprising degree. One could never tell with Ranjit. The emerald grapes were worth a small fortune, but the ring had caught his fancy, and he expressed as much pleasure over it as little Pertab might have done over an ingenious toy.

177

They got away at last. By the following day they were once more encamped on the banks of the Sutlej, and the route back to Simla was planned in detail.

That journey was to prove a miserable one for Fanny. On January 6th, 1839, Emily wrote to Theresa:

'The melancholy catastrophe of the week has been the death of F.'s lemur after two days of illness. It caught cold, like the rest of the camp, in that swamp at Lahore, and died of inflammation of the stomach so violent that no medicine was of the slightest use. Poor little wretch! It was hardly possible to bear its screams at times; though as F. could not stand it, I did my aunty duties to it to the last. It is really a great loss, it was such a clever little animal, and she made such a constant occupation of it, that she misses it very much, and is in a very low state. I own I miss it too, and then its illness has been so shocking. It had such cramps, and held out its little black hands—which are shaped just like ours—to be rubbed, and cried just like a child. That is the worst of a nice pet. However, they are a great amusement for the time they last, and there is, on an average, at least a year's pleasure for a week's grief. A natural death, too, is an uncommon termination to the life of a pet, and Dr. Drummond did everything that could be done for it.'

Rolla's death left an emptiness which Fanny could not talk about. She knew that the only possible thing to do was to find another creature to care for as soon as possible, but she could not bear the thought of another lemur. There were no puppies to be had, except Fairy's babies, and the greyhound's last family had already been shared out. Fanny heard that Barbary goats were pretty, soft, hairy things, and she ordered two through an aide-de-camp. They would be sent on as soon as good specimens could be found.

The first stages of the return journey were made anxious by constant robberies, and the murder of several native servants. It was a bad part of the country; the inhabitants avowedly lived by plunder and were determined thieves. In spite of strong guards, the advance camp was robbed of stores, wine and grain every day, and the army had to lend a company of cavalry to patrol the road in advance.

By the middle of the month they were in the Rajah of Patiala's territories, and the usual exchange of visits took place. An old Sikh chief, the Rajah of Nabha, escorted George back from Patiala's durbar, and asked if the Governor-General and his sisters would like to see his

'HE COVERS HIS HORSE WITH NECKLACES AND HIMSELF WITH CHAIN ARMOUR'
'HE WEARS PLUMES TIPPED WITH GOLD ON HIS OWN AND ON HIS HORSE'S HEAD'
From Fanny Eden's Journals

PRIVATE NATIVE DURBAR.   From a drawing by Emily Eden

gardens that evening. Mr. Macnaghten and Major Byrne were not pleased when George accepted the invitation.

Fanny and Emily thought it rather an ugly garden, but the visit turned out to be well worth while. Macnaghten and Byrne kept charging George not to sit down on any account, as the Rajah was not of sufficient rank to receive a visit from the Governor-General. George declared that he would have to sit down at some time, so he might as well do it first as last. The other two countered this by walking him about the garden on one pretext or another.

Old Nabha now led the way to a garden house, and the Secretaries tried to dissuade George from following, arguing with him in a low voice up to the very steps. The Rajah asked him to look at some paintings in the house, and again the Secretaries protested. Why? asked George. The paintings were improper, replied Byrne. George was interested. He entered the house, inspected the paintings, declared them very pretty, and called Emily and Fanny.

There was a row of chairs in the room, and a select assortment of nautch-girls. George sank down on one side of the Rajah, and told Emily to sit on the other, with Fanny by her side. So ended the advice of the Secretaries, and Nabha now thought himself quite as good as Patiala—which was George's intention. The Rajah gave Emily and Fanny diamond bracelets, which they delivered over to Byrne as soon as they came away, and hoped these would soothe his hurt feelings.

A few days later, the army left the camp, to begin the long march to Kandahar and Kabul. Mr. Macnaghten went with them; he was to be envoy and adviser to Shah Shuja when the business was successfully accomplished. Nobody had the least doubt but that Dost Muhammad would be quickly chased out of Afghanistan and Shah Shuja as neatly escorted in. . . .

The camp seemed much shrunken with the departure of the soldiers. Mr. Wimberley, too, went off; he had left his wife at Simla, and was now returning there by the shortest route so that he could reach her in time for her *accouchement*. He rode away with some cold dinner done up in a napkin in one hand, and *Culpepper's Midwifery*, which he had borrowed from Dr. Drummond, in the other. He was a very practical man, Mr. Wimberley.

Before the end of the week, Emily was taken ill with fever. It was the worst bout of illness she had had so far; she had not known that one head and one set of bones could hold so much pain as hers did for forty-eight hours. 'One ought to be allowed a change of bones in India—it should be part of the outfit,' she wrote to her sister Eleanor.

Dr. Drummond put leeches on her, and she gradually felt better. Her return to the society of the camp was celebrated by cosy conversations on fevers. One magistrate had had the Delhi fever, another the Agra fever, while a third voice spoke up for the dreadful Hansi fever. Emily was sure that every inch of the plains of India had fever on it, only there was not time to catch them all; anybody who wished to make true comparisons would have to live a hundred years.

By the time the camp arrived at Delhi, she was feeling her usual self, but as there was a danger of agues setting in, Dr. Drummond would not allow her to receive or pay calls. She took drives with George, sat with Fanny for an hour or two, then went to bed.

But the camp had to move on. Emily was back in her tent life before long, and the old misery of squelching ground and unceasing rain beating on canvas began again. The agues came back; every night she lay in her cot, shivering under blankets and staring with distaste at the buff and green lining of her tent.

Then fortune turned a bleak smile on her. A package of letters and a box of books arrived. It had in it the complete *Oliver Twist* and *Nicholas Nickleby*. She and Fanny had read some of the monthly parts of each, and now they could finish the stories. There never was such a man as Dickens! Emily thought of proposing a public subscription for him—'A tribute from India.' She was sure everybody would subscribe. He was such an excellent agent for *European* fun; one did not get much of that in this country.

The camp reached Karnal early in March. It was the first station of any size since they had been at Delhi, and the aides-de-camp made the most of it, after the dreariness of marching for weeks in the rains, without the sight of a girl's face. They visited and luncheoned and flirted; they went to dinners and balls and plays. Emily was glad to see them so happy. She felt better, and though she had no desire herself to dance night after night, she liked to see the young ones enjoying themselves.

Only another fortnight to Simla. Emily did not expect anything spectacular now. They were safe from rajahs' visits; balls and dinners lay behind them, the rains had stopped; and though the weather had now turned very hot, Emily could bear it, especially with the prospect of dear, cool Simla before her. What she wanted now was to be *dull*.

It was not easy to be dull in a country where anything might happen. One quiet afternoon she bought two little girls.

'I have made such a nice purchase today,' she wrote to Pamela, 'two little girls of seven years old, rather ugly and one of them dumb. I gave three pounds for the pair, dirt cheap! They belonged to a very bad man. . . . I had tried to get hold of these children at Simla, hearing they were very ill-used and that this man was going to sell them into the palace at Delhi, where thousands of children are swallowed up. Luckily his creditors would not let him go. . . . He sent word I might have the children if I would pay his debts, and the *babu* has just walked in with them. They have not a stitch of clothes on—the man has beat them dreadfully.'

One could do so little for children in this heathen country. But it was well worth three pounds to be able to rescue at least two ill-used scraps, and to take them to the haven of kind Mrs. Wilson's orphanage at Calcutta.

10

'George travels in state'

SIMLA

SIMLA was white with snow. The thermometer had been over ninety a week before; now they were again in a cold climate, and it was delightful. Fanny and Emily felt that they had come home. It was really a jewel of a house that they had taken for the stay in Simla; and they wondered whether they would ever be able to bear the regal mansion in Calcutta again.

Simla society came to call within a few days of their arrival, but Emily did not know how she was going to entertain it in return. A great many husbands had gone off to the war, which left a great many wives with no escorts to balls and parties. There was also a shortage of bachelors; the aides-de-camp were hard put to it on a dancing evening, for they had to figure in every quadrille.

William went tiger-shooting. He was making a more serious business of it than usual, for news had come from a place sixty miles away that a man-eating tiger had recently carried off a number of people, and the *thanadars* of the surrounding villages had begged for a shooting party to find and kill him. William organised a party and set off. The next news which came was that he had been run over by a carriage, and that one of the wheels had gone over his hip.

Fanny at once made preparations to go out to nurse him. It took her over a day, travelling *dak* with Jones and one of the aides. She found William suffering from fever, but no bones were broken. Within two days he had begun smoking again, in defiance of the doctor's orders, and by the end of the week he was on an elephant, directing the shoot. Fanny gave up trying to bring him to common-sense, and returned home.

William wrote every day. He was better, and he had killed seventeen tigers, and a tigress which had carried off twenty-two men and quantities of children. The original man-eater had also been found and dispatched; and within another week a further nine tigers and six cubs. This was a great blessing for the surrounding countryside. Perhaps it was as well that William's obstinacy was stronger than his common-sense.

Now that they were in a house again and likely to stay there for some time, Fanny and Emily were able to plan their days with some comfort. They had a small terrace, on which they could sit and look at the distant snowy range; a sublime sight of which they never tired. There were new pets to look after; Fanny's Barbary goats had come. True, they were rather ugly brutes—large and smooth and *bleak*-looking, instead of being pretty, soft and hairy. But Fanny decided she must like them, and began to train them to know her.

Emily had been given a young flying squirrel; quite a baby. It had sable fur, a tail half a yard long, and wings, and was very playful and gentle. The two little girls whom she had bought were also a constant interest. Wright and Jones were teaching them sewing, and Emily saw them nearly every day and had nearly succeeded in calming their quick-springing fears. When they were normal children again, she would send them to kind Mrs. Wilson; meanwhile their confidence and natural childish spirits were growing.

Early in May Dr. Drummond opened the dispensary which had been built from the proceeds of the fancy fair. George had always tried to encourage the natives to make use of European medical stations, and looked forward to the time when these would be directed by Indians themselves. He had an Indian doctor on his staff, and was pleased when this man asked he if could remain at Simla to take charge of the new dispensary.

It was an odd but satisfying result of a fancy fair, thought Emily and Fanny. So much apparently foolish needlework, and drawings, and side-shows, and small jealousies about who should have this stall, and would not that one be neglected in a corner? But in the end it led to an excellent place, crowded every day by ill people, and dozens of little black children brought to be vaccinated. Emily said that she was quite heartened into trying another fancy fair that year, in spite of the work and the bothers with touchy ladies.

Now came news from Mr. Macnaghten. Besides dispatches to George, he wrote a long letter to Emily, which she read aloud. Shah

Shuja had entered Kandahar, without a shot being fired! Mr. Macnaghten was understandably pleased—even triumphant—over the reception which his protégé had received. Several of Lord Auckland's Ministers in Calcutta had been strongly against the plan of attempting to restore Shah Shuja to Afghanistan; they were sure the people did not want him, having thrown him out twenty years before. But Mr. Macnaghten had been a witness to the welcome which Shah Shuja had received at Kandahar.

'Every great chief with numerous followers came out to meet the Shah, and greeted him with every demonstration of joy,' wrote Mr. Macnaghten. 'The poor strewed the road he was to pass over with roses. Every person, high or low, seemed to strive how they could show their devotion to his Majesty. . . .'

There was no reliable news of Dost Muhammad, but his brothers had fled the country, and Mr. Macnaghten was sure that the Dost would realise he was defeated, and fly, too.

'The country we have been traversing for two months is the most barren and desolate eye ever rested on,' continued Mr. Macnaghten. 'Not a tree, nor a blade of grass to be seen. We were constantly obliged to make marches of twenty miles to find water, [as] the hills were only huge masses of clay. The contrast now is great. The good things of this life are abundant; luxurious crops which will be ready for the sickle in three or four weeks, extensive plains of greensward for the cattle. endless gardens and orchards, fruits of all kinds. Rivulets flow through the valley, the birds are all song birds, and the air rings with their notes. In short, we have reached the oasis at last, and are thoroughly enjoying ourselves.'

It was certainly all very satisfactory; and the whole thing done without bloodshed! An almost hysterical relief swept over Simla. A number of ladies had gone into seclusion on their husbands' departure; and those who had continued with their social frivolities had not always been able to hide their terrors and anxieties. Soldiers and their families had for many years been used to a peacetime army; the only battles they had known were manœuvres. A real campaign against an actual enemy—and a possibly barbarous one at that—was something they had not reckoned on. It had been exciting enough so long as the bugles were blowing and the drums beating. But with the men gone for weeks, and little news seeping back, excitement vanished and fear took its place.

Now it was all over. Sir John Keane wrote most cheerfully to the

Governor-General about the army, saying the soldiers were remarkably healthy. The Shah seemed as comfortably settled as if he had never left his kingdom; all his subjects were happy, and kind to the British. The soldiers' wives saw, in their mind's eye, their husbands eating apricots and drinking sherbet. It would not be long before the dear men were back; or perhaps they would send for their wives to join them in that land awash with milk and honey.

A course of entertaining now set in, and even Emily and Fanny, who had had their fill of social giddiness, felt in spirits to join in.

'We have been uncommonly gay at Simla this year,' Emily wrote to Theresa, 'and have had some beautiful tableaux with music, and one or two well-acted farces. Everybody has been pleased and amused, except two clergymen who are here, and who have begun a course of sermons against what they call a destructive torrent of worldly gaiety. They had much better preach against the destructive torrent of rain which has now set in for the next three months. . . .

'Our parties begin at half-past eight, and at twelve o'clock we always get up and make our courtesies, and everybody goes at once. Instead of dancing every time, we have had alternations of tableaux and charades, and the result has been three aides-de-camp engaged to three very nice English girls, and the dismissal of various native Mrs. Aides-de-camp. . . .'

The return to a moderate climate and the good news from the army had raised her spirits. She and Fanny decided to give a ball in honour of Queen Victoria, and asked a great company to dine beforehand. There were two specially built tents, joined by a flower-bedecked platform, and the decorations included the words 'Victoria', 'God save the Queen', and 'Kandahar', picked out in letters twelve feet high.

Emily's agues were better, and she enjoyed the evening. She wore a gown which had arrived a few days before—such a relief to receive that box of dresses and millinery! There was always danger that gowns she had had for a long time would behave as badly as the pink-striped taffety silk, which appeared to have an odd rent in the sleeve when she had put it on. As she tied the sash there was an odd crack under the arm, and when Chance jumped into her lap there was an odd crack in front. When she sat down to dinner later there was an odd crack behind. In short, long before bedtime, there was hardly a whole strip wider than a ribbon in that pink-striped gown—rather a pretty fashion, but perhaps too uncertain for formal occasions.

Tonight there had been no such mishap; her gauze dress was elegant and remained whole.   After dinner she and Fanny, with their guests, went outside to watch a display of fireworks; then they returned to the tents, which had been cleared for dancing.   Emily led off in one quadrille and Fanny in another.   The aides and other young gentlemen danced away with a will, and the ladies, young and not so young, were in the highest humour; it all looked gay and light-hearted.

Emily grew tired after a time.   She picked up her gauze scarf and went outside, into the moonlit night.   There came into her mind memories of the balls at Bromley when she was a girl.   Perhaps some of her nieces and nephews might be dancing there, or in Kent, or Essex, or Hertfordshire, at this very moment.   Perhaps to this same music.

It was queer how homesickness grew worse, not better, with the passing of the years.   One never got used to it; and she knew it was the same with Fanny, for all her sister's silence about it.   Emily looked at the distant mountains, outlined under the moon: it was restful to gaze at them after the fireworks and the multitude of lamps in the tents.

The music came from behind her; they were beginning another quadrille.   How unreal it was.   Twenty years ago no European had ever been in this place.   Now she and Fanny and the Governor-General and a large company were here, with the band playing 'Masaniello'. They had been eating salmon from Scotland, and sardines from the Mediterranean, and observing that St. Cloup's *potage à la Julienne* was perhaps better than his other soups, and that some of the ladies' sleeves were too tight according to the fashions in the last journals sent from home.   And all this in face of those high hills, some of which had remained untrodden since the Creation.

Here they were, mused Emily, a hundred Europeans surrounded by at least three thousand native mountaineers who were no doubt sitting watching, wrapped up in their hill blankets.   The natives bowed to the ground if a European came near them; the European expected and demanded it.   Emily stood looking out at the mountains, aware of unseen eyes around her.

'I wonder they do not cut all our heads off, and say nothing more about it,' she thought.

*   *   *   *   *

Ranjit Singh was dead.   The wonder was that he had lived so long, after years of such excesses.   When the news came, Fanny and Emily

were genuinely sorry; they had liked the wicked old man, and he had
been very kind and friendly to them.

None could say what would now happen in the Punjab. A
dispatch from George's agent in Lahore described Ranjit's last hours.
He had been paralysed for some time, and had lost his speech towards
the end; but the signs he made with one finger were instantly understood and obeyed. He sent for his treasury of jewels, and directed
them to be sent to different shrines. The Koh-i-nur was to be sent to
the golden temple. His chieftains implored him not to give away the
wealth of his kingdom, and in the end Ranjit said the great diamond
could remain, though the other jewels must go to the shrines as he had
ordered.

Karak Singh had nominally succeeded Ranjit, and Dian Singh was
continuing as Prime Minster to his late master's heir. But there was
trouble stirring. Sher Singh sent his chief adviser to the Governor-
General, asking for advice; he was in a terrible fright, knowing how
hostile Karak had always been. The messenger also brought a letter
from Pertab to Emily, written in Persian, assuring her of his respect
and affection, and asking for assistance should it be needed for his
honoured father.

George was sympathetic, but firm. No degree of confusion in the
Punjab, he said, would keep them in Simla longer than necessary; he
could not embroil himself in the Sikhs' internal affairs. Emily got
Mr. Colvin to write a reply to Pertab in Persian, assuring him of her
affection and kind remembrances. More she could not do. She and
Fanny read accounts sent by George's newswriter in Lahore of Ranjit's
funeral and the dreadful ceremonies which accompanied it. Several
of his wives insisted on immolating themselves on the funeral pyre;
and the beautiful Lotus, too, had committed *suttee*, mounting the piled
wood with the wives, dressed in her most splendid sari and jewels.
She had joined her hands and had not cried out once as the flames
licked upwards.

Fanny had seen in India so much of what she would have considered
unmentionable horrors in England, that the account of the *suttee* did
not make her feel so sick as it might once have done. She wondered
how Pertab would fare in the struggle for power which would now
begin in Lahore.

William was sent off to the Punjab, to take note of what was happening there, but with instructions not to allow himself to be drawn into
any intrigues. Fanny was again conscious of being the third in Emily's

and George's life: odd man out. When William was there, it did not so much matter. Without his companionship, she must sit more with George and Emily. Emily never consciously allowed her to feel an intruder, but Fanny knew herself to be outside, all the same. These two were always sufficient unto each other; their natures were in complete accord. Fanny did not feel aggrieved or hurt that she should not be at one with them; she accepted the fact. They were both typical Edens, with a quick grasp of political affairs: they could think in terms of continents and cabinets. Fanny was more of an Elliot: she favoured her mother's family. Perhaps that was where she got her giddy nature from? William occasionally impressed her giddiness upon her—and as William himself could be very giddy in a man's way, they were in accord, too.

Fanny missed Rolla more and more. The Barbary goats were dull beasts compared to a lemur. She had taken a fancy to one of Fairy's latest puppies, whom she named Matty; but the little dog did not thrive. Puppies born in that country rarely lived long.

And Gazelle, in Meerut. Fanny knew now that she would not be able to have him back; it would never do to keep a full-grown, temperamental deer at liberty in Government House, or even in the gardens at Barrackpore. One had to be sensible about pets. She had grown quite fond of Emily's flying squirrel, which was so tame now that he sat on Wright's shoulder when she was dressing her mistress's hair. He would also sit on George's shoulder when he came into the sitting-room; Emily was sure he whispered secrets into George's ear.

Then the little furry creature died. Fanny shared her sister's wretchedness when he was brought in, stiff and still. If only he had stuck to dry tea—his favourite diet—he would have lived the normal life-span of a squirrel. But he stole a pear from the luncheon table, and ate it before anybody would stop him. A few hours later he was dead.

Fanny was not surprised that Emily was so closely attached to Chance. He was now a full-grown spaniel with a heavy coat of curly hair, and since he had recovered from that alarming illness had been uncommonly well and spritely. Emily declared that as people in India became duller, their animals became more intelligent and interesting, not having such boredom to put up with as human beings had. Here was Chance, getting on in years, but not at all middle-aged in mind; he still took stock of the passing world with his old alertness, and could lead Jimmund, his servant, a dance, too, when he felt like it.

The rainy season came early in 1839. That thinned out the social gaieties a little, for paths and roads became impassable to all but the most determined callers. Fanny liked sitting at her window and watching the rain sheet down; there was something sublime and *water-spouty* about it. In the valley the sun was shining through the rain, and in the extreme distance she could see the Sutlej when it was clear.

Fanny had taken to carpentry. Emily's second fancy fair was to take place before they left Simla, and Fanny had promised to make some dolls for it. She sat at her table under the window, and carved out little jointed arms and legs, and modelled heads which she then painted. Emily wished to leave a substantial sum to carry on the dispensary, and all over Simla, ladies were sewing for this useful purpose. They were glad of the employment; waiting for the army to return was a wearying business.

At the beginning of August news came that the army was fighting. The war had ceased to be a bloodless one. Dost Muhammad had sent a force under the command of one of his sons to hold the ancient fortress of Ghazni, which was a few miles out of Kandahar and on the way to Kabul.

Almost at once the anxieties of wives, mothers and sisters were enveloped in rejoicings over a victory. Ghazni had been taken, and Dost Muhammad's son was a prisoner. Well, said Fanny, so that war was *warred* and done. Ghazni was only seventy miles from Kabul, and the business of seating Shah Shuja comfortably on the throne would not now take long. It took only a matter of days. On August 7th, Shah Shuja-ul-Mulk, shining with jewels and mounted on a white horse, rode into Kabul attended by Mr. Macnaghten, a company of British officers and troops, and straggling lines of the army which he himself had managed to raise.

There were no roses strewn here: few shouts or cheers. The people who pressed into the narrow streets stared inquisitively, as at a show. Dost Muhammad had gone: Shah Shuja was here with his foreign friends. So then? The tribesmen looked on, silent, or shouted remarks to each other. Even Macnaghten had to admit that there was a noticeable lack of enthusiasm in the onlookers; it was different from Kandahar. But he felt that the first part of a long and difficult task was accomplished. Afghanistan was now a part of the north-western rampart. Dost Muhammad had fled from Kabul and was being pursued. Whatever anybody might say, Shah Shuja was the rightful claimant to the Afghan throne, and when the people came to realise what had happened, they must rejoice that the true king had been restored.

If the thought shadowed across his mind that the true king had been

Camel soldiers

a comfortably settled and willing enough exile for twenty years, and that the Afghans had never made any attempt to bring him back, the shadow of a thought was dismissed as irrelevant. The important thing was the accomplished fact of Shah Shuja's return as a king. A puppet king, maybe. Mr. Macnaghten intended to keep his hands on the strings.

Shah Shuja was installed in the royal palace, and clearly enjoyed being the chief personage in the kingdom once more. His natural pomposity stood him in the place of dignity; his lack of intelligence was apparent. He was not a difficult puppet to manage.

Mr. Macnaghten wrote long dispatches to Lord Auckland, saying that he 'intended to propose the following measures to His Majesty'; and his tongue was not in his cheek. He did indeed consult the new king, but it did not enter his mind that Shah Shuja would seriously question any measure suggested by his adviser, the British Envoy.

The dispatches and messages were galloped to Simla, and news of the Afghan success at once sent overland to England. The nation was delighted. What had Russia got to say to Kabul, eh? The Court of Directors of the East India Company, which had been acrimoniously divided on Lord Auckland's forward policy for some time, sent congratulations. Hobhouse and the Secret Committee of the Company were, Charles Greville reported, 'in high glee'. The Board of Control and the Cabinet showed their satisfaction; Macnaghten was made a baronet, and honours were given to the chief officers, political and military, who had taken part in the campaign.

Lord Auckland was made an earl. Simla congratulated him and gave a ball in his honour, with artistically-painted transparencies depicting the taking of the Ghazni fortress, and arches of flowers with the word 'Auckland' framed in them. There was a standing buffet for the company all night, at which one very fat lady was detected in eating five suppers.

The rains had slackened, and dinners and dances were once more in full spate. The army ladies had now come out of seclusion, and were attending all the parties they could, without any danger of their being thought unfeeling. There was an extra reason for going into society, for a new arrival was making eyes turn and tongues rattle.

The newcomer was a girl of seventeen, prodigiously beautiful, and with an interesting history, which everybody knew. She was the daughter of a British army officer, an Irishman called Gilbert, who had died when the child was seven. Mrs. Gilbert, left a widow with a good competence, decided to remain in India, but sent her daughter to be educated in England.

Two years ago she had made the voyage home to see her daughter, now a girl of fifteen, still at school. Mrs. Gilbert had met a young ensign, Lieutenant James, on the ship. He was going home on sick leave, and so aroused Mrs. Gilbert's maternal sympathies that when they landed she kept in touch with him, and even took him with her to visit her daughter at school. The ensign had told Mrs. Gilbert that he was engaged, and had consulted her about his prospects. That did not prevent him from eloping with Miss Gilbert and marrying her.

It was enough to provoke any mother, said the Eden ladies. But it could not be helped, and everybody had been trying for the past year to persuade poor, unhappy Mrs. Gilbert to forgive her daughter and receive her son-in-law, who was back at his India station. She at last gave way, and asked them to come and stay with her for a month.

Fanny and Emily were as curious as anyone else to meet the couple, and readily accepted Mrs. Gilbert's invitation to an evening party. They found the son-in-law a smart-looking man with a bright waist-coat and bright teeth. He was at least fifteen years older than his wife, who was truly lovely, with huge eyes and a flawless complexion. She hardly looked her seventeen years; she seemed to be a merry, un-affected schoolgirl.

Emily could not help feeling sorry for such a young beauty, married to a junior lieutenant with 160 rupees a month pay, and a whole life-time of India before her. She would have been immensely surprised if she could have looked into the future and seen this same merry schoolgirl turn into an enchantress who ranged over Europe, in-fatuating emperor and commoner: a courtesan who was to leave a notorious reputation behind her under the name of Lola Montez.

11

THE KING-MAKER

WILLIAM returned to Simla in the middle of September, bringing news from Lahore. Pertab was as nice a child as ever, and remembered all the English words he had been taught. Karak Singh reigned in Ranjit's place, and wore the old Maharajah's magnificent string of pearls, which he had recovered from the shrine to which it had been sent. He had blunted the edge of Sher Singh's ambitions by an immense bribe of money, and now the two were friends and wept together before Ranjit's picture.

There was a personal message for the sisters, too: a wholly unexpected one. That kind, good Colonel Skinner had begged the Miss Edens, through William, to accept a pair of shawls which he had specially ordered from Kashmir, and not to return them. The Miss Edens were the last people to hurt an old soldier's feelings by refusing such a charming gift; indeed, Emily could have brought herself to accept a scarf to match, if he had only thought of it.

The next *dak* which came from Bombay brought letters, but only one shawl; a marvellously fine one, but still, only *one*. Fanny and Emily took horrid fright, lest the other shawl should have been lost. They had not sufficient nerve to draw lots for this one, and thought it would be less unpleasant to cut it in two. It was a great relief when the second shawl arrived early in October—just as handsome as the first, and so fine it could be drawn through a finger-ring.

With it came a letter from the Agent in Kashmir, who had undertaken to get several shawls made for them to take home in three years' time. These were on the looms, but would still not be completed for some months. He gave a grim account of the oppressive rule of the Sikhs over the Kashmiris. Gholab Singh, who belonged to the same family as Dian Singh, ruled over much of Kashmir, and his cruelties were revolting. He was in the habit of depriving men of their ears or noses for trivial offences, and recently he had flayed alive three hundred Kashmiris who had angered him. It was the practice of Gholab's family never to allow a female infant of their race to live; they married wives from other high Rajput families, but would not give their daughters to inferior princes, or let them live unmarried. So they killed all girl children as soon as they were born.

Reading the letter, Emily wondered that the wives did not get up a little rebellion of their own.

The longer she stayed in India, the more thankful she was not to have been born a woman native to this terrible land. She could laugh and talk about rebellion—but what chance had an Indian woman of rebelling against anything when life was held so cheaply? Men killed their wives for a caprice, a whim, a suspicion, a passing jealousy. Only when they were young and desirable had women any influence over their husbands—and then all must be done by cunning. When they were old, they could command obedience; but this, again, must be gained by devious ways. Emily knew that not for all the emeralds in India could she have borne such a life.

The fancy fair was now ready and Simla turned out to patronise it. Fanny and Emily were in the tent for most of the day, and saw with delight that it was going to be an even bigger success than the last one; money flowed freely. Emily had painted two small pictures of Sikh chieftains, which were raffled, bringing in £75. The aides had got themselves up as gypsies, and told fortunes; the stalls of fancy work were sold out before the morning was over. Fanny's collection of dolls produced over £20, and she wished that she had done more.

The Simla natives came and spent freely, but they were obviously puzzled at the odd amusements of the Europeans. There was a large booth with the sign of the 'Marquess of Granby' over the door, and here luncheon and refreshments were served by several of the Governor-General's staff got up as Sam Weller, old Weller and his wife, and Jingle. The afternoon ended with races round a quite tolerable little course, the gentlemen dressed in satin jackets and jockey caps. There was a weighing-stand, and everything got up regularly. This was a popular end to the day, especially with elderly people who had vague recollections of Epsom in their young days.

Altogether, the fair brought in 6,000 rupees, enough to keep the hospital going for four years. Fanny and Emily were pleased with the result, and with the way everybody had helped to make the affair a success. But then, a very small society was easier to amuse here than in England. Besides, they all had the assistance of numerous servants, who did what they were told, and merely thought the *sahibs* were mad.

At the beginning of November the Governor-General was ready to leave Simla. Fanny and Emily did not want to come down from the mountains. The very idea of Calcutta appalled them now; was one ever glad to walk into a large, well-heated oven? But there was never any point in saying this kind of thing to their brother. What they felt or liked simply did not come into the case where Government was concerned. Though when George told them in his calm, Governor-General way that he intended to stay at Agra for a year on the journey back, they felt like saying a very great deal. Agra was reputed to be one of the hottest places in India, even hotter than Calcutta at its worst. An Agra lady had once said in Emily's hearing that it was better not to think of the hot winds at Agra until they actually came, nor to mention them, but to keep up one's strength and try to live through them.

George wished to stay at Agra in order to study local conditions at his leisure. He was, as usual, anxious to find out how reforms could best be initiated. Something had already been done towards the establishment of schools, and more were being planned. He also intended to press on with judicial reforms; he was determined that Indian judges should have the same authority in the courts as their European counterparts.

He was feeling especially obstinate because of the attitude the Board of Directors had taken over some of the proposed changes which he wished to make. They had begun to be restive at the expense involved when Bentinck and later Metcalfe had carried through improved conditions for educating and training natives. Now they wrote peremptorily to Lord Auckland saying that he must not embark on further legislation without their express sanction. They also wished to cancel several of the measures he had already taken.

George replied to Hobhouse in his usual forthright manner:

'You may almost hold it as an axiom that the folly or the fault next in degree to a folly or fault committed in India, is the attempt to reverse it by an order at nearly a year's date from England.'

After sending that off, he went on with his plans. But he soon found that he was too worried to give his entire mind to social reforms: the one aspect of statesmanship which interested him above all others. He had to think of Kabul.

Macnaghten's dispatches were not so rosy as they had been at first. He made much of Shah Shuja's kingly qualities, but he did not mention that this protégé was beginning to have a swelled head and was making ridiculous demands. The most serious was the Shah's insistence that it detracted from his dignity to have British soldiers so near his palace-fortress, and that they must be withdrawn from the capital. He required the buildings occupied by the 13th Foot for the use of a large harem which he had collected.

Nor did anyone write to inform the Governor-General that Macnaghten, incredibly, had given way. In spite of the fact that the puppet king was actually sitting on the throne because of those very soldiers, Macnaghten had them withdrawn and quartered in a fort outside the city. Henry Durand, the chief engineer of the army, thought it madness. He argued with Macnaghten that the original buildings could be strongly fortified; they commanded the city, and might be of vital importance if Dost Muhammad tried to attack. Already there was fighting going on, raids against outlying posts. It was sheer lunacy to give up a potential strong-point because the king wanted his harem handy. Macnaghten was not to be persuaded. He thought it good policy to humour the Shah; Durand must find other strong-points.

The Envoy did not think these small differences of opinion worth putting into his dispatches to Lord Auckland.

*   *   *   *   *

They were in for it now. Emily and Fanny looked back at distant Simla from the plains in which they were already gently stewing. All the old discomforts, and worse. They had left an autumnal air blowing up there, and a garden full of flowers, and Giles's strawberry beds, properly tucked up, ready for whoever liked to pick the fruit next year.

Now they were in the old camel-dust and noise, the thermometer at ninety degrees in the tents, and punkahs going. But they were glad there were so many ladies in camp; last year, on the way up-country, they had found it tiring to be the only samples of female society. In another week they would be joined by a fresh cavalry regiment, which meant at least another twenty ladies—so useful with the awful number of balls in prospect on their homeward journey.

At Ambala, they found several officers arrived from Kabul who were to march with them as far as Karnal. Reports had been reaching the Governor-General that supplies for the army had not been good on the march to Afghanistan. These officers pooh-poohed the stories. Nonsense, they said. The army had suffered no further distress than a want of wine and cigars; and the 16th were bringing back in safety their pack of foxhounds, which they had taken with them on the campaign in hope of sport. Did that sound like great privations?

They had stopped at Karnal on the way up-country, and the first thing Chance did was to rush to a place he knew and root up the bones he had buried the year before. Emily and Fanny found nothing equally familiar. The bright yellow general who had greeted them last year had taken his liver complaint home, and a pale primrose general, who had been renovating for some years at Bath, had come out to take the other's place.

There was the usual dinner, with an immense party, but the women were all plain—with the exception of that extremely pretty little Mrs. James, who looked like a star among the others. Emily was not surprised that if a tolerable-looking girl came up the country she was persecuted with proposals. There were several gentlemen at Karnal avowedly on the look-out for a wife. There must have been many of them who gazed at the lovely Mrs. James, alas respectably settled in matrimony already.

She really was a charming girl, Mrs. J. Emily and Fanny took to her greatly. She seemed to be so unhappy at their leaving Karnal; her husband was stationed there, and she had to remain. Emily gave her a silk gown, and allowed her to travel a little way with her on her elephant, with Mr. James sitting behind. Mrs. James had never been on an elephant before, and thought it delightful. What a *very* pretty little thing she was, to be sure! A good little thing, too. But they were poor, and she was very young and lively. If she fell into bad hands, thought Emily, she would soon laugh herself into foolish scrapes. At present the husband and wife were fond of each other, but a girl who married at fifteen hardly knew what she liked. Emily saw her enter the *tonjaun* to return to Karnal with regret. It was not often one came across such beauty in India.

The camp moved on. Sergeant Webb's perpetual croaking from his rides ahead: road rough and dusty, or to vary it, road *very* rough and dusty. Then Delhi again, with the usual party to welcome them, and dinners and balls unending.

Fanny had caught a bad cold since Karnal, and Dr. Drummond forbade her to go out. She and Emily could never settle whether they would rather have a slight illness or go through all the festivities of a station. Fanny had not been put to the choice, but now she thought that she preferred enduring the cold, though she ached more than was comfortable to bear. So Emily sat through the dinner and went to the ball, and was pleased to see everybody so busy dancing away. But she felt obliged to speak privately to their engaged aides-de-camp to say how very wrong it was of them to dance three times with the same girl, engaged or not. Such a waste of time to all parties, with female partners in demand.

Fatehpur, and durbars for the Dholepur and Gwalior Rajahs. Neither was remarkable, as Indian princes went, though Dholepur wore eight of the largest pearls Fanny or Emily had yet seen; they must have been laid by a sort of turkey amongst the oysters. And the Gwalior Rajah rode in a kind of two-storeyed carriage, drawn by six elephants.

Emily had a letter from Lady Macnaghten, who had left some weeks before to join her husband in Kabul. She had travelled safely through the Punjab and the Khaibar Pass with her diamonds, her maid, and cat, without meeting any of the dangers with which she was threatened. Neither Lady Macnaghten nor Emily knew that this convenient freedom of passage had been purchased by an agent of Macnaghten's, Captain Mackeson, who had persuaded the plundering tribesmen who controlled the dark gorges of the Khaibar to allow British troops and travellers to pass through unmolested, in return for an annual subsidy of £8,000.

* * * * *

They arrived at Agra a few days before Christmas, 1839, and were pleasantly surprised to find that a good house, which had once been Sir Charles Metcalfe's, had been made ready for them, so they could leave tent life and begin to be moderately comfortable once more.

The place was full of Mogul buildings, all domes and elaborate patterns, and uncommonly trying to Emily's patience when she tried to draw them. Fanny liked intricate designs, and was especially taken with a marble tomb, carved like lace, which, she thought, would make a splendid dairy for Windsor Castle, it looked so cool and royal.

They went to see the Taj, and found it even more beautiful than they had expected, after all they had heard of its fabulous loveliness. But there would be plenty of time for sightseeing; what must occupy them now were plans for building verandahs round the house, and putting in ventilators, so as to have some protection against the hot winds. From the end of March to the middle of June, they were told, these devilish winds blew unceasingly, day and night. Emily tried not to think of that hell which lay ahead.

Agra society turned out to be as full of quirks and absurdities as society anywhere else in India. Some of the officials and their wives were too strict to dance, and Emily and Fanny thought longingly of

the French vaudeville players and their amusing farces; though probably Agra society would have disapproved of *them* just as heartily.
An afternoon garden party which Emily gave would have been very
flat if it had not been for William Osborne.

William had recognised one of the Agra gentlemen, a very stout
individual and the image of Mr. Pickwick, as an old acquaintance;
they had both been to Westminster School. Just when the party had
reached the silent and staring stage, William challenged Mr. Pickwick
to play at hop-scotch, following their old Westminster rules. William
was an active young man and excellent at games, and it was great fun
to see Mr. Pickwick hopping and jumping and panting after him. It
kept everybody in a roar of laughter for an hour, and filled up the
afternoon very well.

George was soon occupied in arousing the interest of the local
governing officials in his plans for new schools. He was trying to
find a suitable man to appoint as Lieutenant-Governor, but the only
likely candidate had to leave Agra because of his wife's illness, and
there was nobody else with the necessary qualifications. George and
Mr. Colvin added two or three extra hours on to their already long
day, and began to work out details of the educational plans themselves.

There was already a pair of schools which interested Emily. These
were orphan schools, set up to take three hundred boys and girls who
had been picked up at the time of the famine two years before. Emily
liked the young German missionary and his wife who were in charge,
and decided to leave her purchased Indian children with them. She
would miss the poor little things, but Myra had mothered them so well
that they were now nearly normal, and they would be well looked
after here during 1840, the year she was to spend in Agra.

The parting was a tearful one; but when Emily and Fanny went to
see them the following day at the orphanage, the little girls were
stuffing rice and curry in large handfuls, and seemed quite reconciled
to their new home.

Another sight which pleased Emily almost as much was the ice-
making which was now going on. At this time of the year the
mornings were cold before the sun rose: cold enough to freeze water.
It was the Agra custom to cover fields with very shallow porous
saucers filled with a little water. When the thermometer came down
to thirty-six degrees in the early morning, the water turned into very
thin ice. The people collected it, broke it up, and stored it in ice-
wells, which were carefully insulated with straw. Some of the ice

melted, but it was reckoned that about a third of it was available in the hot weather. Emily and Fanny would have liked to see the entire district covered with shallow saucers of water. But they were not destined to have ice at Agra.

One morning at the end of the first week in January, George poked his head into Emily's tent and woke her, saying:

"Here is the overland mail come, and all my plans are changed, and we are going down to Calcutta."

Just like that. Emily got out of bed, feeling quite dizzy with delight and relief. By the time she was dressed, she could tell by the pandemonium going on outside that the news had spread. The servants were quite mad, flinging themselves on the ground and throwing off their turbans. When they saw Emily they rushed to her, asking if it was true that they were going home to Calcutta. Ah, how blessed, how wonderful. They would pray to Allah for lordship's health, and thank him for taking them back to their families.

George explained at breakfast. He had received dispatches which made it necessary for him to go down to Calcutta as quickly as possible. Fanny and Emily knew better than to ask too many questions, but they were perfectly familiar with the state of political affairs, and could fill in the picture for themselves.

Another little war, which had been simmering for some time, was now coming to the boil, and George was being forced to take action. For not only was he Governor-General of India, but he was also responsible for the sphere of British influence which swept round to the China seas. The dispatches which had reached him this morning from his Ministers in Council contained news which demanded his presence in Calcutta. The Chinese governors of the ports of Canton and Hongkong were refusing to allow the importation of opium into China. Ships had had their cargoes impounded; others were standing off, unable to come into harbour.

Whatever George thought privately about the opium trade, he was a servant of the Company, and he must act as such. India produced vast quantities of opium; the trade was a very valuable one, and China was one of her best customers. For many years the East India Company had stimulated this trade, in spite of opposition from the Chinese authorities, as well as from members of the government at home. Opium as a necessary ingredient of medicines, yes; but opium as a noxious drug was a different matter. The reformers in London were not at all happy about this part of the East India trade. They could do nothing about it, however; they had as little influence on the Company as had the governors of the China ports, who steadily refused to legalise the importation of opium. There was open smuggling of the drug into their country. The governors had at last taken action, and had refused to allow the Company's ships to anchor.

When this news reached London, instructions were immediately sent to the Governor-General to take counter action. He was to dispatch a warship to China as quickly as possible, to persuade the governors of the ports that it was not wise to interfere with free trade.

The dreaded hot season in Agra would therefore not need to be endured after all; they were leaving as soon as possible. Fanny and Emily joyfully made preparations for the march again. Emily collected her two Indian children from the orphanage to take with her to Calcutta; they could live in the orphanage there, and she would be able to see them. William tried to settle up complicated finances in a few hours. He had spent a thousand pounds on fittings and furnishings for the house he had taken in Agra, and was likely to lose a large amount on reselling. Still, it would be worth it. William was going on the China expedition, and he was looking forward to action.

They began marching two days later, and George and William left the camp at Culpee, together with the aides and Secretaries. They intended to travel fast, so as to reach Calcutta as soon as possible; Emily and Fanny were to come with the others on the route back arranged for them, and to do the honours at the various posts and stations on the way.

Directly George had gone, Emily began to miss him with great intensity. George had always been a sort of idol to her; she admitted it freely. He was, she thought, fonder of her than ever, and more dependent on her even than he had been in the old Greenwich days. She was his only confidante. Though he never spoke to her of what passed in the secret sessions of the Council, he told her enough of affairs to give her an understanding of the complexity of worries which were continually in his mind.

The news from Afghanistan had been troubling him greatly. All was not well in Kabul. In spite of Macnaghten's optimistic dispatches, there were disturbing reports of clashes with both Afghans and Sikhs. Karak Singh was not proving the friend and ally his father had been: it was common knowledge now that he was not to be trusted. It was even said that he was conspiring with some of the Afghans to stop any further passage of British troops through his territories. And now there was the China business. George was a man of peace; he had always hated the use of force, though he had never hesitated when it seemed to him essential to make a show of strongly armed strength. Emily hoped that the appearance of a warship would bring the China governors to a prudent state of mind.

The camp moved on. Allahabad again. Letters came from George saying that he had arrived in Calcutta, and that the green of Bengal was a refreshing sight after the brown and dusty plains. Fanny and Emily, still on those plains, wished they had wings so that they could fly. But the journey was over at last. They arrived back at Calcutta on March 1st, 1840, and not, Emily declared, before it was time. The camp chairs and tables were tumbling to pieces, the china all cracked, the right shoe of her only remaining pair had sprung a large hole, her last bonnet was brown with dust, and the brambles in the jungles had torn her last presentable gown into fringes.

They arrived late in the evening, to find William sitting smoking in his dressing-gown, and George in bed. George said they would find plenty of mosquitoes to welcome them, but Emily did not care; here was a clean and solid house to live in again. Even Fanny admitted to being glad to leave the tent life, after two and a half years of it. Emily found pleasure simply in walking through the vast spacious rooms of Government House.

'Do you not remember the story father used to tell us,' she wrote to her eldest sister, 'of how his friend, the old Duke of Marlborough, went to dine with a neighbour whose house was small, whose fires were low, and whose dinner was bad. And when the Duke drove back to Blenheim and entered that magnificent hall, he said, with a plaintive sigh: "Well! Home is home, be it never so homely." So say I, coming back to this grand palace, from those wretched tents; and so shall I repeat when we arrive at our dear little villa at Kensington Gore.'

*   *   *   *   *

The year 1840 took the course already made familiar by their life in Calcutta three and four years before. The journey up the country had improved Emily's general health, in spite of recurring agues, and Fanny, though thinner and more easily subject to cold, was her usual lively self.

A brutal crime

Fanny hoped that the China expedition would not last too long; she wanted William back. She was also very partial to China silks and had always thought the mandarins made fine figures in their beautiful brocades. It was difficult to think of that neat and smiling people threatening defiance; but, of course, they were not only neat but very clever. Emily expected them to blow up the English ships with their curious coloured fireworks.

Meanwhile, George was again busy with schools. Ten young Hindus had qualified this year to act as surgeons, and the Governor-General was extremely pleased. Some of the boys at the Hindu College had turned into remarkable scholars; Emily was of the opinion that they could beat any Eton sixth-former in history or mathematics. An achievement! Ten years ago neither they nor their relations would have been able to speak a word of English.

It was slow work. George had known it would be slow; all reform was slow in India. But he would have given much to be able to wind up the years with a quick hand when it came to the law and legislation. There was the case of the brute Hughes. George was seized with one of his rare fits of flaming fury when the case was brought to his notice. Hughes, a Calcutta superintendent of roads, had had his house robbed, and suspected some men working on the roads of the robbery. He had a bamboo gibbet erected, tied up a number of these men to it by their hands, their feet not touching the ground, and lit straw under them. This was the least of the horrors; it made George ill to read of the rest.

One of the men was taken down dead, most of the others were insensible. Hughes had his dinner-table brought out into the compound and dined within a few yards of the wretched creatures, saying *that* would teach them to rob his house. He was aware that he was liable to be arrested—and equally sure of the outcome. When he was brought up in court, he made no defence, except to say that he did not touch the natives with his own hands; his overseer had done the actual work.

The judge, Sir Henry Seton, in his charge to the jury, called the crime manslaughter, knowing that there was such a horror of capital punishment in the country that a charge of murder would be thrown out. He intended to give Hughes the maximum sentence within his power—transportation for life. To his astonishment, the jury brought in a verdict of 'Not guilty'. One of the magistrates told George and Emily that the low type of Europeans who generally made up the jury

203

always agreed to acquit any man who was tried for the murder of a native.

George sent for the papers, and wrote a Minute on them which showed very clearly what he thought. When, a short time later, Hughes was again arrested and convicted of some misdemeanour, he was sentenced to two years' imprisonment. It was better than nothing, said George grimly, but this kind of thing was not going on while he remained Governor-General.

Emily took her two Indian girls to the Calcutta orphan school, which she knew well already. Mrs. Wilson, who had started it, was as perfect a character as Fanny and Emily had ever met—and besides being good she was *merry*. She had gathered together 150 black orphans, and was a most loving mother to them. When the little girls reached the usual marrying age of twelve, Mrs. Wilson found native Christian husbands for them, and these built huts round her house and served her as gardeners or labourers. She trusted entirely to Providence for funds, and Emily hoped that the ladies of Calcutta would not leave the entire burden on Providence's shoulders.

The sisters were now collecting pieces of furniture, curiosities and muslins to take home with them. It was wonderful to pack away one small thing after another, knowing that these would be unpacked in the Kensington house which they had not seen, but which was now as familiar to them as if they had measured the curtains for every room. They also sent presents to their sisters and friends whenever a ship was sailing for home. Emily sent Lady Bucks a muslin pelisse by the *Repulse*.

'It has the merit of being worked on such fine Dacca muslin that I thought it would have a sweet, airy effect on a hot summer's day at East Combe,' she told Eleanor. 'And then what nailed me into buying it was that the owner, who certainly had not as much muslin on him as would have made a sleeve to the pelisse, held it up with an air of great vanity, looked over his shoulder with an insinuating smile, and said, "Quite new pattern."'

Fanny and Emily always delighted in native eccentrics, either Indian or Chinese. Old Aumon, the Chinese shoemaker, who glided about Government House with his eyes half-a-mile apart and his long pigtail touching the ground, did not allow the China business to interfere with personal relationships. When opium was seized at Canton, Aumon still made shoes that fitted. When a warship was sent off to China, Aumon fanned himself and knelt in front of Emily with his work and said: "This good satin—this right foot, this left."

On Thursdays they still went to Barrackpore, where they entertained the week-end round of visitors. There were usually one or two clergymen among the guests, and sometimes missionaries. Emily and Fanny had to be discreet over missionaries. It was George's policy not to interfere in any way with the native religions. He knew that he was the target for much criticism over his lack of official support of the missionaries, who, it had to be admitted, *were* trying to interfere with the native religions. George thought it more important to try to win the confidence of Indians of all sects, rather than to take sides publicly with Europeans, however well-intentioned, whose object it was to argue the natives away from their age-old faiths.

Privately, of course, he liked and admired the missionaries, and assisted them whenever he was able to do so within the terms of the policy he was trying to follow. One of the missionaries who came to Barrackpore had made fourteen hundred converts in a month, many of them young high-caste Brahmins. He attributed this to their education as well as to his own religious zeal—an admission which pleased the Governor-General and his sisters.

'It is quite clear that when Hindus allow their boys to be so thoroughly well instructed as they are at the Hindu College, they must see through the horrible absurdities of their own religion,' Emily wrote home. 'Though a single Hindu who loses his caste can hardly withstand the persecution of his countrymen, yet if any number change their religion, they become a refuge to each other, and make the conversion of more much easier.'

Letters came from William. The Chinese were already saying that they hoped there would be 'a good deal of talkee before fightee', which looked as if they did not mean to come to the fightee at all. This was a great relief.

At last came some solid news. The fleet had taken the island of Chusan, the Admiral was going to see the Emperor, and the Chinese had decided to be sensible. William wrote that he was on his way back, that the bazaar at Chusan was open again, and he was bringing some little knick-knacks.

The Chinese affair looked to be on the way to a satisfactory settlement, but the news from the north-west kept the Governor-General on edge. Afghanistan was no conquered colony. Shah Shuja sat on the throne—with Sir William Macnaghten conveniently near—and

Dost Muhammad had submitted and was an honourably treated prisoner in Hindostan. But the wild, warlike tribes of the Afghan states had no intention of welding themselves into a peaceable parcel of subjects under a so-called king whom they despised for his weakness and laughed at for his vanity. Neither had they much stomach for an army of occupation belonging to a Power which had forced a war on them that they had not wanted.

The plundering Ghilzai clan of the hill-country began to block the roads between Kabul and Kandahar; the Baluchi tribes attacked fort after fort. There were risings in the Durani country. The forts and garrisons were defended by brave officers, but news reached George of one small disaster after another. It was clear that Afghanistan was in a state of ferment.

Then came orders from the Court of Directors in London which redoubled George's worries. The occupation of Afghanistan was costing a fantastic amount of money. There were twenty-five thousand troops in the country; the Shah's court was kept up on British gold, and large sums were being paid to the chieftains to keep them friendly. How long was it going on?

The Russian bogey was fading. The Russians had actually attempted an invasion against Khiva, but it had been such a failure that no-one now expected them to march against India. Russia's strength had been broken against the frozen, desolate mountain country; cold and starvation had decimated what remained of the troops who straggled back to their base. With that satisfactory news in front of them, the Court of Directors wrote to the Governor-General that there was no longer any need for such vast expenditure in Afghanistan. There must be immediate and considerable retrenchment.

Lord Auckland sent instructions to Macnaghten, telling him to reduce expenditure in every possible way. Sir William Macnaghten had been in the East long enough to know what would be the effect of withdrawing large bribes to chieftains whose main interest in life was plunder. He wrote to the Governor-General saying that he was cutting down expenses at the Shah's court and among the administration, but he thought it unwise to reduce the subsidies to the tribesmen. Lord Auckland, harried by dispatches from London, replied with firm orders to cut down in *every* direction; the Shah must now look to maintaining his own kingdom.

Macnaghten had no choice but to obey. He summoned the chiefs together and explained that the flow of British gold was to be turned down to a trickle; the Shah was now to be responsible for his own treasury. The chieftains, who owed no loyalty to a king they had not wanted in the first place, salaamed to Macnaghten, and went off to stir up trouble against the British and Shah Shuja.

In Calcutta the Governor-General sat with Mr. Colvin, reading letters and dispatches from Afghanistan. Those from Macnaghten still insisted on the popularity of Shah Shuja. Every other account—from civilians and soldiers alike—made it clear that Shah Shuja had no influence whatever. He was a broken reed. Without the British force in Kabul and the surrounding forts, they said, he would be swept off his throne in a moment.

George had always trusted William Macnaghten's judgment; his adviser seemed, by mentality and experience, well suited to the task he had been given in Afghanistan. One could not withdraw one's trust now, because troubles were arising. Macnaghten was sure those troubles were transient: that the country was really in the process of settling down into peace. So reasoned the Governor-General.

The Court of Directors in London did not take that view. Their dispatches came by the overland mail, specially expedited. It was necessary, they insisted, either to increase the military force in Afghanistan quite considerably, or to retreat from that country. For their part, they said, they would prefer the entire abandonment of Afghanistan, and a frank confession of failure, to the folly of attempting to maintain peace within the Shah's dominions, and prevent aggression from outside, by a small British force.

The dispatch gave the Governor-General a chance to withdraw without losing face. He did not take it. Macnaghten looked on the very notion of withdrawal as 'an unparalleled political atrocity'. The dispatch came up before the Ministers in Council at Calcutta in March, 1841, and they supported the Governor-General and Macnaghten. The occupation of Afghanistan was to go on, in spite of every ominous sign that the forces there were living on the crust of a volcano that might erupt at any moment.

12

THE EDGE OF CATASTROPHE

AND now the fishes would probably be wearing the new gowns which Mary Eden had sent out six months ago. So provoking! It was not what Emily had understood in the old days as 'dressed fish'.

When Captain Hill announced that a box the size of a pianoforte had arrived, Emily exclaimed that it was about time, and regretted that the box was not the size of a church organ. But when it was unpacked, Emily and Wright were puzzled by articles which they had never asked for—and found a note at the bottom to say they were for Fanny.

Emily was sure that *her* box had been drowned. Captain Hill was sympathetic, and said he would make enquiries about overdue ships. But Emily had little hope of seeing her box again. Robert had not mentioned in his letter what vessel Mary was sending the clothes by, so any enquiry could only be a general one. And there had been so many ships wrecked during the past year: burnt down to the water. Emily forgot her box of gowns when she thought of the terror of the unfortunate people trapped in flames on those vast, empty seas.

Captain Hill had succeeded the efficient but unlamented Major Byrne as Controller to the household; the *Spoke* had gone home on leave. Captain Hill was as helpful and accommodating as the other had been rigid and Spoke-ish, and Emily and Fanny liked him.

The latest news from the Punjab saddened the two sisters. Ranjit Singh's death, like that of Alexander, had shattered his kingdom into chaos. His soldiers had turned on their European officers and murdered them, and were marauding wildly over the country. Emily and Fanny thought of General Ventura and General Allard, who had given up long years of their lives to help train Ranjit's Sikhs. . . .

Karak Singh, too, was dead. Some said he had been poisoned by his son; he had been ailing, and had been given medicine mixed with powdered emeralds—evidently not wholesome, thought Emily. Sher Singh was now king, and little Pertab the Heir-Apparent. But who knew if that charming and intelligent boy would live to sit on the throne of the old Lion?

Fanny and Emily were glad to occupy themselves with thoughts of a more agreeable kind; a wedding, more or less in the family. Fanny's maid, Jones, after a sedate courtship which had been going on during all the time they had been in India, had agreed to marry Mars, George's personal servant. The sisters were pleased, as they always were when they heard of any matrimonial venture that bid fair in its prospects. Mars was a trustworthy individual and would make an admirable husband, and Jones was a nice young woman in every way. Fanny wondered where she was going to find another Jones, but there were several English servants who wished to return to England, so she would have some choice. The wedding took place in March, and the couple were given a week's holiday. Scarcely had they gone when Emily's pleasure in their happiness was wiped out by a calamity which she had always dreaded, but which she knew would have to come some time.

Chance had to be put to sleep. He had been ill for some time, but they had not been unduly worried; he had recovered from worse illnesses before. Then his mouth became diseased, and after a few agonised days of watching him grow more and more distressed, Emily could bear it no longer and at last agreed to have him shot. He was, of course, quite an old gentleman, even for a spaniel, a long-lived breed. But Emily and Fanny had somehow come to look upon him as immortal, and they were wretched at his passing. It was not only that he had been such a dear companion, but he was a link with the old, carefree days at Greenwich and Grosvenor Street. He had been closer to their hearts than any pet they had ever had.

Jimmund, his bearer, sat crying all day. On the night of Chance's funeral, Emily found Jimmund and his wife sitting on the little grave, weeping sorely. They did not see her, but their genuine sorrow somehow brought a sense of comfort to her own.

A few days later, a doctor who had just arrived from England sent Emily a spaniel puppy, one of two which he had brought out with him. He had heard of her loss and advised her filling Chance's place as soon as possible. He hoped Duke would find a corner in her affections, and so on. Emily appreciated his kindness, but she could not take to Duke. He had immense ears, a short nose, and all the right points. It might have been better if he had had a few of the wrong ones. By nature he was wild and riotous, and ran off like a mad thing with the servants streaming after him all over the house calling "Juck, Juck!" That name was his only merit, thought Emily; she did not suppose anybody ever had a dog called Juck before.

Fanny had her dog, Matty, but it was surprising for both sisters to have to try so hard to love new pets. At one time Fanny would have been able to take any animal into her affections—with the possible exceptions of tigers and alligators—but she felt strangely apathetic these days. The Barbary goats were in the park at Barrackpore and remained there; that experiment had not been a success. More and more she thought of Gazelle, and her beloved Rolla. . . .

They were both growing weary, and they knew it. George had written to the Board of Control saying that he wished to have a successor appointed by February, 1842. In the present state of the home government—judging by the last mail—Emily and Fanny would not have been surprised at an earlier recall. But that was too much to hope for. They fixed their hopes on the next February, and wondered how they were going to get through these last months of waiting.

William was subdued these days, too; his old high spirits had gone. Something unfortunate had happened to William. He had rarely taken more than polite notice of the young ladies whom he met at parties and balls; mothers and aunts had given him up as a determined bachelor. Now he had fallen in love with a married lady: deeply and desperately in love.

It was a hopeless attachment. It was the first time Fanny had seen William really unhappy, and when he withdrew to his own quarters and ceased to sit with her, or take her driving, as in former days, she did not attempt to force her company on him, but left him alone.

Fanny herself was quietly relapsing into worse health. She did not know what was the matter with her. She did not feel actually ill, and nothing hurt. But a weakness, a continual exhaustion, had begun to set in which alarmed Emily and made her insist on sending for the doctor. It was not, alas, Dr. Drummond. He had been in failing health himself for some time and had had to go home. The new doctor was polite and attentive, and took all the pains he could over Fanny. But he was evidently an ignorant man on the subject of medicine, which was, thought Emily, unlucky for a doctor. In every other respect he was the greatest bore she had ever encountered, and she had met a great many. He was the sort of man who made one wag one's ears and stamp, he was so tiresome and slow.

George frankly detested him. Not on account of his boringness: George, too, was used to dullards. What damned the doctor in George's eyes was his attitude towards the natives. Nothing would induce him to treat the servants or their families, and one day Emily had a grand blow up with him over a boy who had been bitten by a dog. He maintained that he was there to attend only to Europeans, and Emily could not move him. George wanted to dismiss him on the spot, but Emily realised that such an action would be put down to his failure to cure Fanny, and would ruin him in his profession. She dissuaded George from anything so definite, and sent for old Dr. Nicolson.

Everybody abused Nicolson but they all sent for him in a crisis. He was not able to do much for Fanny, but at least he brought back a little of her old verve, and made her laugh. A sea-voyage would blow some good air into her, he said: she must go on a sea-voyage.

This was a suggestion which fitted in with an idea Emily had already had of getting Fanny away from Calcutta during part of the hot weather. There was cholera in the city; Emily's tailor had died, and there were tales all round of people being struck down with appalling suddenness. In Fanny's weak state of health there was danger of picking up the infection. A sea-voyage was a good idea.

William was going to China again, and Fanny could go with him as far as Singapore, and return on the first vessel from that port. She could not go as far as China because a war was going on there. Not a painted-on-a-screen, firecracker war, but the real thing.

The China affair had not turned out to be as simple as Emily and Fanny had first thought. The talkee had come to nothing in the end, and now it was a case of fightee in good earnest.

The Emperor had refused to sign the treaty, and the fleet had taken the Bogue forts in the Canton river. Later the Admiral had unaccountably evacuated his positions, much to Emily's fury; she did not think her national pride had ever been so hurt before. But the Admiral continued the war after a policy which took no notice of Miss Eden's patriotic feelings, and Fanny embarked on the Commodore's warship with William on May 23rd, with no notion of discussing anything more belligerent than the weather.

'I think those great war tea-kettles, which go rolling on through storm and calm, wonderful inventions,' she wrote to Eleanor Grosvenor. 'The paddles are not irritating, and though the powder magazine was under my cabin, and cannon-balls would break loose and run about the deck, that was preferable to the noise of ropes and the creaking of bulkheads. A gale of wind to which, now it is over, I can never be sufficiently obliged, made us put in to the Prince of

Wales Island—the most beautiful sample of an island you can fancy, and with a hill where the climate is perfect. And there I remained, instead of going on to Singapore. They gave up the Government House to us. . . . We were chiefly waited upon by convicts, some branded on the forehead for murder. But it was the sin of their youth, and we were evidently expected to think it venial. . . .'

Fanny stayed on the island for sixteen days, walking and resting and enjoying the glorious views in all directions. Then the steamer *Cowasjee Family*, bound for Calcutta, stopped to take her up, and Fanny stepped on board feeling quite in her old excellent health.

She arrived back at Calcutta to find the hot weather more sweltering than ever, and Emily with another pet spaniel. This one was a success. It was an absurd little creature with no talents and no temper, but it cared for nothing and nobody but Emily, and required constant petting —a familiarity Chance had not approved of. It was difficult not to give in to it. Juck, with all his physical perfections, was presented to an aide, Captain Mackintosh, who had taken a fancy to him, so that business was satisfactorily settled.

Fanny wished that the business of governing India could have been arranged with so little trouble. George was weighed down with fearful responsibilities. It was not only China. Afghanistan was never out of his thoughts—or out of the arguments of his Ministers in Council. Macnaghten wrote about the 'cheering prospects' which everywhere met his gaze in Kabul. The commanders in the field outside Kabul sent reports of bloody clashes with the clansmen. Macnaghten wrote: 'All is content and tranquility, and wherever we Europeans go, we are received with respect and attention.' The soldiers wrote of a strong convoy of British troops fighting their way through to their fort, their guns and bayonets outmatching the wild rush of multitudinous swordsmen. 'The impudence of a few hundred rascals' blocked the way through a pass within fifteen miles of Kabul, but Macnaghten wrote a private letter that the country was perfectly quiet. Indeed, many of the officers had already got their wives with them, and were looking upon Kabul as an Indian hill station, the climate was so delicious.

There was much that Macnaghten still left out of his letters to the Governor-General. He did not think it necessary to pass on the story that a Captain Grey had told him, of the friendly chief who had warned that the Afghans were determined to murder or drive out the hated foreign invaders. Macnaghten was used to that kind of threat in the

East. Nor was there any need to mention that a number of chieftains inside the capital itself had disappeared, and were reported on good evidence to have joined one of the many bands of rebels which had been falling on British forces wherever these were to be met with.

The Governor-General heard some of the stories, all the same. Sir Robert Sale, in charge of a brigade, wrote of barely being able to beat off strong attacks launched by hordes of the insurgents. General Nott, a blunt soldier of the Bengal Army, made no secret in his letters of what he thought of the political agents whose bungling had bared the throat of every European in the country to the sword of the Afghan and the knife of the bloody Baluch.

The torrid summer wore slowly on in a Calcutta which had not known such a hot season for years. Fanny's renewed good health was fading into lassitude, but she and Emily were lifted into high feather by the arrival of the July post, which told them that there was a change of government at home. The Whigs were now out and the Tories in. That made their home-going certain. Emily remarked that she was still an excellent Whig, but there was much pleasure in Opposition.

She had already written some months before to Captain Grey, asking what accommodation he could give them if they returned to England in February. A reply reached her, to say that Captain Grey now commanded the *Endymion*, which was smaller than the *Jupiter*, but he thought he could make them comfortable. So that was settled!

It would not be so difficult now to endure the remaining few months in India. Emily looked at George, grown so withdrawn and silent—except for the great bursts of rage which were coming upon him more frequently now.

"I wonder how we are allowed to keep this country a week!" he said one day, in the greatest fury. He had just been told by Dr. Nicolson of a young European who kept a bulldog which ran at the natives. The doctor drove the dog away from one terrified bearer, and later, seeing it at the heels of a young man, stopped and told him about the dog's ferocity, and how he had had to drive it away from the bearer.

"Oh, did you?" said the young man. "Why, I keep this dog and another for the sake of hunting them. I had a famous run this morning after a black fellow on the course, and brought him down."

George's anger was such as Emily had never seen. He made immediate enquiries, and found that the man was an indigo planter. The Governor-General offered a reward from his own private purse to anyone who could catch the planter at his morning sport, and Emily, through one of the aides, established an understanding with the superintendent of police which she hoped would procure the desired result.

'But is it not enough to make anybody foam with rage?' she wrote home. 'I wonder what natives must think of the Christian religion, judging by its effects here? An indigo planter the other day murdered his wife, a girl of sixteen, in the most horrible manner—beat her to death—and, because she was half-caste, the other planters in the neighbourhood helped him to get away, and the magistrates took no notice of the murder till the papers got hold of it. Then the Government interfered, but the murderer had gone off to France. "Indeed, indeed, I'm very, very sick."'

She and Fanny had already begun to pack some of the things they had bought to take home. Fanny had brought back a boxful of Chinese articles from her sea-trip; an American whom she had commissioned to purchase small ivories and inlaid pieces had carried out the work well. There were souvenirs of the journey up-country; workboxes and stuffs and hangings. Wright folded them away in the tin-lined boxes so that there should not be too much to do on the eve of departure.

December came, and they said, "The last Christmas." Never had they faced the prospect of balls and dinners with such equanimity. If only George would look less harassed. There was bad news from Afghanistan. General Sale had been obliged to retreat to Jalalabad, leaving cannon behind him. Some of the Shah's troops had gone over to the insurgents, and General Sale had few provisions, in a country full of mountain passes. Captain MacGregor was with him as political agent. MacGregor's father, mother and sister had been at Government House to a party, and had been so proud of him. Poor people! They had an anxious time before them, thought Emily.

The accounts came in all through the first days in December—and the news took a turn for the worse. There had been a rebellion in Kabul. Lady Sale had managed to get a letter through to her husband, who was in Jalalabad, wounded; and General Sale had sent the letter on to Calcutta. Lady Sale had always been an active, strong-minded woman, and she wrote in a plain manner. The Shah was able to do nothing to stop the wild Afghan rebels. She was not optimistic about help coming from India; the snow was beginning to fall on the passes, which were dangerous at the best of times. She could only pray and hope.

Fanny and Emily were appalled. The very last letter from Sir William Macnaghten had been full of gratification at the state of the country, how prosperous it was becoming, and how much the Afghans were beginning to appreciate the equitable laws of the British, after their own harsh rule. Captain Burnes, the Agent in Kabul, had held the same views.

Now news came that Burnes had been murdered. A letter had been got through to General Sale from Kabul, imploring him to come to their rescue. Sale's wife and daughter were in Kabul, but he could not risk an attempt on the city; his men would be overwhelmed.

December dragged on, and after the quietest Christmas they had known in India, Emily and Fanny saw 1842 dawn. It was difficult to attempt to rejoice. Calcutta was waiting for news. A letter came from the heroic Lady Sale. There were only three days' provisions left, she said, and then, she went on calmly, they were to eat the few ponies and camels left alive. The enemy had proposed a capitulation. The married men and the women were to be left as hostages, Shah Shuja given up, and the soldiers to lay down their arms and be escorted to the frontier—in other words, to come out and be massacred. They had not agreed.

The fiery Muhammad Akbar, Dost Muhammad's eldest son, had thrust himself into the command of the rebel Afghans. Dost Muhammad had shown himself in the past to be a man of his word, and his son Akbar was deemed to be less treacherous than his fellow-chieftains. Macnaghten realised at last that the puppet kingdom had collapsed, and that thousands of British lives were likely to be crushed under it. He went out to Akbar's tent to treat with the Afghan.

A week later the news of that meeting reached Calcutta. Macnaghten had been murdered. Akbar himself had shot him, after an angry scene in which Macnaghten had flung taunts at him. The officers with him had been disarmed and maltreated; the Envoy's body had been hacked to pieces and displayed to the howling tribesmen in the city.

George's face was haunted as he went about his usual business in Government House. Everybody was waiting for further catastrophe: it seemed certain now. Reports and rumours trickled in—dreadful reports, but they were not so terrible as the broken pieces of real news, when these were assembled and the whole story made clear.

The military commanders in Kabul had managed to make a treaty with the Afghan leaders, in which they were to be allowed to retreat in exchange for a large sum drawn on the Indian Treasury, and the surrender of guns and equipment. On January 6th, a force of over four thousand men, together with *dhulies* carrying many women and children, and hundreds of camp followers, began picking their way through deep snow across the wastes beyond Kabul. The retreat had begun. It became a nightmare. Cold and hunger took its toll. And the tribesmen on the heights of the grim Khurd gorges were waiting.

The nightmare went on, as sepoys and British soldiers struggled over the rocky country. Everywhere they were met by sword and match-lock fire; every mile was strewn with its dead. A few score officers were able to cut their way through the carnage and gallop on, but these were picked off, one by one. Behind, tribesmen had been following the stricken army, taking the women prisoners, hacking down the wounded.

A week later a military doctor, Dr. Bryden, fainting from wounds, hunger and exhaustion, was assisted into the fort of Jalalabad, which General Sale still held. He was the only survivor, except Akbar's prisoners, of nearly five thousand souls who had come out of Kabul on that bitter January night.

13

HOME AGAIN

THE *Endymion*, Emily was told to her disappointment, would not be coming to Calcutta after all. While she had been at Bombay, a number of her sailors had caught a fever, and Captain Grey had thought it best to put out to sea again. The next homeward-bound ship was the *Hungerford*, and though she was old and slow, she was reputed to be comfortable. The Captain assured Emily and Fanny that as his vessel had been newly encased in teak, she was quite safe. In any case, she was sailing early in March—which was the next best thing to February—so they settled to go in her.

The cabins were dark and small compared to those in the *Jupiter*, but they would have a good sitting-cabin, next to George's, on the poop. After the first three weeks they would be sailing into cooler air, and then they could really begin to look ahead to home. Emily hoped that the voyage would do George good; he seemed to have aged ten years in three months.

He had collected some pieces of jade and china for Lady Bucks and his other favourite relations, and Emily tried to get him interested in packing them. George was ready enough to fall in with suggestions she made about taking things home, but he never seemed to be really listening.

Fanny was enjoying herself writing her last Indian letters to Eleanor.

'I please myself about once a week making lists of linen, gowns, books and things in general. Just now I have seen the woman who is to take the place of Jones, who I hate the notion of parting with. However, the woman I have got is in the constant habit of voyaging backwards and forwards, and may know how to make a ship comfortable; I am sure I don't. She looks like an albatross in her cap and artificial flowers; she had no front teeth, and I am longing to know whether they dropped out naturally, or whether a very young husband she has knocked them down her throat.'

Lord Ellenborough, the new Governor-General, landed in Calcutta shortly before their departure, and George and his sisters prepared to leave Government House; they had taken a small house not far away for the few remaining days before the ship sailed. But Ellenborough was insistent that they should not be discommoded, and they remained in their quarters. It was pleasant to be guests for a week, and to be entertained instead of having all the work to do. The new Governor-General struck them as being extraordinarily active and English in all his ideas and plans. Ah, well, the climate would settle a good many of *them*. They enjoyed his hospitality and his good nature, and wished sincerely that he might not lose his enthusiasm too soon.

The last few days passed in leave-takings, social and official. Fanny and Emily were surprised to find how sorry they were to go, when it came to the point; how used they had become to people who had seemed at first to be antipathetic. It became quite painful to say good-bye, especially when so many faces were sad. One could hardly meet anyone who had not had a friend or relation in Afghanistan.

There was some small consolation in a letter from Lady Sale, saying that she and Lady Macnaghten and the others were being well treated. But the shadow of the disaster lay heavy over everybody.

Early in the morning on March 12th, the great hall at Government House filled with the Bishop, the Chief Justice, the Ministers in Council and other officials. George and his sisters came in, dressed for travelling, and took their places in front of the gathering. Emily and Fanny knew what George must be going through: what a burden he was carrying back with him to England. But he showed nothing save his usual façade of unassuming dignity. He listened to the speeches and replied to them with appreciation. Then a procession formed to escort him down to the *ghaut*.

There was a great crowd on the Strand, and at their genuine cries of regret, George was visibly touched. Emily saw tears in his eyes— and she knew that they were real tears, pricked on not by sentiment but by suffering. He had landed here with such high hopes six years ago.

It was over at last. The aides and several of the permanent staff accompanied the departing Governor-General on the State barge as far as the steamer which was to take them down the river. Fanny and Emily stood at the rail and tried to think of home. All they could really manage to focus in their minds was the prospect of the *Hungerford* up-and-downing across the oceans, with themselves tossing about inside, and four months of misery between them and Southampton. No amount of casing in teak could change the *Hungerford* into a flyer which would scamper across the waves and keep steady.

"It has eighty thousand cockroaches on board. That I know as a fact," declared Fanny.

But at least they would not need to live with the cockroaches after they reached England. They stood by George and talked to the escort; they spoke of Indian things, of Indian people and places. Behind them lay Calcutta, and Gazelle in his field at Meerut, and Rolla in his grave, and Chance in his endless sleep beneath the urn Emily had put over him in her special garden.

There was another spaniel in Emily's arms now; Zoë was going home to England. Zoë had the same markings as Chance, and for that both Emily and Fanny were glad. England was the right country for dogs. Zoë would grow from a black roly-poly into a proper spaniel, and when she learnt to swim there would be no alligators to look for.

The steamer pushed on; and there, at last, tall-masted and stolid, was the ship which was to take them home.

★   ★   ★   ★   ★

The first weeks in England were strange. The sisters had imagined that they need only step ashore at Southampton, and everything would be as before; they could pick up the thread of English existence as easily as an embroidery needle picked up the next stitch in the design on a piece of work which had been folded away six years before.

It was not so easy as that. It was not easy at all. To begin with, they had not expected to feel so *cold*. After a four-months' voyage—the *Hungerford* had actually been faster than the *Jupiter*—they had arrived in a warm July and had begun to shiver. It was absurd, but they knew that it was logical. They had been accustomed to such heat that a pleasant warmth now made no impression; they had to call for shawls.

At first it was odd not to have half-a-dozen joints in a tail of servants hurrying off to find the shawls. But Wright as well as her mistress quickly recovered her sense of humour along with a proper perspective, and within a few days the sisters were finding it a relief not to be followed about by black bowing shadows. They did not at once settle into the house in Kensington which had been the centre of their conversation on many an Indian afternoon. The villa was as delightful as they had anticipated, and well placed on a corner of Kensington Gore. They left the furnishings they had brought from India for Wright to unpack, and set off on visits to their family and friends. Emily would have liked to go to Theresa Lister first, but on her arrival she had been met with the news that Theresa's husband had suddenly died. All she could do was to send her friend a loving note. Pamela, too, she longed to see, but she was not sure if her friend was in Ireland or Scotland; one never knew with the Campbells.

It was good to go down into Kent again; to drive round their old home, and then on to Eleanor at East Combe. It was all as they had remembered it; nothing had changed. The gardens, the orchards, the house with its comfortable little rooms: all were the same. It was they who had changed. Fanny walked through the rooms, touching familiar things, and paused before a mirror on the wall. She was the colour of a buttercup. Did one lose that Indian shade in time? And her hair was greying, though that was natural at her age. She felt her forty years, every one. Perhaps it was because she had not lost the tiresome symptoms of her Indian illness, which still left her exhausted by the end of the day. The voyage home had done something to restore her former well-being, but she again felt low.

A long round of visits soon raised her spirits. Lord Clarendon declared that all three of them looked younger and fresher for the sojourn in India—which meant that he was the same George Villiers of yore, always ready to say something kindly and heartening, and meaning it.

Fanny went to stay with the Grosvenors, and soon forgot her grey hairs. Her letter-journals from India had been carefully kept, and it was amusing to go over them and fill in details in answer to her friends' eager questionings. For they really were interested in all she had seen, and been thinking, and doing, these past six years. It was in an atmosphere like this that Fanny bloomed: she felt so *wanted* here. Just as she felt at her eldest sister's.

Emily began to pick up the old threads, too, as soon as she felt active enough. It was astonishing the way India softened one's very bones. How long it took to adjust oneself again to a moderate climate! Her friends admired her Cashmere shawls, and Emily was thankful that these were as warm as they were beautiful.

The round of visits went on. Emily found, to her own rather amused surprise, that she had grown more tolerant of fellow-guests who turned out to be uncongenial.

'One good thing of age, and of hard practice in India, is that one does not mind being bored so much as one did in one's youth,' she wrote to a friend. 'The sediment at the bottom of the cup is decidedly thicker whenever I am reduced to swallow a spoonful; but still, I am more used to the taste of it, and as Dickens says of orange peel and water, if you make believe very much, it is not so very nasty.'

There were, however, no bores at Bowood. Emily and Fanny had always been extremely fond of the Lansdownes, and had often visited Bowood. They had always enjoyed themselves amazingly. It was generally rather superior society in point of conversation; Emily liked it because there was less said there about people, and more about books and affairs going on in the world. The one subject she was becoming tetchy about was politics. George had returned home to face censure and abuse in the newspapers, and searching questions from the Board of Control. The statesmen who had rejoiced in the first successes in Afghanistan now blamed him for the later disasters. He knew he must bear the responsibility, and listened to the politicians calmly.

Emily tried to urge him to defend his Indian policy, but no-one could move Lord Auckland against his will. The new Governor-General had taken firm measures against Afghanistan within a few weeks of his arrival in India. A punitive force had been sent to Kabul, the prisoners there had been rescued, Shah Shuja deposed, and Dost Muhammad restored to the throne. Ellenborough had then clearly indicated that it was going to be no part of British policy in the future to interfere with Afghan affairs. The Cabinet in London agreed. There was a meeting at Lord John Russell's to determine whether a vote of thanks to Ellenborough should be opposed or not. It was attended by the most conspicuous of the Opposition of both Houses.

'They resolved with only two dissentients,' wrote Charles Greville, 'that the vote should not be opposed. Auckland took no part, of course, but entirely concurred. His sister, Emily Eden, who has great influence over him, and who is a very clever and wrong-headed woman, was furious, and evinced great indignation against all their Whig friends, especially Auckland himself, for being so prudent and moderate, and for not attacking Ellenborough with all the violence which she felt and expressed.'

Charles Greville had not always thought Emily wrong-headed. The truth was, the last two years in India had shaken her very badly. Her intense loyalty to George had not allowed her to judge him; she could never bring herself to admit that he had made such terrible errors of judgment.

The storm went on, and presently died down. George and his sisters were now living in the Kensington house, which looked bright with its Indian curiosities, jade and china. The garden was soon made into an *Eden* garden, with flowers and shrubs; and there were a number of fine trees, too. Over the way was Hyde Park, so Emily and Fanny had plenty of space in which to exercise Zoë, and Fanny's new little dog.

Theresa Lister married Sir George Cornewall Lewis in 1844, and began a new life of happiness, much to Emily's contentment. She still wrote long letters to Theresa and Pamela; they were still the two human beings, after George, who mattered most to her. She loved her family dearly; nothing could ever lessen the Eden family affection. But Theresa and Pamela were like detached pieces of her own self. When she was irritated she could dash off a line to one or the other; if she was happy in any good fortune, they were the first to rejoice with her. She was growing irritated more frequently now, she found, and was forced to recognise that her health was failing. Fanny, too, had grown very thin and quiet. The doctors prescribed, but medicine seemed to do little good.

They went to the Isle of Wight for a long holiday, and George joined them. Lady Bucks came for a time, and astonished them by her activity. She had never before travelled on a railway, nor had she been on the sea since their father had been Ambassador in Holland, fifty years before. Then Robert came with Mary and their seven children, who raced about and livened up the Indian aunts. It was all very jolly while it lasted. But back again in London, Fanny grew listless once more, and Emily's agues grew worse.

They had plenty to occupy them. Emily had made hundreds of drawings and paintings in India, and she and Fanny began sorting them into order. All their friends begged for copies, and Emily decided to publish a collection. It came out under the title of *Portraits of the Princes and People of India*, and the edition was soon sold.

Emily had much enjoyed writing the descriptions under each portrait. She thought of the novel she had begun at Ham Common, years ago; it was put away in a box, somewhere. One day she would find it, and perhaps go on with it. Theresa had a gift for writing, and had published two novels, though under a pen-name. Emily thought it would be quite a charming occupation for her own old age.

★   ★   ★   ★   ★

William was home; a very subdued William. His unfortunate attachment in India had had a melancholy end, for the lady had died of one of the sudden fevers so common in India. He had left her in perfect health but an hour before, and then had come news of her death the same evening. After the first months at home with his parents, William's unnatural reserve wore off; he swung to the other extreme of wildness and boisterous spirits, flinging himself into every amusement that offered, to the anxiety of his mother. He found it impossible to settle down to anything. If he went to see Fanny and Emily at Eden Lodge, he would not stay long; he seemed distressed at any mention of India. At other times he wished to talk of nothing else, and they could not get him to stop.

Gradually his nerves became steadier, and he began to go out into normal society, much to his family's relief. He was now nearly forty. If only he would marry a nice girl. That was the solution which everybody urged—though not to William's face. Then, in 1844, he did what everybody hoped he would do. He married Caroline Montague, Fanny's friend, and settled down to be happy.

Emily and Fanny had also settled down, and were as happy as far as was possible, now that they both found they could not lead the varied and active existence which had been so full of zest before they went to India. Eden Lodge was admirable; they fitted into it.

And then they had to leave it.

Lord John Russell formed a new administration in 1846, and made George First Lord of the Admiralty. Emily and Fanny were naturally pleased for George's sake—but the kitchens at the Admiralty! And the enormous reception rooms! However, outsize apartments held no terrors for people who had been used to living in the marble halls of Government House. Emily let Eden Lodge, and they moved to the First Lord's quarters at the Admiralty.

It was pleasant to be in the centre of political life again, and comforting to see George in office. He thrived on work, and made nothing of going down to review at Portsmouth, sailing on to Jersey and Guernsey in appalling weather, giving great dinners at bad inns, and generally doing all his duties with his usual might and main. It was better for him to get about, even in rough weather, than to sit writing all day. Emily believed that if the use of pen-and-ink had been denied to public men, public affairs would have got on better.

There followed a few years of the kind of quiet contentment which Emily had often imagined in the sleepless nights of her Indian tent-life. She had so often looked into the future, to themselves reunited with their friends, to the stimulating tug and thrust of the political scene. This was the life George liked best, and the life she liked best. And here it was. She had not anticipated becoming an invalid; that had not entered into the picture. But if it was the will of Providence, she must make the best of it. George was sensible enough to go off on visits without her, if she was unable to accompany him. Or he took Fanny, when their younger sister felt well enough. They both wrote full accounts of everything they did, so that Emily should not feel neglected; and there was always plenty to talk about on their return.

At the end of 1848 they spent Christmas together at Eden Lodge. George had been invited to go for a New Year shooting week-end at The Grange, Lord Ashburton's house in Hampshire. Emily had been unable to get up for Christmas, but on the day of George's departure she made a great effort and got dressed, tucking herself up on the sofa and appearing to be in better health and spirits than she felt, so that George could go off with a cheerful last impression of her.

As he said good-bye to her on that Friday afternoon, Emily thought how well he looked; better than he had done since he had come home from India. He wore a cloak over his travelling suit, and as he turned in the doorway to wave, he seemed much younger than his sixty-four years.

He arrived at The Grange in good time, and was in excellent spirits that evening. The following day he went out shooting with the other guests, and shot well. It was late afternoon when they returned to the house.

George went to his room, and on the way he was struck down by a fit of apoplexy.

Hampshire was several hours' journey from London; it was impossible for Emily to be taken there. Fanny set off at once, and reached The Grange to find her brother still unconscious. On the Sunday evening, he looked long at her as she sat by his bedside. Presently recognition came into his eyes. That meant hope.

They watched all through the night. George had fallen into a coma now, and he never came out of it. He died early the following morning, the first day of the new year, 1849.

14

'BARBARIC GOLD AND PEARL'

'I F anyone has a right to feel for you and with you,' wrote Emily to Pamela Campbell, 'it is I.'

How kindly Pamela had written to her in those first bitter hours. Emily had hardly understood what comfort could mean, but her old friend's affection had somehow got through the numbness. They had always found it easy to speak to each other; early ties, the memories of happy days shared, all helped when calamity came. Emily was attempting to find words that would help Pamela. It was not a month since her own loss, and now Pamela was bereaved of a husband who had been the love of her life. Of what use were words? Yet Emily wrote on, seeking for those words which would strengthen.

She herself was in a constant state of ill-health. Fanny, too, was not well. Like a wraith, Fanny seemed to move without substance. The doctors had found signs of a definite malady in Emily, but with Fanny it seemed to be something of the spirit. She appeared to be *dwemming* away: dwindling, fading. Emily said little to her about her lack of appetite, her listlessness. One had never been able to argue or reason with Fanny; she had always listened, smiling, and then had gone on in her own Fanny-ish way.

Emily had got used to her younger sister's long silences, and did not notice any change. But by April the bright spirit in that lamp was burning low. It flickered, and went out.

Fanny had been forty-eight. Emily was fifty-two, and she felt an old woman. She was very tired. And she had not thought it possible to be so lonely.

What a blessing nieces were. Nephews, too, of course; they were often in the interesting state of trying to engage a young lady's affections. Satisfactory young ladies, too: some with several thousand pounds a year of their own. Though where true love was not present, Emily was sure that no fortune, however handsome, was any compensation whatever for the lack of happiness. Her nephew, Maurice Drummond, dear Mary's son, had married Lord John Russell's step-daughter, and that was a marriage which seemed to Emily to be a model. Maurice's manner to Addy was perfect—not only full of tenderness and attention, but sensible and kind. Emily liked having them come to stay with her.

But it was her nieces who were such a comfort. Caroline's girls, Robert's girls—they took it in turns to pay her visits at Eden Lodge, or accompanied her for long holidays, when she travelled to Ramsgate or Broadstairs, to seek for an improvement in her health.

Emily liked Broadstairs. She took a cottage there called Villette; quite a small place, but soon made convenient by turning the greenhouse into a bathroom, which opened out of her sitting-room. She could lie on her sofa by the window and look out at the busy sea, always covered with ships of various kinds. The quietness of the tiny coast village soothed her, and its bracing air gave her an illusion of her old vitality coming back. But it was only an illusion. There was something really the matter; her doctor, whom she disliked but trusted, said it was gout in the stomach. All through 1851 she had recurring bouts of dreadful pain, until she found her courage slipping away at the thought of any more.

There was only one thing to do, said the doctor, and the other advisers whom he called in agreed. Emily realised that she must face an operation, and thanked Providence for the invention of chloroform. The operation was successful so far as it went; the trouble was not gout, but stone. Emily woke up after a week of shuddering pain to find that though she was as weak as a baby, her mind was quite clear. She turned to her letters, and to the political news in the papers, and began to pick up the threads of her old interests.

Much of the news made her angry, and the political comments made her angrier still; she found that *The Times* had become perfectly drivelling, writing the sort of trash which might be expected from a rheumatic old lady who had been left out of the Cabinet. However, it served a useful purpose, for when she became too furious she flung it to the other side of the room, and had to get up to fetch it again— which was good for exercise.

She would have liked to stay in Broadstairs a great deal longer, but decided she would have to return to Kensington. Eden Lodge had been let to what had seemed an eligible tenant, a rich widow with one daughter. A few days before the business was to have been finally settled, the widow's friends had frightened her about the Exhibition in nearby Hyde Park, and the great crowds who would be prowling about. The letting had fallen through, and Emily did not suppose anyone would take it now, so late in the year; inconvenient to her from a pecuniary point of view, but it could not be helped. She had better go back there herself.

Her niece, Lena Eden, came to stay with her. Lena was Robert's daughter, and now nearly thirty: a kind, earnest girl with a deep religious sense. Lena had been writing a novel with a strong evangelical theme, modelled on Miss Yonge's excellent books, and as Aunt Emily was always sympathetic to anyone with literary ambitions, Lena liked staying with her. Emily herself had begun to write a book. Her body was weak; she spent most of her time now lying on a sofa. But her mind had regained its old vigour, and she had to keep it constantly occupied.

Her friends visited her often. The sitting-room at Eden Lodge became a kind of salon in the mornings, where the Whig statesmen dropped in to drink coffee and to talk. It became the recognised thing to call at Miss Eden's when one wished to meet a prominent politician; there was a chance that he would be there.

By luncheon time Emily was tired out, and needed to rest during the afternoon. Then came a renewal of vitality: Lena or one of the maids brought writing materials, and Emily sat up and began on her letters. She wrote regularly to Theresa Lewis, to Pamela, to the Drummonds and Colviles; exchanging news about births and marriages, congratulating mothers on the betrothal of their daughters. 'Their young happiness will do good to all our old unhappinesses,' she had once written to Theresa, and for her own part she had never lost her zest for a romance in the family circle, or among her friends.

She wrote to Charles Greville and to Lord Clarendon, criticising the latest political manœuvres with her accustomed point and prejudice. The place-hunting in the new Aberdeen administration of 1852 roused her ire to boiling-point. Grey's daughter-in-law had been grumbling that the Grey family had not been given all the high places to which they were undoubtedly entitled.

'I wish these wives of political men would hold their tongues or elope,' Emily wrote to Clarendon, and would have written a great deal more had she not decided that she had said enough.

It was less heating to turn to her novel, which was beginning to take shape. She could not work at it for long at a time, and sometimes she put it away for months together. There were long interruptions when she went to stay with her relations, or had one or other of them staying with her. She had, too, other literary irons in the fire; at least, she was thinking of heating them up. She had some thought of publishing the journals and correspondence of her father, William Eden, the first Lord Auckland, and was collecting family papers, and writing to people who might have documents which should be included in the book. George Hogge was to edit them, under her supervision.

Then there were her own letters from India. Her sisters and Robert had kept all theirs, and Theresa and Pamela had treasured every one she had written to them. The Indian story was unique, her friends said; the jewels, the elephants, the shawls! And the strange life in that half-known continent, where so many younger sons disappeared into the Company's service, and were not seen again. Emily should tell the story through her letters.

It was 1858 before Emily and Hogge had got her father's journals ready for Bentley, the publisher, who had expressed himself anxious to have them. Emily had taken a house at Richmond in Surrey, Fountain House, situated on the rise of Richmond Hill. She had always been fond of Richmond; ever since the summer spent on Ham Common she had considered the air there fresh and sweet. It was quiet at Fountain House, and when she had sent off the *Journals and Correspondence* to Bentley, she went back to her novel and worked steadily at it, so that it should be ready for publication the following year. She was giving it the title of *The Semi-detached House*, and she was really enjoying writing it. A lifetime of devotion to the works of Jane Austen had, she knew, made some impression on her own literary style; but she had no idea of attempting to copy Miss Austen. The absurdities of social snobbery, the arrogance of wealth trying to climb into high places—she had seen enough of these in her own day to be able to write about them from life.

'Semi' grew, week by week, even when progress was slow because of her lack of strength. Theresa Lewis had promised to godmother it through the business side of its publication. It was finished by the end of 1858, and Emily waited for her father's Journals to come out before sending 'Semi' to Bentley. But he dawdled over the Journals. In the end it was too late for spring publication; he said it must wait until the autumn. But this was the best time for a work of fiction, and he would like *The Semi-detached House* at once.

Emily was angry. She needed money, and she had had offers from other publishers for the Journals. She told Bentley so in a 'coldly savage letter'. Besides, he only offered £250 for 'Semi', and Emily felt she could not take less than £300. 'So mind you stick to £300 and a very early publication,' she wrote to Theresa.

Bentley was anxious to have the novel, and agreed on both counts. *The Semi-detached House* was an immediate success. The influential *Globe* newspaper gave it a good review which was soon reflected in the sales, and Bentley, all smiles, called on Emily to suggest another book to follow up one success with what he was sure would be another.

Emily was surprised as well as pleased at the praise which 'Semi' evoked. Mary Eden wrote to say that Robert, who was normally punctual, was missing at breakfast the morning after 'Semi' arrived. He was discovered in bed, declining to get up until he had finished the book. Robert had succeeded to the Auckland barony, and was now also Bishop of Bath and Wells; but he was the same Eden-ish Robert in the bosom of his family.

Sydney Herbert and his wife called at Eden Lodge on their way to dine with Florence Nightingale at Hampstead. Mr. Herbert wanted to congratulate Emily in person, and to say that 'Semi' had taken his fancy prodigiously. They talked for a little about Miss Nightingale, now undoubtedly come quite to the last days of her useful life, and dying of disease of the heart. Mr. Herbert said that every breath she drew could be heard through her closed doors. But she could still speak, and speak persuasively, he told Emily. The great nurse liked to talk to him about ways of improving soldiers' hospitals and barracks. There was nothing the matter with Miss Nightingale's mind, invalid though she might be.

Emily was not in the habit of comparing herself with other women —she had ever thought comparisons odious—but she felt that her own mind was still in quite good working order. She had an idea for working up that novel she had begun long ago, at Ham Common. She had recently found the package of papers, containing a number of chapters, and now she began to revise them. That gave her a good start, and she was soon launched on her second novel. It was to be a story about a young pair who spent the first year of their married life misunderstanding each other, and she was going to call it *The Semi-attached Couple*.

Bentley was well pleased at the prospect of a successor to the first 'Semi', and advertised it well. Emily wrote most of it by hand, when she felt well enough to sit up, and dictated the rest to Lena. It was completed in time for Bentley to publish it in 1860, and was taken up by the newspapers on account of its predecessor. But it never attained the popularity of the first 'Semi', and Emily herself did not like it nearly so much as the other.

The Auckland *Journals and Correspondence* still hung fire, but the book came out at last in 1862. It had been a work of filial piety, and Emily did not expect it to reach the public which rushed to buy the latest novels. She got a great deal of quiet satisfaction out of the appreciation of her father which came from the political world, the world which mattered in this connection. But it was painful to look down the list of her parents' children. Her beloved sister Mary had just died.

'Is it not strange,' she wrote to Theresa, 'that with my health I should have outlived my six sisters—all, except Lady Godolphin, in perfect health when I came from India?'

Yes, they were all gone now. Only Robert remained to her, only they two were left to share memories of long-ago, sunlit days at Eden Farm, with brothers and sisters playing in the meadows, and pigeons flying overhead, and George cantering in after an early morning ride, and Fanny cluck-clucking to the hens and running under everybody's feet. Quicksilver Fanny, who could never keep still—until India put a fiery hand round her and brought her to an unwonted quietness.

Emily now began to edit her Indian letters, those which told of the great journey to see Ranjit Singh. Most of them had been written to Eleanor, and after her sister's death they had been sent back to Emily. There were hundreds of letters, and selection was not easy. Some of the people mentioned in them were still alive. Emily spent a great deal of time deleting names and substituting initials—mostly wrong ones—to disguise European personalities. She had no intention of giving the vulgar food for tittle-tattle. The book was finished in 1865, and Bentley published it in two volumes the following year. Theresa did not live to act as literary godmother to this book; she died in 1865, and that wonderful friendship came to an end.

Up the Country was a bigger success than *The Semi-detached House* had been. It was true, and its astringent descriptions of people and places brought the Indian scene to life as no book of travels had done for years. Many letters came from the family: from the Edens, the Colviles and Vansittarts, the Drummonds and Godolphin Osbornes. Dozens of other people, who had been in India or who had relations there, also wrote to her praising the book; she was glad to have Lena's assistance as a secretary.

Emily felt more than usually exhausted after that effort, and during the next few years she knew that she was slipping downhill. In the spring of 1869, she insisted on being taken to Richmond, though the doctors said it was too long a journey for her. She had grown very fond of Fountain House, and the view from the hill at Richmond, and the peace of it all. It was a fine spring that year, and a delicious summer came after. The kind of summer Emily and Fanny had talked of so often in India; not hot, but warm, with the scent of flowers floating in on the breeze, and birds piping in the garden.

Emily died in August. She was buried in the family vault at Beckenham, in her beloved Kent, and many came to mourn her. Surviving Edens of her own generation, and nieces and nephews in the next; and friends whom she had sometimes annoyed and often amused, and those elect few whom she had warmly and unreservedly loved. But perhaps it was William Osborne who thought of her longest that day. Perhaps he sat reading once again the dedication printed at the beginning of his aunt's last book, *Up the Country*. She had addressed it to him.

'My dear William,

I know no-one but yourself who can now take any lively interest in these letters. She, to whom they were addressed, they of whom they were written, have all passed away, and you and I are now almost the sole survivors of the large party that in 1838 [1837] left Government House for the Upper Provinces. . . .

Now that India has fallen under the curse of railroads, and that life and property will soon become as insecure there as they are here, the splendour of a Governor-General's progress is at an end. The Kootub will probably become a railway station; the Taj will, of course, under the sway of an Agra Company (limited, except for destruction) be bought up for a monster hotel; and the Governor-General will dwindle down into a first-class passenger with a carpet-bag.

These details, therefore, of a journey that was picturesque in its motley processions, in its splendid crowds, and in its "barbaric gold and pearl", may be thought amusing. So many changes have taken place in Indian modes of travelling, that these contrasts of public grandeur and private discomfort will probably be seen no more, on a scale of such magnificence.

Believe me,
Ever your affectionate Aunt,
Emily Eden.'

231

APPENDIX 1

THE FAMILY OF WILLIAM EDEN, 1ST BARON AUCKLAND

(*Extracts from Eleanor Eden's Diary*)

1776. Married September 26th to my beloved Husband at St. Margaret's Church, by Markham, Archbishop of York.

Birth of My Children

1777. Eleanor Agnes, *b.* London
1778. Catherine Isabella, *b.* America
1780. Elizabeth Charlotte, *b.* London
1781. Caroline, *b.* Ireland
1783. William F. Elliot, *b.* London
1784. George Eden, *b.* Kent
1786. Henry, *b.* Paris
1788. Mary Louisa, *b.* Spain
1791. George Charles Frederick, *b.* The Hague
1793. Mary Dulcibella, *b.* Kent
1795. Morton, *b.* London
1797. Emily, *b.* London
1799. Robert John, *b.* Kent
1801. Frances, *b.* London

(William was drowned in an accident in 1810, Henry died of a fever at the age of eight, Charles died after a long illness at the age of four, and Morton died at the age of 26.)

APPENDIX 2

GLOSSARY

Ayah—Indian nursemaid or lady's-maid (from Portuguese '*aia*').

Babu—'a clerk who writes English'. Properly a term of respect attached to a name, but has come to mean a superficially cultivated Bengali.

Bara (fem. *bari*)—large or big.

Bhawani—Kali, Goddess of Destruction.

Bibi (Persian)—a lady. The word was later superseded by 'Memsahib'.

Chaddar—a wrap or sheet.

Chhota—small.

Chobdar—a stick bearer. An attendant on officials of rank who carries a stick overlaid with silver.

Chowrie (*chauri*)—Yak's tail set in a handle and used as a fly-whisk. Part of the insignia of ancient Asiatic royalty.

Dacoit—robber belonging to an armed gang.

Dak—transport by relays of men or horses. The post.

Dhuli—a covered litter.

Ghaut (*ghat*)—landing place.

Gucheras—probably connected with the Hindi 'Ghorcharha', meaning rider or trooper.

Havildar—sergeant: sepoy non-commissioned officer.

Jeel (*jhil*)—a mere.

"Jeldee, kubbadar" (*Jaldi Khabar-dar*)—quickly, take heed.

Jemadar (*jamadar*)—a chief servant. Also rank of native officer in a company of sepoys.

Jonpon, jonpaun (Hindi, *jompon* or *janpan*)—chair rather like European sedan-chair with two poles, borne by sticks between the poles; for use in hilly districts.

Khansama—chief table servant.

Kitmutgar (Hindi, *Khidmatgar*)—Muhammadan servant who waits at table under the Khansama.

Mahout—elephant driver and attendant.

Mali—gardener.

Muharram—period of fasting and mourning held during the 1st month of the Muhammadan lunar year, terminating in the ceremonies known as 'the Muharram'.

Murray—Fanny had probably heard the word '*mara*', meaning 'hit', when the beaters shouted out that a tiger had been hit. From this she must have deduced (wrongly) that the word was synonymous with 'carcase'.

Nautch—dance performed by women. Also any kind of stage entertainment.

Nazir—a kind of sheriff in the courts.

Peon (Portuguese)—orderly; messenger; foot-soldier.

Sirdar—a chief, or leader.

Suttee (sati)—rite of widow-burning.

Syce (sais)—groom.

Tatti—screen or mat made of roots of fragrant grass, with which doors and windows are filled in the hot season, usually kept wet, for purposes of evaporation and therefore cooling.

Thanadar—chief of police station.

Tonjon, tonjaun—portable chair carried like a palanquin by a single pole and four bearers.

Zeafut—a gift.

(*Compiled from information kindly supplied by Mildred Archer.*)

SELECT BIBLIOGRAPHY

Letters from India. By the Hon. Emily Eden, edited by her Niece. 2 vols. Bentley, 1872.

Miss Eden's Letters. Edited by her great-niece, Violet Dickinson. Macmillan & Co., 1919.

Up the Country: Letters written to her Sister from the Upper Provinces of India. By the Hon. Emily Eden. Bentley, 1866.

Portraits of the Princes and People of India. By Emily Eden. London, 1844.

The Semi-detached House. By Emily Eden, edited by Lady Theresa Lewis. Bentley, 1859.

The Semi-attached Couple. By Emily Eden. Bentley, 1860.

The Journal and Correspondence of William, Lord Auckland. Edited by G. Hogge. 4 vols. London, 1860.

★

The Earl of Auckland. By Captain L. J. Trotter. O.U.P., 1893.

John Russell Colvin. By Auckland Colvin. O.U.P., 1895.

The Life and Correspondence of Charles, Lord Metcalfe. Edited by J. W. Kaye. 2 vols. London, 1854.

The First Afghan War and its Causes. By Sir H. M. Durand. London, 1879.

History of the War in Afghanistan. By J. W. Kaye. 2 vols. London, 1851.

The Court and Camp of Runjeet Singh. By the Hon. W. G. Osborne. London, 1840.

★

Wanderings of a Pilgrim in Search of the Picturesque. By Fanny Parks (or Parkes). London, 1850.

Curry and Rice. By G. F. Atkinson. London [1856.]

★

The Administration of the East India Company in India. By J. W. Kaye. London, 1853.

The East India Company, 1784–1834. By C. H. Philips. Manchester University Press, 1940.

★

The Greville Memoirs (Second Part). Edited by H. Reeve. 3 vols. London, 1885.

Life and Letters of the 4th Earl of Clarendon. By Herbert Maxwell. 2 vols. Arnold, 1913.

The Cambridge History of India, Vol. 5. British India, 1497–1858. Edited by H. H. Dodwell, M.A. C.U.P., 1929.

The Men Who Ruled India. Vol. I. The Founders. By Philip Woodruff. Cape, 1953.

PAMPHLETS

The Great Game in Asia (1800–1844). By H. W. C. Davis (Raleigh Lecture), Proceedings of British Academy, 1926.

Lord Auckland and Lord Ellenborough. By a Bengal Civilian. London, 1845.

Catalogue of Exhibition of Paintings by the Hon. Miss Eden. (At Victoria Memorial Exhibition, Belvedere, Calcutta.) 1916.

MANUSCRIPT SOURCES

Letters from Board of Control of the East India Company, 1833–42 and *Letters from the East India Company to the Board of Control, 1833–42.* C.R.O., Indian Records Section.

Letter Books and Minute Books of George Eden, 2nd Baron Auckland, Governor-General of India. Add. MSS. 36789–37714, B.M.

Letters in Panshanger Collection. (Hertford County Archives.)

The Internal Policy of Lord Auckland in British India from 1836–1842. By D. P. Sinha. (Unpublished thesis for Ph.D., 1953, consulted by kind permission of Dr. Sinha and the Goldsmiths' Librarian, University of London.)

Fanny Eden's Journals. (The private letter-books of the Hon. Frances Eden, written from India, 1836–1842.) Now acquired by the Commonwealth Relations Office, India Office Library.

Various letters in private collections.

There is a great deal of correspondence and official records preserved at the Commonwealth Relations Office, India Records Section, relating to Lord Auckland and the Afghan War.

INDEX

Index

Ranees of Benares, 102–5; visits the Baiza Bai, 113–14; in Simla, 143–7, 160–4, 182–94; entertains Ranjit Singh's envoys, 145–7; visits Ranjit Singh, 164–178; in Agra, 198–201; returns to Calcutta, 202; prepares to leave India, 214, 217, 218; life in England again, 219–21; publishes *Portraits of the Princes and People of India*, 222; moves to the Admiralty, 223; moves to Richmond, 228; *The Semi-detached House*, 228–9; *The Semi-attached Couple*, 229; *Journals and Correspondence* of 1st Lord Auckland, 228, 230; *Up the Country*, 230; death, 231; *et passim*

Eden, Frances (Fanny): early years, 1–2; moves to London, 3; moves to Greenwich, 7; moves to Ham Common, 10; prepares to leave for India, 12–13; leaves for India, 14; on the voyage, 15–25; arrives in India, 26–7; social life, 29–31, 33–4, 51–7; goes tiger-shooting, 58–81; leaves on the journey to Simla, 92; life on the 'flat', 94; visits the Rajah and Ranees of Benares, 102–5; visits the Baiza Bai, 113–14; in Simla, 143–7; 160–4, 182–94; visits Ranjit Singh, 164–178; in Agra, 198–201; returns to Calcutta, 202; visits Prince of Wales Island, 211–12; prepares to leave India, 214, 217, 218; life in England again, 219–21; moves to the Admiralty, 223; death, 225; *et passim*

Eden, George—*see* Auckland, Lord (George Eden, 2nd Baron, afterwards 1st Earl of Auckland)

Eden, Lena, 227

Eden, Louisa (Mrs. Colvile), 3

Eden, Mary (Mrs. Charles Drummond), 6, 230

Eden, Robert (afterwards 3rd Baron Auckland and Bishop of Bath and Wells), 1, 5, 229

Eden, William—*see* Auckland, Lord (William Eden, 1st Baron)

Ellenborough, Lord (1st Earl), 217–8, 221

Famine, 123, 160
Fane, Sir Henry, 30, 53
Fatehpur, 198

'Gazelle', Fanny's pet, 91, 94, 98, 107, 120, 129
Ghazipur, 100–1
Ghazni, 189
Gholab Singh, 193
Ghoopi Gunj, 109
Giles, George's manservant, 14, 143
Government House, Calcutta, 28, 44, 88
Govin Ghur, 172

Greenwich Hospital, 7
Greville, Charles, 9, 82–3, 162, 221
Grey, Capt., 12, 17, 20, 21, 22, 23, 26, 42, 213
Grosvenor, Eleanor, 4, 24
Gurkhas, 138

Hamond, Sir Graham Eden, 19
Henry, Prince of Orange, 116–17, 118, 119, 123
Herat, 128, 129, 144, 157, 161
Herbert, Sidney, 229
Hill, Capt., 208
Himalayas, 137, 139
Hobart, Lady Eleanor—*see* Buckinghamshire, Eleanor, Countess of
Hobhouse, Sir John Cam, Bart., 40, 90, 191

Irish Church Bill, 9

Jalalabad, 214, 216
James, Mrs. Marie (*née* Gilbert, afterwards known as Lola Montez), 192, 197
Jones, Fanny's maid, 14, 59, 63, 70, 74, 209
Jupiter, the, 12, 14, 15–26, 43

Kabul, 83, 90, 129, 156, 189, 212, 214, 216, 221
Karak Singh, 166, 171, 176, 187, 193, 201–202, 208
Karnal, 134, 180, 197
Khaibar Pass, 198
Koh-i-nur, 151, 158–9, 170, 187
Kutb, the, 131–2

Lahore, 156, 175–7
Lister, Theresa (*née* Villiers, afterwards Lady Lewis), 3, 10, 219, 222, 228, 230
Lotus, Ranjit's favourite, 152, 153, 166, 187

MacGregor, Capt., 52, 86, 139, 148, 214
Macnaghten, Mrs. (afterwards Lady Macnaghten), 93, 107, 113–14, 133, 135, 164, 198, 218
Macnaghten, William (afterwards Sir William, 1st Baronet), 90, 93, 103, 107, 119, 145, 148–9, 151, 153–4, 155, 156, 161, 175, 179, 183–4, 189–91, 195–6, 206–7, 212–13, 215
Madeira, 16–17
Maharajpur, 118
Mars, George's valet, 14, 20–1, 139, 209
Meerut, 129–30
Melbourne, Lord (William Lamb, 2nd Viscount), 6, 11, 13
Metcalfe, Sir Charles (afterwards 1st Baron Metcalfe), 25, 29, 32, 42
Mirzapur, 109
Mohan Ke Sarai, 105, 106

Index